I0824362

# WITHOUT PRECEDENT

# WITHOUT PRECEDENT

## How Chief Justice Roberts and His Accomplices Rewrote the Constitution and Dismantled Our Rights

LISA GRAVES

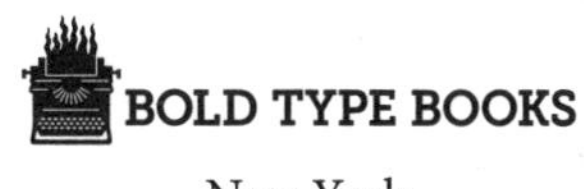

BOLD TYPE BOOKS

New York

Cover design by Ann Kirchner
Cover images © Universal History Archive/UIG/Bridgeman Images;
© kosmofish/Shutterstock.com; U.S. National Archives and Records Administration


Bold Type Books
Hachette Book Group
1290 Avenue of the Americas, New York, NY 10104
www.boldtypebooks.org
@BoldTypeBooks

Printed in the United States of America

First Edition: September 2025

Published by Bold Type Books, an imprint of Hachette Book Group, Inc. Bold Type Books is a co-publishing venture of the Type Media Center and the Hachette Book Group.



Print book interior design by Bart Dawson

Library of Congress Cataloging-in-Publication Data
Names: Graves, Lisa author
Title: Without precedent : how Chief Justice Roberts and his accomplices rewrote the Constitution and dismantled our rights / Lisa Graves.
Description: First hardcover edition. | New York : Bold Type Books, 2025. | Includes bibliographical references and index. |
Identifiers: LCCN 2025003656 | ISBN 9781645030676 hardcover | ISBN 9781645030690 ebook
Subjects: LCSH: Roberts, John G., Jr., 1955– —Criticism and interpretation | Roberts, John G., Jr., 1955– —Social and political views | United States. Supreme Court—Officials and employees—Biography | Political questions and judicial power—United States | Constitutional law—United States | Civil rights—United States | Conservatism—United States | LCGFT: Biographies
Classification: LCC KF8745.R63 G73 2025 | DDC 347.73/2634—dc23/eng/20250202
LC record available at https://lccn.loc.gov/2025003656

ISBNs: 9781645030676 (hardcover), 9781645030690 (ebook)

LSC-C

Printing 1, 2025

*For Don, whose boundless love uplifts me*

Power concedes nothing without a demand. It never did and it never will. Find out just what any people will quietly submit to and you have found out the exact measure of injustice and wrong which will be imposed upon them, and these will continue till they are resisted. . . . The limits of tyrants are prescribed by the endurance of those whom they oppress.

—Frederick Douglass, 1857

# CONTENTS

## PART V
## DOMINATION

# INTRODUCTION

A FEW DAYS before the Fourth of July in 2005, John Roberts advanced a big step toward his ambition to be appointed to the Supreme Court of the United States. On that sweltering Friday, the end of the Court's 2004–2005 term was far from my mind when I awoke early to get ready for our annual holiday pool party that weekend at my home near Rock Creek Park, in Washington, DC. By late morning, news broke that President George W. Bush would get to fill a momentous vacancy on the nation's highest court.

This vacancy came just a few months after I had left the staff of the US Senate, where I'd been chief counsel for nominations for the Senate Judiciary Committee for Senator Patrick Leahy, when he was the chair and then ranking member. It was the first time in almost a decade that I wasn't working for the federal government. I had left behind my government-issued BlackBerry after Bush began his second term. When my new cell phone chimed the theme song from the HBO hit *Sex and the City*, I had no idea my father was calling with surprising news.

Sandra Day O'Connor (a Ronald Reagan appointee) had just announced she would be stepping down to spend more time with her ailing husband, John. I was not a big fan of O'Connor, though she was the first woman appointed to the high court. I knew having a woman in a powerful role would not advance justice and equality in and of itself. It was her rulings that mattered, and I was not fond of how often she sided with her Stanford Law School classmate and former romantic partner William Rehnquist (a Richard Nixon appointee to the position of associate justice and a Reagan appointee to the post of chief justice).

I did appreciate O'Connor for keeping the promise she made during her nomination: to follow precedent and not impose her personal views about abortion. During her tenure on the Court, she joined a ruling known as *Planned Parenthood v. Casey*, which affirmed *Roe v. Wade*, and emphasized that "liberty finds no refuge in a jurisprudence of doubt." Her ruling rested firmly upon the foundational principle of fair jurisprudence known as stare decisis, a Latin term meaning "to stand by decided matters." In that ruling she and her colleagues in the prevailing plurality quoted Justice Potter Stewart (a Dwight Eisenhower appointee) to explain the profound importance of stare decisis in a democracy: "A basic change in the law upon a ground no firmer than a change in our membership invites the popular misconception that this institution is little different from the two political branches of the Government. No misconception could do more lasting injury to the Court and to the system of law which it is our abiding mission to serve."[1]

Perhaps her prior experience as a state legislator, at a time when politics had been seen as the art of compromise, made O'Connor more of a centrist than I thought she was, especially as the Court moved further to the right. However, in 2000, she voted with four other Republican appointees to the Supreme Court to stop the recount of ballots in Florida, which had the effect of making the Republican candidate, George W. Bush, the president of the United States. Bush lost the popular vote and, by many accounts, would have lost the Electoral College vote if all the ballots had been counted, but for the Rehnquist Court's ruling. The recount had been triggered by the closeness of the initial vote count. John Roberts, then an appellate lawyer in private practice, had traveled to Florida to advise Florida Governor Jeb Bush, Bush's brother, on how to navigate the recount. Less than a week before the Court issued its partisan 5–4 ruling in *Bush v. Gore* stopping the recount, Jeb sent a personal note to Roberts thanking him.

Three years later, as a staffer on the Senate Judiciary Committee, I had written a game plan for how to respond to the next Supreme Court vacancy; in the wake of O'Connor's announcement in July 2005, people were calling for my advice on the battle to come. O'Connor had played an essential role in Bush's ascent, and now her resignation could extend his impact—along with the GOP's control of the Court—for decades. Plus, Bush would likely get another vacancy to fill soon, given Rehnquist's failing health.

I had tendered my resignation from my job with the Judiciary Committee shortly after the 2004 presidential election. Sitting in a beautiful office in the Russell Building with the high ceilings and lovely western sunlight, Senator Leahy kindly urged me to stay on. Despite how much I loved working for him—a senator tall in stature and integrity (and a devoted Batman fan)—the Democrats had lost four Senate seats in that election, making it unlikely we could sustain our filibusters of Bush's controversial appellate nominees, let alone a potential Supreme Court nominee. I just could not stomach looking like human wallpaper behind the senators at the hearings to come, bearing silent witness to history on C-SPAN, unable to stop the Republican-controlled Senate's confirmation of whomever Bush chose.

I told Senator Leahy I could not accept his entreaty to stay, and a few months later I started a job as the senior legislative strategist on national security for the American Civil Liberties Union. In 2005, I had spent the weeks before the July 4 holiday working with former Congressman Bob Barr (R-GA) and others on a bipartisan effort to reform the USA PATRIOT Act. That Friday, July 1, after the calls about O'Connor's announcement subsided, overwhelmed with worry about what the Court and America would become, I stopped to grieve and to paint. Almost two decades earlier, I'd entered college focused on prelaw but with an art scholarship. When I was working for the Senate, my dear friend Yolanda encouraged me to return to painting as a way to do something totally nonverbal while fighting Bush's judicial nominees. I began painting huge, colorful abstracts to reignite my joy, but that day, for the first time, I painted only in black-and-white, mostly black. It was the most mournful piece of art I've ever made.

The speculation began immediately about who would replace O'Connor and whether it would be another woman. Through countless conversations, I held firm to my contention that Bush would nominate John Roberts, whom I had tried and failed to stop from getting appointed to the US Court of Appeals for the DC Circuit in 2003. A few weeks after O'Connor's announcement that she was leaving the Court, I got a call from Phil Toomajian, a talented staffer working on Senator Leahy's judiciary team, telling me Bush was going to announce Roberts as his nominee. He "congratulated" me for correctly predicting since early in Bush's first term that he would pick Roberts. Phil's congratulations reflected the gallows humor common among those in the political trenches, but it did little to lighten my mood.

I was convinced Roberts would be a disaster for the Court and for the country. Despite his polite demeanor and the endorsements of establishment Republicans and some Democrats, I was certain he would devote himself to advancing a right-wing political agenda through the judiciary. To make matters worse, in September Rehnquist died, and Bush nominated Roberts to become the chief justice instead of filling O'Connor's vacant seat.

A week later, the Republican-controlled Senate Judiciary Committee began hearings on Roberts's nomination and quickly pushed through a committee vote. Only two weeks after that, on Thursday, September 29, the Senate voted to confirm him. That accelerated timeline left little time to muster opposition. To my dismay, even

Senator Leahy voted for him, which is a powerful testament to how terribly effective Roberts's performance before the Senate had been.

When I heard Roberts had been confirmed, I wept.

---

This book explains how John Roberts ascended to the Supreme Court and for nearly two decades maintained a reputation as a fair referee despite using the Court to advance a reactionary political revolution in the law to undo widely popular policies. It details the network of billionaire-funded groups engaged in a radical crusade to remake American society through the courts and shows how Roberts is both a cause and a consequence of their efforts. This corrupt and corrupting effort is not merely an aspect of Roberts's legacy: It *is* his legacy. This reactionary agenda and the means used to achieve it are, in a word, unprecedented.

Most people really have no idea who Roberts is, what a destructive force he is to American jurisprudence, and how he has helped fracture our political system and our society.

In 2002, as part of my work for the Senate's Judiciary Committee, one of my first tasks was to evaluate Roberts, whom Bush had nominated to the US Court of Appeals for the DC Circuit. Roberts would impress some of the senators with his amiable confidence, his calm reassurances, and his easy smile. He looked like a Norman Rockwell–style embodiment of judicial restraint and rectitude. But a thorough examination of his record and career path convinced me that, his carefully constructed résumé and polished persona notwithstanding, he would make a seriously detrimental addition to the federal appeals court. In the Senate hearings on his elevation to the Supreme Court, he demonstrated his gift for disarming opponents when he proclaimed, "I will remember that it's my job to call balls and strikes, and not to pitch or bat."

The image of Roberts as an impartial umpire proved to be persuasive and durable, but instead of being a genuine expression of his temperament and approach, it was a meticulously planned and effectively delivered public relations strategy. He presented himself as a dedicated institutionalist who sought to uphold American judicial traditions. Far from being a protector, however, he has used his position as chief justice to orchestrate a pattern of extreme decisions that have unmoored American democracy from its foundations—and that was before Donald Trump's three appointees joined the Court. Despite Roberts's claims that there are no Republican or Democratic federal judges, he has established himself not as a fair referee but as a diabolically effective player rewriting the Constitution and remaking America in accord with his reactionary political agenda, as he strategizes how to move the ball forward and disarm the opposition.

Roberts's approach to constructing his public persona is best understood in light of, and in contrast to, the experience of Robert Bork, President Reagan's failed nominee to the high court in 1987. The two Roberts are not so far apart when it comes to their dark and repressive vision for American law, but John Roberts's moon face and striking blue eyes have never communicated the sort of villainy that Bork's arched brows and matching goatee conveyed to cartoonists and the public at large. But, more than that, Bork's extremism was loud, voluble, confrontational, and aggressively public, while Roberts has enacted much of the same right-wing agenda with stately civility. Roberts's reserved demeanor and projection of affability have helped enable his Court to undermine our rights without raising as many alarms as warranted. While he often aligns with the results sought by his shriller brethren, Clarence Thomas (a George H. W. Bush appointee) and Samuel Alito (a George W. Bush appointee), Roberts has until recently managed to maintain credibility with the public and the press by minding the pace of the extremist takeover of our laws and culture. His calm style—with a close-lipped kind of Cheshire cat grin—somehow made the outcome seem more palatable, or even reasonable, to many in the press. Litigants on the other side of his agenda have continued to hold out hope they will be the ones to somehow persuade him to capitulate and rule in their favor, which is actually quite rare.

Roberts's reactionary docket has included destroying environmental rules that protect our planet from predatory billionaires, overturning legal precedents that limited access to deadly guns, forging the shield of religious freedom into a sword to attack equality and access to health care, decimating labor unions' power to bargain for workers' rights, and unleashing waves of billionaire spending in our elections in ways that corrupt our representative democracy and sever public institutions from vital traditions of impartiality. Democrats credited him with, and Republicans lambasted him for, saving the Affordable Care Act (dubbed Obamacare), but Roberts is playing for team GOP, and his occasional nods at moderation allow him to more effectively realize his long-term agenda. Kicking millions of Americans off of health insurance could have caused the GOP even bigger losses in 2012, and embracing the dubious legal theories against Obamacare would have undermined the power to enact tax policy that favors the rich.

Devastatingly, Roberts has systematically altered the very structure of our democracy by sabotaging voting rights and permitting illegitimate and undemocratic electoral maps that have all but eliminated incentives to seek compromise, fueling extremism and division. But Roberts's masterstroke was alchemy: turning gold into speech by judicially rewriting the First Amendment to allow mountains of gold in the form of dark money to distort our elections. His Court did so by barring Congress from regulating the corrupting influence of unlimited cash supplied by billionaires seeking to manipulate our elections. The result in that case, called *Citizens United v. FEC*, was orchestrated by the Roberts Court, which ordered an out-of-season oral argument on new questions to clear the decks for a surge in secret cash for the 2010 midterms—just in time to try to rein in America's first Black president, Barack Obama. That tsunami of cash has been deployed to distort the ensuing elections, epitomized by the actions of the richest man in the world, Elon Musk, who spent $288 million to procure the presidency for Donald Trump (and an unelected copresidency for a while) in 2024. Big money has also altered the makeup of the nation's highest court and, with it, how our Constitution and laws are interpreted, creating a self-reinforcing circle of corruption. Roberts's success in dismantling the guardrails needed for fair elections and fairness in general has greatly weakened—and, in fact, imperiled—our democracy.

Through action and inaction, Roberts has also allowed a culture of corruption to run rampant. For more than a decade, he has worked to stall congressional efforts to require an enforceable code of conduct for the Supreme Court, even though every other judge in the nation is subject to such rules. He has not taken any public action to redress the numerous investigative reports about the mountain of secret gifts and serious ethical failures associated with Clarence Thomas and others. Roberts stood silent as Thomas sat on the case involving Donald Trump's immunity claims in a criminal case about Trump's efforts to subvert the 2020 presidential election, even though Thomas's wife, Ginni Thomas, actively sought to stop the count and even to secure fake electors. Roberts adopted the same do-nothing approach toward Samuel Alito, despite evidence that flags tied to the January 6 insurrection were flown over his homes. Why? Roberts needed their votes in order to accomplish his most reactionary agenda to date and to cement the most unprecedented edict of all: to effectively pardon Trump and pave the way for his return to power, emboldened by kinglike immunity from prosecution for any of his "official acts" as president.

The pattern of conduct is clear: Roberts has made extraordinary efforts to ensure that those with great power and wealth have the opportunity to corrupt every aspect of our politics and society, and when the long-festering corruption of his Court has become front-page news, he has refused to clean up the mess. On the surface, his response has been singularly feckless and an insult to the institution of the Court, but on a deeper level he understands that actually cleaning up the Court would undermine his overarching political agenda to remake the law. On Roberts's watch, the Court has become a creature more beholden to the influence of the richest few—and their political operatives—than at any time in the past century. This is not a bug; it is the design.

For many years, Roberts had the highest approval rating of any federal official. Now that there is a 6–3 right-wing majority, the mask has fallen. Roberts's single-minded determination to give Trump unwarranted and anticonstitutional immunity for the serious criminal activities alleged in federal indictments reveals just how untethered John Roberts really is from the text of the Constitution and so-called originalism. His orchestration of the trifecta of 2024 rulings involving the January 6 cases shows that his jurisprudence does not arise from a principled interpretation of the Constitution but rather is guided by his desire to exert power for both himself and the political party he hails from, even as the latter has grown more extreme. His dogged allegiance to a regressive political agenda poses grave threats to our democracy and our freedom.

Calls for genuine, bold reforms are growing and may grow even stronger in response to further efforts by the Right to dismantle democracy, serve billionaires while hurting ordinary people, and impose deeply unpopular and even dangerous policies. The Roberts Court cannot be trusted to save us from all of the dictatorial impulses of Trump that Roberts and the MAGA justices on the Supreme Court have emboldened. Until he leaves the Court or is removed, Roberts will continue to obstruct vital ethics reforms and essential repairs to the Constitution that he has so grossly distorted with the immunity edict and other deeply damaging rulings. Meanwhile, I am committed to doing everything in my power to expose John Roberts for the regressive politician in judicial robes that he really is and, in doing so, ultimately to help restore—and expand—the constitutional rights, privileges, immunities, and power of We the People in these United States.

# PART I

# INCEPTION

## CHAPTER 1

# CONFIRMATION

ON THURSDAY, SEPTEMBER 29, 2005, the Republican-controlled Senate confirmed John G. Roberts Jr. to become the chief justice of the Supreme Court. The vote was 78–22. He was forty-nine years old—the youngest chief justice since John Marshall took the oath of office in 1801.

The vote to give Roberts a seat on the nation's highest court happened just two weeks after the hearings on his nomination before the US Senate Judiciary Committee. The hearings were held in the Senate Caucus Room, which is now called the Kennedy Caucus Room in tribute to the late Senator Ted Kennedy (D-MA). The room is historic, akin to a majestic theater, flanked by twelve enormous Corinthian columns. Its walls have sheltered the somber hearings on the disastrous sinking of the RMS *Titanic* and the titanic hysteria of some of Senator Joe McCarthy's tirades against supposed communist plotters in federal agencies.

It was also the chamber where, in May 1973, Senator Sam Ervin (D-NC) gaveled in the Watergate hearings investigating the crimes and cover-up of President Richard M. Nixon. While these congressional hearings dominated the news cycle, John Roberts was about to graduate from his private prep school and head to Harvard

College. A year later, Nixon resigned in disgrace after public opinion turned strongly against him and the US House of Representatives began impeachment proceedings. Nixon later claimed, "When the president does it, that means that it is not illegal." His claim that a president has kinglike powers that immunize his actions from criminal prosecution was met with widespread revulsion and was summarily dismissed.[1]

Roberts entered that historic chamber in September 2005, after President George W. Bush initially nominated him to replace Justice Sandra Day O'Connor. She admitted she was disappointed that Bush did not nominate a woman, although she lauded Roberts's oral advocacy skills. She had first met Roberts after President Ronald Reagan nominated her to become the first woman on the Court in August 1981, when Roberts was assigned to help her prepare for her Senate hearing that September. In August of that year, Roberts began his new job at the top of the US Department of Justice (DOJ), as a special advisor to Attorney General William French Smith. Roberts documented his game plan for O'Connor's confirmation process, writing, "The approach was to avoid giving specific responses to any direct questions on legal issues likely to come before the court, but demonstrating in the response a firm command of the subject area and awareness of the relevant precedents and arguments." The essence of his scheming memo was to explain "how a nominee could deflect senators' questions while appearing to answer them."[2]

Twenty-four years later, Roberts was preparing for his own Senate hearing to replace O'Connor, but when Bill Rehnquist died on September 3, Bush swapped Roberts into the chief's vacancy. So it was, in that famous Senate theater on September 12, 2005, that Roberts deployed a distinctly American analogy to assure the American people that he would be fair. He claimed, "I have no agenda, but I do have a commitment. If I am confirmed, I will confront every case with an open mind . . . and I will remember that it's my job to call balls and strikes, and not to pitch or bat."[3]

On that sunny day in September, Roberts's baseball umpire metaphor proved to be a brilliant bit of public relations. But the spin he manufactured was not just for the public: It helped him win the nomination. Though Roberts did not invent the analogy, he contrived to deploy it first on the initial decision maker: President Bush. "W," as he was known, was the oldest son of President George H. W. Bush and had been a co-owner of the Texas Rangers. The younger Bush later wrote that when he interviewed Roberts as a finalist for the Supreme Court—along with Judge Michael Luttig of the US Court of Appeals for the Fourth Circuit (an appointee of the elder Bush)—Roberts had impressed him by saying, in W's recollection, "A good judge is like an umpire—and no umpire thinks he is the most important person on the field."[4]

Roberts had played sports in the Indiana High School Athletic Association—but not baseball. At the private preparatory school he attended, so small that there were only twenty-two young men in his class, he competed in wrestling and track, and he was one of the captains of the football team. In 2005, his defensive line coach, Dave Kirby, told a right-wing political group backing Roberts—called Progress for America—that Roberts had "loved the process of studying the game and creating strategies to beat an opponent." Kirby also told legal biographer Joan Biskupic that Roberts, a few inches short of a six-foot stature, was a small linebacker but "feisty and sort of ferocious, sort of like a mean little dog, always at the right place." That ferocious leader of the football team who strategized about how to tackle his opponents was not on display during his nomination hearings, where Roberts sought to project the image of a gentle, learned jurist.[5]

A little-watched speech that Roberts gave in 2013 to the graduating class of his prep school, La Lumiere, sheds light on his enduring approach to his grand ambitions. Standing behind the podium in a pin-striped suit and red tie sans judicial robes, he focused on "one value"—"the discipline of persistence." Roberts elaborated,

> No quality is more essential to achieving your hopes for the future. And unlike many other keys to success—intellect, talent, physical ability, health, looks, where you were born, into what sort of family, luck—persistence is entirely, *entirely*, within your control. . . . As President Calvin Coolidge once remarked, "Nothing in this world can take the place of persistence. Talent will not. Nothing is more common than unsuccessful people with talent. Genius will not. Unrewarded genius is almost a proverb. Education will not. The world is full of educated derelicts. Persistence and determination alone are omnipotent."

Roberts credited this formative advice to the founders of La Lumiere. That private Catholic boarding school opened in Indiana in 1963, just a few years after US marshals famously shielded Ruby Bridges from an angry crowd as she integrated a public school in New Orleans and numerous private schools were launched across the country. In 1968, John Roberts applied to La Lumiere, writing precociously at age thirteen, "I've always wanted to stay ahead of the crowd." It was an odd sentiment for a child of that age, who, already a salesman, wrote that he did not want only a "good job" someday but wanted "to get the best job by getting the best education."[6]

Since then, that value he hailed as central to his training at La Lumiere—persistence—has proven to be central to his success and his strategy for remaking American law. Persisting is what John Roberts does. It is deeply part of who he is. Persistence can be a valuable trait, but being relentless can have real adverse consequences for others, especially if combined with a rigidity of ideas. That trait can be a potent weapon, especially for someone with a lifetime appointment. Roberts won the best job in the US legal system, atop the Supreme Court, a job with the power to issue far-reaching rulings while insulated from most checks and balances.

True to his ambitions, Roberts was determined to get the best job when President George W. Bush came calling. Key members of Bush's inner circle, such as Brett Kavanaugh, who was then the White House staff secretary, also vouched for Roberts. They knew he would be a sure thing, a bankable vote, for the Right's political agenda, with its hostility to key legal precedents. In other words, Roberts was no David Souter; operatives like the Federalist Society's Leonard Leo had assured right-wing activists that Roberts could be trusted on issues they cared about. After all, the Bush administration had taken to heart a plea made at a major Federalist Society event in 2000: "No more Souters!"[7]

Souter, who had previously served on the Supreme Court of New Hampshire, had been appointed to the US Supreme Court by Bush's father, George H. W. Bush, at the urging of his chief of staff John H. Sununu. Souter's sin was that he was a traditional Yankee conservative, one who kept his word when he pledged to follow legal precedents. During the fifteen years before John Roberts was chosen for the Court—and the four years he served after—Souter earned a reputation as a fair-minded, thoughtful judge who was not a rigid ideologue but had empathy for the plight of others. Souter was willing to put the law before partisan political outcomes, as he did when he followed the Court's precedent in *Roe v. Wade* and voted to uphold it, alongside Sandra Day O'Connor, Anthony Kennedy (a Reagan appointee), John Paul Stevens (a Gerald Ford appointee), and Harry Blackmun (a Nixon appointee who had written the majority opinion in *Roe*). In other words, Souter behaved like a traditional judge, serving the cause of justice with real political impartiality, which to right-wing hard-liners was a failure.

The "No more Souters" mantra has continued to animate the Right. In 2016, seven years after Souter's retirement, Leonard Leo's right-hand man, Jonathan Bunch, called Don McGahn, a key legal advisor to Donald Trump's campaign, to discuss potential US Supreme Court picks. McGahn deadpanned that he had already tapped Sununu to draw up a list of potential nominees because he had played such a decisive role in recommending Souter. Bunch was taken aback, until he realized that McGahn was joking. To Bunch's relief, Trump would not make the same "mistake" of appointing fair-minded justices like Souter to the nation's highest court.[8]

There is another telling contemporaneous example of how the "No more Souters" mantra cleared the path for John Roberts. Just four days after Roberts was confirmed with 100 percent of the Republican senators voting for him, Bush nominated his White House counsel, Harriet Miers, to fill the vacancy left by O'Connor's retirement. Miers's nomination was met with howls that she was not "conservative" or doctrinaire enough. Unlike Roberts, she apparently could not be counted on reliably to take their side and use the Court to advance the right wing's political agenda. She was perceived to be another Souter: too fair. Leonard Leo briefly tried to save her nomination by citing her antiabortion efforts in the American Bar Association, even as his close compatriots were encouraged to mount the campaign against her, to make way for Leo's friend, US Court of Appeals for the Third Circuit Judge Samuel Alito (a George H. W. Bush appointee).

Right-wing VIPs like Robert Bork—whose nomination to the Supreme Court was defeated after his extreme views of the law were exposed to the public—also opposed Miers. He called her selection a "slap in the face" to loyalists "who've been building up the [right-wing] legal movement for the last twenty years." It took only three weeks of pressure to get President Bush to bail on his old friend and withdraw Miers's name. The very next day Bush called

Alito about O'Connor's vacancy and then offered him the nomination to the nation's highest court.[9]

Leo strongly backed Alito, a fellow Roman Catholic and a former Reagan-Bush administration lawyer known for his devotion to the objectives of the right-wing legal movement. Neither Alito nor Roberts was assailed as a "Souter" for the simple reason that both were clearly more Bork than Souter, the difference being that Alito was less soft-spoken than Roberts and garnered more no votes. In contrast, in the hearings on his nomination, John Roberts effectively conveyed to most senators and the American people that he had "no agenda." I strongly suspected that assertion was not true then, and it is demonstrably untrue now.

Back in 2005, some Democratic senators saw through Roberts's act and voted against his confirmation. Senator Chuck Schumer (D-NY) voted against Roberts in the Senate Judiciary Committee, along with Senators Dick Durbin (D-IL), Dianne Feinstein (D-CA), and Ted Kennedy. Senator Joseph R. Biden Jr. (D-DE), who would later be elected vice president and then president, opposed Roberts too. They were joined by seventeen other Democrats in voting against Roberts's confirmation by the full Senate. All fifty-five of the Republican senators voted yes, which made the final vote that put Roberts on the high court 78–22.

My former boss, Senator Patrick Leahy (D-VT), voted to confirm Roberts. Leahy later came to deeply regret that vote, remarking, "I think in [Roberts's] actions and the actions in which he has joined, he has made the court an arm of the Republican Party." At the time of the confirmation vote, I was no longer chief counsel for nominations, a position where I could have closely pursued efforts to persuade him. I had lost that battle the first time around, in 2003, when Senator Leahy voted to discharge Roberts's nomination from the committee after Republicans took over the majority in the Senate. Back in 2003, Leahy did agree to let me ask Senator

Harry Reid (D-NV), who was then the Democratic minority whip (the party's lieutenant whose task was to marshal votes), to not have a recorded vote on Roberts's circuit court confirmation. I wanted to give the Democrats the chance to vote against Roberts when he was elevated to the Supreme Court, as I was certain he would be if Bush nominated a white man. That is why John Roberts was confirmed to the US Court of Appeals for the DC Circuit by "UC," or unanimous consent. It did not mean he was unanimously supported. UC is the process the Senate uses to move a bill or nomination without members voting yay or nay by name in a roll call vote.[10]

Although my heart was broken when Roberts was waved through in 2003, I was still in the fight to keep as many other right-wing operatives off the bench as I could. My work was not going to be just a "speed bump," as a Democratic operative envious of my title sneered after the Republicans won control of the Senate in the midterms in 2002 and I began making the case for filibustering some of Bush's nominees. That was a seemingly impossible objective while facing a wartime president in the aftermath of the midterm Democratic losses, but as rocket scientist Robert Goddard wrote, "Everything is impossible until it is done." I led the staffing of the first filibuster of DC Circuit nominee Miguel Estrada in 2003 and helped spearhead and aid all the other judicial filibusters we mounted through the end of 2004, despite vicious attacks against us.

On September 29, 2005, though, Roberts was sworn in as the new chief justice in the East Room of the White House, where Bush observed that "the nomination power is one of the most serious responsibilities of a president." Bush said, "When a president chooses a Supreme Court Justice, he is placing in human hands the full authority and majesty of the law." Bush also recognized that the chief justice "has added responsibilities as the leader of the court and the presiding officer of the Judicial Conference of the United

States," which oversees federal court policy, such as ethics rules for federal judges.[11]

Bush described Roberts as a nominee of "uncommon talent," "humility," and "integrity." He also assured the American people that Roberts would "be prudent in exercising judicial power . . . and above all a faithful guardian of the Constitution." Perhaps President Bush did not really believe that Roberts would "be prudent," a phrase his father George H. W. Bush used so often that it became a signature line in *Saturday Night Live* skits featuring comedian Dana Carvey. After all, the younger Bush was reading a speech filled with ceremonial words written by a speechwriter for a ceremonial occasion: the swearing in of the seventeenth chief justice of the United States, a powerful role with a tenure that always exceeds the appointing president's term in office. With John Roberts being only forty-nine years old, the duration of his power was expected to exceed Bush's tenure by decades.

Tellingly, however, Bush also said Roberts would act as a judge in the tradition of the man Roberts had clerked for in the 1980–1981 term, Bill Rehnquist, whose sudden death just three weeks earlier had created the vacancy that Roberts now filled. In certain ways, Bush was presciently right about that. Rehnquist was one of the two justices who dissented in the 7–2 ruling in *Roe* and had repeatedly voted in favor of weakening *Roe* over his next three-plus decades on the bench. Rehnquist was known for being affable and also for pushing a regressive view of the law, including voting rights. The chief's song-filled holiday parties were legendary, but his legal rulings were devastating to the lives of ordinary Americans.[12]

In 2005, with Bush looking on and Roberts's wife, Jane, holding a Bible, Supreme Court Justice John Paul Stevens administered the oath. Roberts wore a red tie—as he had at his hearings. Although Roberts swore that "judges are not politicians," he had chosen the political color that signified his team, the party he had aligned with for the preceding quarter century or more. His wife chose a dress in the shade dubbed "Nancy Reagan red," after Reagan's wife. The GOP, its party loyalists, and its fans have widely embraced that cadmium red color, which newscasters have used to mark the Republican Party since the 2000 presidential election.

---

Just two days after his confirmation, Roberts—again wearing a red tie—attended the Red Mass at the Cathedral of St. Matthew the Apostle, a Romanesque revival–style church in Washington, DC. The event gets its name from the deep red color of the vestments of the Catholic clergy, with the red representing "the tongues of fire symbolizing the presence of the Holy Spirit." The Red Mass has been a religious and political event celebrated in DC since 1952. During that early period, "red" also symbolized something dangerous, the communist "Red menace." Republican Senator Joseph McCarthy, a prominent Roman Catholic from Wisconsin who gathered power by smearing civil servants and others as communists or "homosexuals," was elected that year while the United States was waging a cold war with the Soviet Union in the name of eradicating communism. From the very beginning, the Red Mass included prescriptions on law and politics delivered from the pulpit. One of the first homilies, in 1954, when the hysteria of McCarthyism was at its peak, included a condemnation of "communist propaganda" in DC.[13]

The cathedral was also the site of the funeral mass for Rehnquist in 2005, even though he was raised Lutheran, and later the mass for Arne Panula, a powerful priest who led the US arm of a secretive society called Opus Dei. In 2001, before "google" became a verb, *Newsweek* named Justices Antonin Scalia (a Reagan appointee) and Clarence Thomas (a George H. W. Bush appointee) as members of Opus Dei, a right-wing personal "prelature" of the Catholic Church endorsed by Pope John Paul II. One of its long-standing objectives was getting its inner circle and allies into positions of political power. Its roots, as detailed by Gareth Gore in his 2024 book *Opus*, trace back to Josemaría Escrivá, a high-powered and zealous Spanish priest with deep ties to the Fascist regime of Francisco Franco. Escrivá was the ruthless dictator's spiritual advisor.

The Red Mass at St. Matthews is held every year on the day before the US Supreme Court's opening session, which is the first Monday in October. Supreme Court justices are invited to attend along with other bold-faced names from the political world, although not all of the justices do so. Pictured on the steps after the Red Mass that day, on October 2, 2005, were John and Jane Roberts. Also in attendance were Supreme Court Justices Scalia and Kennedy, both of whom were born into Catholicism and were followers of that faith.

Who else was there? Justice Thomas, who had attended private Catholic schools as a child and then Catholic colleges and who returned to that faith after his confirmation to the Court. Notably, billionaire Harlan Crow would later commission a seven-foot-tall bronze statue in tribute to Thomas's favorite teacher, Sister Mary Virgilius Reidy, among the many valuable gifts from his billionaire benefactors that Justice Thomas did not disclose to the public until pushed to do so. Also in attendance that day were other prominent figures from other faiths, including Justice Stephen Breyer, President George W. Bush, First Lady Laura Bush, Secretary of State Condoleezza Rice, and White House Chief of Staff Andy Card. John Roberts was photographed inside the event with his arm around Laura Ingraham, a former Thomas clerk and fellow Catholic who later became a FOX entertainment host known for defending Trump.

The Red Mass, "a Solemn Mass of the Holy Spirit," is sponsored by the John Carroll Society. The group is named for an enslaver who founded the Catholic Church in America, as well as Georgetown University, after the American Revolution. In addition to that sponsorship, the society also gives medals to "distinguished

Catholics in recognition of lifetime achievement, public service, outstanding leadership, and commitment to their faith." The list of recipients includes six Supreme Court appointees (and sometimes their spouses): Justice Thomas, Justice Scalia and Maureen Scalia, Justice Kennedy and Mary Kennedy, Justice Alito and Martha-Ann Alito, Chief Justice Rehnquist, and Chief Justice Warren Burger and Elvera Burger.[14]

Jane Sullivan Roberts, John Roberts's wife, is the historian of the John Carroll Society. That leadership role was previously held by Mary Ellen Bork, the wife of failed Supreme Court nominee Robert Bork. Jane Roberts apparently joined the society's board of governors after her husband's appointment to the Court. In 2009, she became the society's parliamentarian. In 2011, she was listed as its historian when it published a pamphlet with excerpts from past sermons, like this one from 1989 assailing abortion, divorce, and the US Supreme Court's legal precedents on the separation of church and state:

> This separation will necessarily lead to moral decay. Indeed, it already has, as evidenced by the number of abortions, divorces, and teenage pregnancies. Church and state should engage in a dialogue to rediscover those moral values founded on the Judeo-Christian tradition and on the natural law, specifically those values which defend the dignity and value of every human being, that are embodied in the Constitution.[15]

On October 3, 2005, the day after his first Red Mass as chief justice, John Roberts's formal investiture at the Court took place. Roberts—again wearing a red tie—took the official judicial oath to "faithfully and impartially discharge and perform all the duties incumbent upon [him] as Chief Justice under the Constitution and laws of the United States." Despite Roberts's sworn oath, he has broken those promises over and over as he has deployed his skillful partiality in rulings that demonstrate a superseding allegiance—a seeming omertà or secretive devotion—to the reactionary political objectives of the Reagan branch of the right-wing movement: to the lost causes that even a majority in Congress would not dare impose, like dismantling the landmark Voting Rights Act.

As chief justice, Roberts has also helped steer the Court to take up annual slates of political issues at the behest of right-wing groups fueled by Leonard Leo and his benefactors on the outside and aligned with Senator Mitch McConnell (R-KY) and others on the inside. (At one point, McConnell gave a speech to a chapter of Leo's Federalist Society, criticizing President Barack Obama for daring to pledge to appoint judges who have "empathy." McConnell objected to such compassion: "Well think about that for a minute. If you are the litigant for whom the judge does not have empathy that's not so good.") Under Roberts, the Supreme Court's hand-picked cases look more like a McConnell-style legislative agenda than the docket of a truly independent court. Indeed—despite Justice O'Connor's strong admonition that a "change in the law upon a ground no firmer than a change in our membership" makes the Court look like a political arm—just months after he was confirmed to the Supreme Court, Roberts took up a case to begin to change the law on abortion. It was one of his first acts as the chief: his first tell.[16]

CHAPTER 2

# CONCEPTION

IT TOOK LESS than five months from the beginning of his first term for John Roberts to take up the issue of abortion, but the decision to do so actually came only three weeks after the Court was fully staffed with nine members. Samuel Alito replaced Sandra Day O'Connor on January 31, 2006. Just twenty-one days later, the Roberts Court announced it would accept a petition in a case about banning late-term abortions, *Gonzales v. Carhart*. The Roberts Court took up that case even though less than six years earlier, the Supreme Court—with O'Connor in the majority of a 5–4 ruling—had found that such bans, like the one in Nebraska, violated people's constitutional rights, in a case called *Stenberg v. Carhart*.[1]

In *Gonzales*, the Roberts Court ruled 5–4 that such bans did *not* impose an undue burden, precisely the opposite conclusion reached by the Supreme Court when O'Connor was a justice. Even though Roberts and his supporters went to great lengths to convince the US Senate and the public at large that he would adhere to the principle of stare decisis and rule based on sound judicial principles, *Gonzales* showed that this was untrue. Understanding how the Court came to decide *Gonzales*, thus striking a serious although not lethal blow to *Roe v. Wade*, is essential to grasping how Roberts advanced his political agenda from the start of his tenure as chief justice.

Republicans had long sought to use the infrequent instances of late-term abortions—a medical procedure used when a woman's life is in grave danger or there are severe fetal defects—as a wedge issue to undermine reproductive rights. Their claim that parents and their doctors are murdering newborns is absurd, offensive, and outrageous. About a decade before the Roberts Court intervened in the so-called partial-birth abortion issue, President Bill Clinton twice vetoed such bans, surrounded by women whose lives and reproductive futures were saved by rare late-term abortions. But Republicans continued to rage about access to this procedure.

Antiabortion groups worked to get Nebraska and a few other states to adopt such bans, which the Supreme Court found unconstitutional in *Stenberg*. Then, after Republicans took back the US Senate in 2003, President George W. Bush signed a federal version of such a ban into law. The Roberts Court could have refused to hear the case because the lower federal courts had followed the Supreme Court's recent precedent in *Stenberg*, affirming *Roe*. But if Roberts and Alito treated the Supreme Court as political arm of the Republican Party, they could swing the tally *against* abortion access since Alito had replaced O'Connor, who had safeguarded that access.

O'Connor had been the key swing vote reaffirming *Roe*. That legal precedent limited the power of states to restrict access to abortion in the months before a pregnancy was viable. It also recognized the constitutional imperative to protect women from state restrictions in later stages of a pregnancy that threaten their life or health. O'Connor had protected *Roe*, even though the man who appointed her, Ronald Reagan, ran for the presidency in 1980 on a political platform that called for adopting a constitutional ban on abortion and overturning *Roe v. Wade*.

The Republican Party platform that Reagan ran on expressly pledged to "work for the appointment of judges at all levels of the judiciary who respect traditional family values and the sanctity of innocent human life." This plank of the platform, essentially an abortion litmus test, constituted an unusual politicization of the judicial appointment process. It was "the first time in a major party platform that such an express pledge has been made," and it provoked condemnation by the House of Delegates of the American Bar Association, the largest group of lawyers in the United States. It also reflected the party's intention to ban abortion from the moment of conception, a political doctrine that now goes by the phrase "fetal personhood." That formulation is an attempt to use the Constitution's Fourteenth Amendment to give an embryo or fetus equal rights to those of a woman, even though that constitutional amendment expressly provides that the privileges and immunities of citizenship accrue to those who are "born" here, not upon conception.[2]

As a judge sitting on the US Court of Appeals for the Third Circuit, Alito had dissented in a major case about abortion access just eighteen months after President George H. W. Bush appointed him to that post. Alito's dissent in that 1991 ruling by the Third Circuit argued that it was *not* an "undue burden" for the state of Pennsylvania to require that a husband be notified before a married woman could obtain an abortion—unless, for example, she invoked a statutory exception by certifying that he had raped her. Alito asserted that this notification requirement was consistent with the Constitution and that states have a legal "interest in furthering the husband's interest in the fetus" and "the fate of the fetus."[3]

In 1992, O'Connor spearheaded the Supreme Court's plurality decision in *Planned Parenthood v. Casey*, which reaffirmed *Roe* though modifying its analysis. Her ruling—coauthored with Justices David Souter and Anthony Kennedy—explicitly rejected the position Alito took. In contrast to Alito, they found that Pennsylvania's notification rule imposed a "substantial burden" on the exercise of a constitutional right by placing a "substantial obstacle in the path of a woman seeking an abortion before the fetus attains viability."

Unlike Alito, the majority of justices in that case honored the US District Court's factual findings that millions of American women are in abusive relationships whose perils do not fit the narrow statutory exceptions to the notice requirement permitted by the state. The majority of justices properly deferred to the lower court's factual findings that Pennsylvania's statutory exceptions from the notice requirement

> could not be invoked by a married woman whose husband, if notified, would, in her reasonable belief, threaten to (a) publicize her intent to have an abortion to family, friends or acquaintances; (b) retaliate against her in future child custody or divorce proceedings; (c) inflict psychological intimidation or emotional harm upon her, her children or other persons; (d) inflict bodily harm on other persons such as children, family members or other loved ones; or (e) use his control over finances to deprive [her] of necessary monies for herself or her children.

While Alito had disregarded such factual findings, the justices issuing the ruling against Pennsylvania had the empathy and wisdom to acknowledge that notice could unfairly impede women from exercising their constitutional right to abortion.

Two other Republican appointees, Justices John Paul Stevens and Harry Blackmun (who authored the *Roe v. Wade* decision), also voted against Pennsylvania's notification law and issued separate opinions. Chief Justice William Rehnquist—along with Justices Antonin Scalia, Clarence Thomas, and Byron White (a John F. Kennedy appointee)—dissented.

Souter, Kennedy, and O'Connor—the only woman who had been appointed to the Court at that point—declared, "Liberty finds no refuge in a jurisprudence of doubt. Yet 19 years after our holding that the Constitution protects a woman's right to terminate her pregnancy in its early stages, *Roe v. Wade*, 410 U. S. 113 (1973), that definition of liberty is still questioned. Joining the respondents as amicus curiae, the United States, as it has done in five other cases in the last decade, again asks us to overrule *Roe*."

Although this case was about a Pennsylvania abortion restriction, President George H. W. Bush's administration—representing the "official position" of the United States—involved itself by sending the solicitor general of the United States to support Pennsylvania. Shortly after Bush was inaugurated, he had nominated Kenneth Starr to be the solicitor general, the official who represents the federal government before the US Supreme Court. Upon his confirmation to that post, Starr resigned from his judgeship on the powerful US Court of Appeals for the DC Circuit—a position he had held since 1983, when Reagan nominated him to become a federal judge at the age of thirty-seven. Because he was appointed at such a young age, just six years after he completed a clerkship on the US Supreme Court, Starr had spent very little time as a lawyer, let alone as a litigator. Why would he step down from a judgeship? Serving as solicitor general could help burnish Starr's reputation by giving him experience arguing before the high court, filling out his résumé to help pave the way for a future nomination to the Supreme Court.

I had worked for Ken Starr as a summer associate at the DC offices of Kirkland & Ellis, where he landed after President George H. W. Bush's only term ended and Bill Clinton entered the White House. The talk of the firm that summer of 1993 was how Ruth Bader Ginsburg (a Clinton appointee) had taken the Supreme Court seat that should have been Starr's. Clinton chose her to replace Justice Byron White, the last Democratic appointee then on the Court and a conservative on most issues other than racial equality. As President Kennedy's deputy attorney general, White had moved to Alabama "to take charge of federal efforts to prevent violence against Freedom Riders," a legal campaign against racial segregation and discrimination that Attorney General Bobby Kennedy sent federal marshals to help protect. If Bush had won, White's seat could have gone to Starr, although Starr was not the only horse in the race, and some Bush officials thought he was "too malleable."[4]

When Justice William Brennan (a Dwight Eisenhower appointee) retired after suffering a stroke in 1990, Bush had passed over Starr and chosen David Souter, to the great disappointment of some hard-liners. Then, when the civil rights icon and first Black man appointed to the Court, Thurgood Marshall (an appointee of Lyndon B. Johnson), retired due to illnesses in 1991, Bush chose to replace him with Clarence Thomas, a forty-three-year-old Black man who had made a name for himself in the Reagan and Bush administrations as a critic of affirmative action.

A surprising but rarely acknowledged reality of the last half century is that almost 75 percent of US Supreme Court appointments were made by Republicans. In my lifetime, since 1967, only six justices have been appointed to the US Supreme Court by Democratic presidents, compared with sixteen by Republicans. Between President Johnson's appointment of Thurgood Marshall in 1967 and President Clinton's appointment of Ruth Bader Ginsburg in 1993, there was a stretch of twenty-five years with eleven Republican appointments to the nation's highest court in a row. The notion that liberals packed the Supreme Court is completely and utterly false. Republicans have dominated it and, in recent years, have refined a program to capture the Court to reverse our rights by handpicking young ideologues to advance their agenda from the bench.

During the 1992 presidential election, court watchers had been anticipating that two more seats could become vacant in the next presidential term due to the aging of the Court. Solicitor General Starr and Senator Orrin Hatch (R-UT) were said by some to be the top two contenders for the vacancies that Clinton instead got to fill. According to the word around Kirkland & Ellis in the summer of 1993, the only question had been which of them would get the first vacancy. That would prove to be Ginsburg, who was confirmed in 1993. Then, in 1994, Clinton nominated Stephen Breyer, the former counsel to Senator Ted Kennedy, when Harry Blackmun (a Richard Nixon appointee) stepped down. Blackmun was eighty-six when he retired.

Senator Hatch later wrote that he had brokered the deal between the Republican Senate caucus and Clinton to get Ginsburg and Breyer confirmed. They were well respected and they were older, sixty and fifty-six, respectively, and so likely to serve less than thirty years—a prediction that turned out to be accurate. With Thomas as the prototype, Republicans would, at the next opportunity, choose younger appointees who would have a longer-lasting impact.[5]

When I accepted that summer associate job in Kirkland's DC office, I knew it would be challenging for me because it was considered a Republican firm. Robert Bork had been a partner there. I had interviewed at big law firms all over the country, because public interest groups had proven to be more elitist than the private sector in response to my having worked my way through college clerking at small law firms and waiting tables. I had callbacks with prestigious white-shoe firms on Wall Street like Shearman & Sterling, but I had interviewed with only three law firms in DC because I was worried Bush would get reelected. During the interviews in the fall of 1992 at Kirkland's offices on 15th Street overlooking the White House, I was screened for political alignment. The interviewer asked if I had read Robert Bork's *The Tempting of America* about his failed nomination and his views on the law. I told him I had and that I had written notes all over the margins. He was so pleased. I did not tell him that I was glad Bork had failed or that many of my notes were on passages I had annotated as "B.S.!!" with double underscoring.

Even though I had voted for someone other than Clinton in the Democratic primary, when he won the election and brought an end to what I called the "Reagan-Reagan-Bush era," I leapt at the chance to work in DC. I accepted the offer from Kirkland because, I rationalized, if I was going to work at a corporate defense firm, I wanted to see firsthand how one of what I called the "big bads"—the most right-wing law firms in the country—operated. Since then, Kirkland has become one of the biggest, most lucrative law firms in the world.

I was nervous about passing as a conservative for a whole summer, and when I learned that Starr had joined the firm in the spring of 1993, I became even more concerned. The announcement arrived at my home in Ithaca, New York, during the spring of my second year of law school. It was printed on heavy cotton paper, and as I read it, my hands shook. That is because, as an avid court watcher, I knew the controversial positions Starr had taken as solicitor general in the Bush administration. They included defending regressive policies like the "gag rule," which barred federally funded nonprofit groups from using their own funds to provide abortion counseling, in a case called *Rust v. Sullivan*. I was active in the Cornell Women's Law Coalition and would later help lead it, as a passionate defender of women's reproductive rights.

In person, though, Starr was unfailingly polite to me, the law librarian, and the janitors—a quintessential politician. In the platonic sense, he was a "sweet-talking son of a preacher man," the son of a minister of the Church of Christ. The evangelical sect he grew up in demanded baptism for salvation and barred musical instruments, a little like the preacher in *Footloose*.

I ended up working with Starr on a potential case for the US Supreme Court that involved the application of a precedent he had argued in *United States v. Verdugo-Urquidez*, which had allowed evidence from a foreign search conducted without a warrant. Our meetings were always cordial. After one dinner party at his home in northern Virginia with the Thomas and Scalia clerks who had joined him at Kirkland, he showed me his library. It had a brag wall I later privately called the "wall of horrors." There were photos of Starr with Bork, Nixon, and other right-wing lawyers and, though I would not have recognized him then, probably John Roberts.

Despite Starr's good manners and warm hospitality, when he was later named independent counsel to probe a real estate deal involving the Clintons, I doubted that he would be a fair prosecutor to the man whose election effectively denied him a seat on America's highest court. Starr's conduct as independent counsel confirmed my suspicions; indeed, it is fair to say that he greatly exceeded my fears. Starr redirected the resources of the Office of Independent Counsel to pry into Clinton's sex life, and he allowed the probe to pursue rank conspiracy theories, prodded by one of his young associates, a lawyer named Brett Kavanaugh. Starr's salacious report led to the Republican-controlled House of Representatives adopting two articles of impeachment against Clinton: alleging perjury and obstruction of justice regarding his affairs, with a particular focus on the relationship he had with White House intern Monica Lewinsky. With Newt Gingrich (R-GA) as its leader, the House appointed thirteen impeachment managers, including Representatives Lindsey Graham (R-SC) and Bob Barr, to prosecute Clinton in the Senate trial, which Chief Justice William Rehnquist almost seemed gleeful to preside over. Several of the Republicans pursuing Clinton's impeachment, including Gingrich, had themselves had extramarital affairs with younger women, some of whom had worked for or with them. The politicization of the solemn impeachment process and the hypocrisy of so many of the Republicans pursuing what was largely a political smear campaign contributed to the failure of the Senate trial to convict Clinton on either count. Clinton served out his full second term as president until the Court's *Bush v. Gore* ruling swept George W. Bush into the White House.

When I first met Starr, I did not know of his ties to John Roberts or who Roberts was, but I later learned that Roberts was Starr's principal/political deputy in the Solicitor General's Office from October 1989 until January 1993. Roberts would later try to downplay his work for the Reagan and Bush administrations during the hearings on his nomination for the Supreme Court. He claimed that he was just "a staff lawyer" and "no one cared terribly much" what his personal views were but, despite that spin, his powerful posts were no ordinary jobs.

In the decades before Roberts was hired as the principal deputy, the US solicitor general had been considered "the tenth justice." That is, the solicitor general was not considered a political arm of the president but was generally counted on by the Supreme Court to weigh in on cases fairly and to make trustworthy legal arguments on behalf of the United States. The Justice Department had been especially mindful of its mandate to operate with independence from the White House in the years after Watergate and Nixon's efforts to weaponize the department to protect himself. Both Republican and Democratic administrations had embraced internal rules about who from the White House could speak with whom at the Justice Department, for example, to limit political interference in the administration of criminal and civil justice. The independence of the solicitor general as more adjunct to the Court than to the president was a treasured tradition, although of course the solicitor general represented the administration.[6]

As a practical matter this meant that the president did not fully control the solicitor general, whom the Court essentially entrusted with grounding its position in the law more than politics. President Reagan's first solicitor general, Rex Lee, argued dozens of cases before the Court. As solicitor general, Lee was regarded by many as an honest advocate. Justice O'Connor "recalled that when right-wing Reagan supporters blasted him for not adhering at all times to Reagan's policies, Lee replied, 'I'm the solicitor general, not the pamphleteer general.'" Lee's seeming independence led the Reagan administration to create a new top post in the Solicitor General's Office: the "political deputy," although the official title was principal deputy. That deputy's job, from its inception, was to ensure that the positions of the Solicitor General's Office reflected and advanced the administration's full "political agenda." The White House wanted to make sure a true believer was installed in that Justice Department office to fully advance its goals and the flavor of its politics. Tellingly, during the Reagan administration, when John Roberts decided to join the White House Counsel's Office to aid and advise President Reagan, he privately wrote to Judge Henry Friendly, the judge for whom he had clerked before Rehnquist, to report that he was "delighted [to] serve an Administration whose objectives I share."[7]

In 1989, Roberts was chosen to be the political deputy in the Solicitor General's Office of Reagan's successor, George H. W. Bush, specifically because he was trusted to fully advance an agenda he shared, unlike Rex Lee. Although Ken Starr later joked that Roberts purportedly kept his personal views close, Roberts's support for the right-wing agenda was well known to insiders: For example, when Roberts was later being considered for the Supreme Court, President George W. Bush's deputy counsel, David Leitch, told Karl Rove, Bush's top political advisor, that John Roberts was "not David Souter. He's going to be reliable" on the issues important to the GOP. (Roberts later appointed his friend Leitch to chair the Supreme Court Fellows Commission.)[8]

The Republican platform that Vice President George H. W. Bush ran on in 1988 echoed Reagan's platform in declaring that "the unborn child has a fundamental individual right to life which cannot be infringed." Sometimes planks in political platforms are merely hortatory or written as a salve for a particular constituency, but others are intended to be actualized by official policy, affecting budgets, bills, regulations, and litigation. For the Bush administration, with John Roberts as the political deputy in the Solicitor General's Office, that office's positions and claims demonstrated that advancing the antiabortion agenda was not just a platform; it was policy.[9]

Roberts was the man entrusted to implement that policy before the US Supreme Court, and he did not disappoint. For example, in the *Rust v. Sullivan* litigation over the gag rule, Roberts signed a brief arguing, "The Court's conclusions in *Roe* that there is a fundamental right to an abortion and that Government has no compelling interest in protecting prenatal human life throughout pregnancy find no support in the text, structure, or history of the Constitution."

When Roberts was confronted with this brief during the hearings on his nomination to the Supreme Court, he claimed that it was just "the position of the administration" and thus not necessarily his. He underscored that the Solicitor General's Office had taken the same position in four other briefs. O'Connor similarly noted in the *Casey* ruling that the Solicitor General's Office had repeatedly made that attack against *Roe*, and the Court rejected it. But because it was Ken Starr who presented the oral argument in favor of Pennsylvania's husband-notification provision, not Roberts, Roberts was able to distance himself from the case at his nomination hearing, presenting himself as just an attorney representing a client. He successfully deflected responsibility for his words and deeds as a savvy player in the right-wing political movement.

Notably, in *Casey*, Starr had argued to the Supreme Court that the government has a "compelling interest in the potential life, in fetal life, and that interest runs throughout pregnancy," that is, from conception. During the oral argument, Justice John Paul Stevens pressed Starr on that assertion, noting that there was no "textual basis in the Constitution" for that claim. Justice Scalia intervened in the argument by acknowledging that *Roe* had said that "the Constitution does not protect the fetus under the

Fourteenth Amendment," but, he prodded, *states* could do so, right? Starr agreed. Planned Parenthood's lawyer, Kathryn Kolbert, replied that accepting the solicitor general's position "would denigrate and restrict the ability of women at all stages of pregnancy to have an abortion" in states that adopted such restrictions. In *Casey*, the Court rejected the notion that states should have such power over women's medical decisions.[10]

---

The *Gonzales v. Carhart* case on so-called partial-birth abortion was John Roberts's opening salvo from the Court on the agenda to abrade *Roe*. Some in the Republican Party had been demanding for decades that *Roe* be overturned. As the new chief justice, Roberts not only took up the *Gonzales* case to overturn the lower courts and O'Connor's last ruling on abortion as soon as Alito replaced her. Roberts also scheduled the oral argument in the case on the day after the 2006 midterms, thereby guaranteeing that press coverage about the case would be part of the news cycle as Americans were voting. The false narrative around late-term abortions, despite the rarity of the procedure, is one of the political arguments Republicans have long thought of as one of the strongest in their arsenal against *Roe*. On April 17, 2007, the Roberts Court issued its 5–4 ruling overturning the *Stenberg* precedent, a ruling made possible only by a change in Court personnel.

Roberts's calculation appears political, reflecting his understanding that overruling *Roe* quickly and fully would satisfy some of the Republican base but could hurt the party's electoral prospects. Doing so would make it harder for the GOP to fundraise off of *Roe* and motivative get-out-the-vote efforts. A shrewd political operator would recognize that it could be risky for Republicans' political future to overrule such a popular legal precedent outright, to become "the dog that caught the car." Better for the GOP to have *Roe* to rally against than to incite voters to unite against the antiabortion movement. If Roberts could instead methodically grind down *Roe*, the Supreme Court could help avoid galvanizing opposition against the political party that opposes women's reproductive freedom, a freedom that a majority of Americans support.[11]

How could Roberts accomplish that?

It was surprisingly easy. That is because each year the nation's highest court handpicks almost all of the cases it wants to rule on. Antiabortion groups have developed a well-funded pipeline to deliver an array of options for the Court to choose from to change the law on abortion access. One of the underreported realities about the US Supreme Court is that its docket is almost entirely discretionary, a fact that should be reported *every* single time the Court takes a case or issues a ruling. Under our Constitution, the Supreme Court has mandatory jurisdiction only over litigation between the states and a few other types of cases that are relatively rare in modern times. Roberts had a hand in that too: In 1984, after his mentor, Justice Rehnquist, endorsed a bill to limit the Court's mandatory jurisdiction, Roberts helped sign off on that measure when he was Reagan's associate counsel.[12]

As a consequence, almost all of the cases that the nation's highest court hears are ones it chooses out of thousands of what are called "cert petitions." That is shorthand for writs of certiorari, which comes from the Latin phrase *certiorari volumus*, meaning for a thing to be made more certain. Four out of the nine justices are needed to "grant cert," which is short for agreeing to hear a case seeking judicial review; this is often called the "rule of four." Each year, between 8,000 and 9,000 cert petitions are filed with the Supreme Court, and under the Roberts Court only 60 to 80 are granted. That is, the Roberts Court hears fewer than 1 percent of the cases where its review is sought. Who votes for taking those cases is not published, although sometimes justices will dissent from the denial of cert, making their position visible. Or, years after a justice dies, handwritten notes about who voted for cert might become publicly accessible.[13]

The key point to remember is that the Roberts Court is not issuing rulings on issues because it *has* to. It is taking up cases on those issues because a majority of justices are all but certain that they have the votes to move the law in their desired direction, like legislators but without the check of facing another election. This discretionary process has historically been focused on resolving "circuit splits" where there is some disagreement among the thirteen federal appellate courts below the Supreme Court (that is, the eleven numbered circuits, plus the DC Circuit and what is known as the Federal Circuit, which has jurisdiction over certain cases, like patent cases). Groups can manufacture a circuit split by filing similar claims in different circuits.

With the Supreme Court's capture, the Court's discretion is being deployed to advance a highly developed agenda: What laws are at the top of the right-wing faction's priority list for this year? What cases are right-wing groups signaling to be important through amicus (or friend of the court) brief filings, which Senator Sheldon Whitehouse (D-RI) has described as a "flotilla" of dark-money groups? In turn, the Roberts Court has taken up cases on abortion, voting rights, and presidential immunity where it could have let lower-court rulings based on existing precedent stand. The pattern we are seeing of the Roberts Court inserting itself into so many controversies reveals how the Court's Republican appointees do not *want* American law—and culture—to remain as is. They were handpicked to overturn popular legislation and rules and to reverse key precedents of the twentieth and even twenty-first centuries, not to uphold or follow them.

On *Roe*, Roberts signaled his game plan for doing just that, at his confirmation hearings. When asked about the *Casey* decision—the one O'Connor wrote striking down the husband-notification requirement, in addition to other abortion restrictions—he repeatedly refused to disclose whether he agreed with that decision. Instead, he took refuge in assuring senators that he would follow the doctrine of stare decisis, repeatedly deploying that Latin phrase as a kind of incantation to lull senators into accepting the suggestion that he would follow legal precedents like *Roe*. Roberts used the term to suggest he would follow precedent, but while, on the surface, that Latin term of art means "to stand by things decided," the actual doctrine is more complex and provides an escape hatch to overturn precedents under purportedly narrow circumstances. Roberts used the phrase specifically to dodge many questions about *Casey*, which had reaffirmed *Roe* as binding precedent while providing a new way to calibrate a woman's constitutionally protected liberty interest in obtaining an abortion against a state's interest in a potential birth.

In *Roe*, Justice Blackmun—who for years had served as the resident counsel for the Mayo Clinic—had approached balancing the interests at stake in abortion access by using a trimester analysis, weighting the state's interest the highest when a fetus could survive outside the womb. *Casey* affirmed *Roe*'s recognition of the constitutional right to access abortion but recalibrated the standard for assessing the constitutionality of a restriction on whether it imposed an "undue burden" on a woman's rights and her ability to terminate a pregnancy.

In response to Senator Dianne Feinstein's question about whether the *Casey* ruling affirming the *Roe* decision was good precedent and remained workable, Roberts testified, "That determination in *Casey* becomes one of the precedents of the Court entitled to respect, like any other precedent of the Court, under principles of *stare decisis*. I have tried to draw the line about not agreeing or disagreeing with particular rulings, but that is a precedent of the Court." Roberts was agreeing only that the prior ruling was precedent, not that he *had* to follow it. Here Roberts was scrupulously following the advice he had given to Sandra Day O'Connor to use during her hearing in 1981, which was to "deflect senators' questions while appearing to answer them." Or, as he put it in a cover note to a document he drafted for the Reagan administration, to avoid taking a public position while appearing responsive: "Does it succeed in saying nothing at all?" Roberts went on to explain to the senators and people watching the hearings on his nomination to the Supreme Court, "Adherence to precedent promotes evenhandedness, promotes fairness, promotes stability and predictability. And those are very important values in a legal system. Those precedents become part of the rule of law that the judge must apply." Although that statement appears reassuring, he avoided making any promises to be bound by precedent.[14]

Roberts followed up with a well-phrased addendum, which really amounted to a take-back: "Stare decisis is not an inexorable command. If particular precedents have proven to be unworkable, they don't lead to predictable results, they're difficult to apply, that's one factor supporting reconsideration. If the bases of the precedents have been eroded . . . that's another basis for reconsidering the precedent. At the same time, you always have to take into account the settled expectations that have grown up around the prior precedent. *It is a jolt to the legal system to overrule a precedent*" (emphasis added). Just months after his confirmation, Roberts joined in the majority decision in *Gonzales v. Carhart*, which was designed to advance the antiabortion agenda incrementally, while avoiding a "jolt to the legal system." The tactic proved remarkably effective, as the decision received little critical attention outside activist circles and did not diminish in the least the reputation Roberts was constructing as a fair-minded institutionalist.

Roberts has used his two decades on the Court to pick away at the constitutional right to access abortion and other rights. He accomplished this through his favored value: persistence. Patience is a virtue Roberts deploys to accomplish his agenda when he seemingly judges that going slowly would yield the best results. But in other areas—like gutting the Voting Rights Act and concocting unprecedented immunity from criminal prosecution for Donald Trump—he has moved quickly, even recklessly, to secure his political agenda. Ultimately though, even with his considerable advocacy skills, Roberts could not bridle the base instincts of the other Republicans on the Court, and that resulted in the abrupt and complete undoing of *Roe* in 2022. Their edict prompted the very backlash he had worked to avoid. Republicans now have the right-wing Court they have lusted after for decades, but their triumph may contain the roots of their downfall.

PART II

# CAPTURE

## CHAPTER 3

# AMBITION

The roots of the disastrous, politically motivated decisions issued since John Roberts took the helm of the Supreme Court can be traced back to the Court's ruling in *Bush v. Gore* in 2000.

Even among the most cynical court watchers, no one really expected an act of judicial fiat by Republican-appointed judges to install a fellow Republican as president by intervening in the 2000 election and preventing Americans' votes from being recounted in Florida. Such an act was singular in US history, and it caused massive disruption, including putting a man in the White House who was easily swayed to start a ruinous war in Iraq, a war premised on lies. The Supreme Court's 5–4 partisan ruling made George W. Bush an incumbent and a wartime president in 2004, when he was legitimately elected for the first time rather than effectively installed by partisan Republicans on the nation's highest court. That electoral victory gave Bush not one but two vacancies on the Court to fill, and he filled them with staunch partisans.

As I watched the situation in Florida unfold, I held a career post in the US Department of Justice (DOJ). The initial reporting had basically declared Bush the winner, even though the initial tally indicated that he had won by less than 0.5 percent of the votes out of the millions cast by Americans living in Florida. That statistical reality in some counties triggered a recount under Florida law, which initially reduced his margin to just over 600 votes out of millions cast.

A Republican named Katherine Harris, who was both the Florida secretary of state and the cochair of Bush's state election campaign, had refused to waive a November 14 deadline for vote tallies despite the fact that the recount was ongoing in the state's most populous counties, in and near Miami. Harris, an antiabortion Christian evangelist, had earlier overseen the purge of more than 58,000 purportedly illegitimate voters, a maneuver with disproportionate and adverse effect on Black Floridians, who were likely Democratic voters. As the US Commission on Civil Rights later found, for example, "In Miami-Dade, more than 65 percent of the names on the purge list were African Americans, who represented only 20.4 percent of the population."[1]

Separately, there were also problems with how the names of candidates were listed in some "butterfly" ballots, which resulted in white Catholic nationalist Pat Buchanan, who was running for president under the Reform Party, getting a statistically improbable number of votes in Palm Beach County. That county had a large Jewish population of predominantly Democratic Party voters. Another third-party candidate, consumer advocate Ralph Nader, received more than 97,000 votes. Many Democrats blamed Nader for Bush's victory, but had any of these factors not been in play, Democratic nominee Al Gore would likely have won Florida with no recount at all.

As the battle over Katherine Harris's decree on the recount continued, lawyers from Washington, DC, aligned with both the Republican and Democratic parties, flew into Florida to aid the litigation. One of those lawyers was John Roberts, whose ambition was to get the best job and become a federal appellate judge and perhaps get seated on the Supreme Court like the man he had clerked for,

Justice William Rehnquist. Roberts helped Bush in the *Bush v. Gore* litigation, which in turn propelled his career ambitions. It gave him additional bona fides to be trusted with a precious and powerful judgeship. If George W. Bush were to win the White House in 2000, it seemed likely that Roberts would be on a path to get what he had long desired.

In 1988, Roberts had aided Bush's father in his electoral goals by providing "opposition research." Roberts was also on the Executive Committee of DC Lawyers for Bush-Quayle, which burnished his credentials to be named the political deputy solicitor general after that ticket won. Roberts was rewarded for his political loyalty again, in January 1992, when, as Bush began the primary season, he nominated Roberts to the prestigious US Court of Appeals for the DC Circuit, after Clarence Thomas's elevation to the Supreme Court created that new vacancy. His loyalty had paid off: Just thirteen years after graduating from law school, Roberts had the chance to follow in the footsteps of his mentor, Ken Starr, who joined the DC Circuit at the same age, thirty-seven.

During that presidential election year, in 1992, the chairman of the Senate Judiciary Committee, Joe Biden, moved eleven of Bush's circuit court nominees to a confirmation vote, but Roberts was not one of them. It is safe to assume that in 2000, he was hoping for an earlier nomination.

Who asked John Roberts to come to Florida to help?

During his 2005 nomination to the Supreme Court, Roberts told the Senate Judiciary Committee that in November 2000, Ben Ginsberg, the national counsel to the George W. Bush–Dick Cheney presidential campaign, asked him to help Bush fight the recount in Florida.

Ginsberg's deputy on the campaign was Ted Cruz, a Harvard Law School graduate who also clerked for Rehnquist on the Supreme Court (in the 1996–1997 term). Cruz then briefly joined Chuck Cooper and Mike Carvin at Cooper & Carvin, whose motto is "Victory or death." Cooper clerked for Rehnquist right before Roberts. (Cooper is known for defending California's Proposition 8, which banned marriage equality before such bans were later overturned.)

Cruz left that law firm in 1999 to join Bush's presidential campaign as a policy advisor. In November 2000, Ginsberg asked Cruz to help assemble the legal team for the Florida recount battle. Cruz later said his first call was to Carvin, a Republican lawyer who worked with Roberts in the Reagan administration. Cruz said his "second call was to a Washington lawyer named John Roberts. 'John had been a friend and a Rehnquist clerk—I've known John a long time,' Cruz said. 'Everyone we called, without exception, dropped everything and came down.'"[2]

Roberts was also enlisted to help with the recount by Dean Colson, with whom he had clerked for Rehnquist. A prominent personal injury lawyer in Miami, Colson recommended Roberts to Frank Jimenez, the acting general counsel of Florida Governor Jeb Bush. Roberts flew down to Tallahassee to meet them on his own dime, a small investment for the rewards to come. Roberts advised them on a governor's responsibilities under federal law if a presidential election is in dispute and on the "constitutional and statutory provisions" implicated by the recount.[3]

Who else was working with Cruz to recruit lawyers for Team Bush?

Leonard Leo.

Leo was then the director of the Federalist Society's lawyers division. He later told a history project that he had spoken "quite regularly" with the Bush campaign and become "very actively involved" in the fight against the Florida recount. Implying he was unpaid by that nonprofit, Leo said, "In fact, I took a brief leave from the Federalist Society, in order to help organize teams of lawyers to go to Florida. For the purpose of helping with canvassing and some of the challenges that were taking place there." He also said,

"Because of my work, at the Federalist Society, I knew a lot of people who . . . who would be willing to volunteer some time to do this kind of thing . . . which was really the sort of guts of the whole recount process." He also described how "on the media side of things, we . . . probably worked with . . . about a dozen key lawyers and scholars. And then for the litigation teams, it would be even fewer than that." (Other characters who were aiding Bush in other ways would become more famous later. For example, Roger Stone helped coordinate congressional staff shouting at election workers in what became known as the "Brooks Brothers Riot" because the agitators were well-dressed GOP operatives from DC. There is no sign that Roberts participated in those activities.)[4]

Which GOP players recruited which Republican loyalists for which tasks remains a little opaque, but at the end of the day, one thing is known for certain: As of early 2025, three of the six justices in the majority faction of the US Supreme Court—John Roberts, Brett Kavanaugh, and Amy Coney Barrett—all helped fight the recount and aid the litigation that resulted in *Bush v. Gore*, helping to make George W. Bush the forty-third president of the United States.[5]

What is also known is that Roberts helped prepare his old friend Mike Carvin for oral arguments before the Florida Supreme Court in Tallahassee. Roberts flew back to DC to argue a patent case on November 29, 2000, before reportedly returning to Tallahassee to continue helping Team Bush. When Roberts was later nominated to the US Supreme Court, "neither Governor Bush nor other Republicans involved in the recount would say . . . just what advice Judge Roberts, then a lawyer at Hogan & Hartson in Washington, shared."[6]

After hearing oral arguments from Carvin and others, on December 8, 2000, the Florida Supreme Court ordered a manual recount because the evidence showed that the vote-tabulation machines had not properly counted more than 60,000 ballots. The

Bush campaign appealed, and the very next day, five of the Republican appointees to the US Supreme Court issued a stay, temporarily stopping the recount until the Court could rule on it. Incredibly, in their order to halt the recount, that bare majority, led by Justice Antonin Scalia, claimed a recount would cast "a needless and unjustified cloud" over the legitimacy of Bush's win and cause him "irreparable harm." Two Republican appointees, Justices John Paul Stevens and David Souter, joined the Democratic appointees in dissent. As Stevens rightly noted, "Counting every legally cast vote cannot constitute irreparable harm" in a functioning representative democracy.

Two days later, the US Supreme Court held oral arguments in the case. The very next day, on December 12, 2000, the Court issued a 5–4 decision stopping the recount, effectively making Bush the president-elect. The result of that partisan edict was that Bush was declared the winner by 537 votes out of 5,963,110 votes counted, or 0.009 percent. In almost half the states, including Florida, a recount is automatically triggered if the margin is as close as 0.5 percent.

Many were shocked by the partisan nature of the Court's decree, but the next day Al Gore announced that he accepted "the finality of the outcome" though he disagreed with it. He had won the popular vote by more than 500,000 votes but, with no way to get the Florida votes recounted, he could not win the state's twenty-five Electoral College votes and become president.

A few days later, on December 17, President-Elect Bush announced he would nominate John Ashcroft to be attorney general. I was on the phone with Attorney General Janet Reno's chief of staff, the indefatigable Ann Harkins, when the news broke. We both gasped.

Ashcroft was antiabortion, held extreme views on gun laws, and had opposed the racial integration of schools. He had even orchestrated a racist dog whistle campaign to tank President Bill Clinton's nominee to the US District Court in Missouri—Ronnie White, the first Black American to serve on the Missouri Supreme Court—by smearing him as "pro-criminal." I remember walking Reno out of the building on the evening of January 19, with my beloved mentor, Eldie Acheson, who had served as assistant attorney general in the Office of Policy Development / Legal Policy for both of Clinton's terms. That was their last day. At noon the following day, Bush was sworn in as president. The next day I returned to a very different DOJ, with all the Clinton political appointees on the fifth floor above me gone. As a career deputy assistant attorney general, I was now tasked with aiding in the "orderly transition" of government.

One of the first people I met from the incoming team after the inauguration was Ted Cruz. Since he was then only thirty and had barely practiced law, his reward was not a judgeship but a plum job as associate deputy attorney general. Some of the career attorneys still left at the main Justice building were Republican operatives who had burrowed in and got very busy churning out new memos on how Bush should dismantle key policies. Some of the new political appointees had come into DOJ with printouts of the Heritage Foundation's 2000 Mandate for Leadership, a predecessor of Project 2025. The 2000 blueprint was filled with changes that the right-wing group, launched by Christian nationalist Paul Weyrich, wanted implemented pronto.

In 2001, when a friend asked what it was like seeing the fox guard the henhouse, that analogy gave me pause. I replied then what I still believe: It was more like putting termites in charge of a treehouse, because they were intent on dismantling progressive advances piece by piece from the inside out—at least with a fox, you still had a henhouse at the end of the day. (But that was just a prelude to the destruction of Justice Department ideals by Trump 2.0 appointees.)

I suspect that Cruz assumed I was a Republican because I was still working in DOJ's policy office. He would come to my office to probe for intel, such as asking whom he should trust. I found his hunger for power repellant. I was tasked with briefing him on gun policy and judicial nominations. One day, after I walked down the hall to his office overlooking Constitution Avenue to bring him a file he had requested, a glass paperweight sparkling in the afternoon sun caught my eye. I took a closer look at the object on a side table while he was on the phone and was shocked to see that it said "Bush-Cheney Florida Recount Team 2000" and that the sparkling bits were chads—those little pieces of paper scooped up off the floor after some Florida voters used a small punch to puncture the ballot next to their choice for president and other offices. Republicans tried to disqualify ballots where the chad was still "hanging" and had not torn fully away from the perforations in the ballot. It was jarring and enraging to see that paperweight celebrating what, in my view, was the partisan theft of that election. I immediately turned and left Cruz's office, although there are days when I regret not throwing it out the window.

Instead, I left DOJ in May 2001, just as John Roberts was being repaid with a nomination to a far more powerful job than Cruz had won. Within a few months after Roberts assisted the Bush family with the recount, President Bush chose to reward him with a nomination for the judgeship on the DC Circuit that he had wanted for so long. Bush had moved quickly on Roberts's nomination and ten others, announcing them on May 9, 2001. The elder Bush's administration had managed to vet and propose only eight circuit nominees in his entire first year in office—the first new judicial nominee who was not a renominated Reagan pick came in August 1989. Though Roberts had been nominated by Bush's father nearly a decade earlier, a new nomination required new forms, including an updated FBI background check form and a new Senate Judiciary Committee questionnaire.

In early 2001, the Bush administration had removed the American Bar Association (ABA) from its role in the evaluation process prior to nomination, which it turns out was partly Leonard Leo's doing. After Leo helped Clarence Thomas get confirmed to the US Supreme Court in 1991, despite Anita Hill's testimony about his repulsive conduct—including asking her if there was a pubic hair on his can of Coke, which he denied—Leo was hired by the Federalist Society, reportedly as its first paid employee. That group had been created almost a decade earlier, in 1982, as a pipeline to power for "conservative and libertarian" law students. It held its first conference shortly before President Reagan nominated Antonin Scalia to the US Court of Appeals for the DC Circuit. Scalia helped launch the group by getting it a $20,000 grant to fund recruitment.

One of Leo's main roles as a Federalist Society employee was recruiting lawyers to organize city and state Federalist Society groups, building on its presence at law schools. Leo's other role back then—before he became the "moneybags" man for the Federalist Society—was running an attack operation called "ABA Watch." Through that program, Leo targeted the nation's largest bar association, whose members included thousands of corporate lawyers, for supposedly being too liberal. The ABA had given Thomas a mere "Q," or qualified rating, for the Supreme Court. The ABA had issued that rating because Thomas had only been a judge for seventeen months before being tapped for the nation's top court, and he had no experience arguing cases before the Supreme Court (the ABA's rating was finalized before Anita Hill's testimony about Thomas).[7]

Few people know that, in 2001, the Bush administration outsourced part of the evaluation process for potential federal judges not to a politically neutral group like the ABA but to the right-wing Federalist Society. This was years before Donald Trump announced that he had asked Leonard Leo and the Federalist Society to create the list of potential Supreme Court nominees. Back in 2001, Federalist Society leadership had asked some potential judicial candidates if they had voted for Bush in 2000 and told them that, if they had not, their names would not go forward.

The Federalist Society did not have to ask John Roberts whom he had backed in the 2000 election. He had already taken Bush's side in the recount litigation. They did not have to ask him anything at all. Leonard Leo and other right-wing insiders already knew he was a sure bet on the big things they wanted to change by judicial fiat, through the plan to capture the Supreme Court.

CHAPTER 4

# OLD MONEY

John Roberts is the real successor—and first success—of the "No more Souters" campaign to transform the US Supreme Court. Its goal was not just to accomplish the "Reagan Revolution." Its objective was to manifest judicial rulings hostile to the civil rights, women's rights, environmental movements, and legal precedents that democratized America and made the Constitution's promises of freedom and equality more real than rhetorical. Therefore, it should come as no surprise that Roberts—whose ascendancy marked the triumph of the "No more Souters" mantra—is also the first beneficiary of the twenty-first-century political machine funded to pack the Supreme Court with right-wing operatives. Here is what I witnessed as Roberts was being promoted to be cloaked in judicial robes.

On May 9, 2001, President George W. Bush announced his first slate of federal judicial nominees, and John Roberts was on the list. At a White House event, Bush announced his first eleven circuit court candidates. Of course, they were all beaming, including Roberts with his standard red tie. Bush and his allies, such as Federalist Society leaders, expected these nominees to be speedily confirmed by the Republican-controlled US Senate. For some of the May 9 candidates, the objective was to get them some experience as federal judges—to briefly kiss the bench—so they could be in the running for the potential Supreme Court vacancies that court watchers were predicting Bill Clinton's successor would have the opportunity to fill.

But, in a surprising turn of events, Senator Jim Jeffords of Vermont threw a wrench into those plans. He decided to leave the Republican Party, become an Independent, and caucus with the Democrats. Jeffords made that announcement on May 24, 2001, just two weeks after John Roberts was nominated, effectively disrupting Roberts's trajectory toward the federal bench. A month later, on June 24, 2001, in what now seems like a backup plan in case the most prized of those initial nominees did not get confirmed to the circuit court in time, White House Counsel Alberto Gonzales interviewed judge Samuel Alito for a potential Supreme Court seat.

Jeffords's move also had the effect of allowing me to assist in gumming up the works.

As a career appointee at the DOJ, I could have stayed in the George W. Bush administration and worked with its political appointees, like Ted Cruz, but I had no desire to help them appear more reasonable than they were. In early May 2001, I left my post as deputy assistant attorney general and went to work as a leader in the federal court system. My new office was in the light-filled Thurgood Marshall Federal Judiciary Building, near Union Station. The job offered more pay and a slower pace. The work included aiding anticorruption initiatives in addition to overseeing the staff of the Financial Disclosure Office, which reviews annual disclosure reports required of Supreme Court justices and the rest of the federal judiciary. It was there that I first learned how, as chief justice, Bill Rehnquist stacked the most powerful or plum committees in the federal court system with his favored Republican judicial appointees.

Meanwhile, I focused my efforts on the legitimate oversight of federal judges, for example, by objecting to my boss, the amazing Mike Dolan, about the slow-walking of public requests to review judges' financial disclosures. One particularly egregious situation emerged when a lower-level manager suggested that requesters, like Doug Kendall's Community Rights Counsel, only be allowed to view the forms while sitting in an actual closet, which contained a chair and a small table with an uneven leg. I was making good trouble, but by the fall of 2001, I knew the oxygen was too thin for me to continue working in what I came to call "the adminisphere."

In a joyous turn of fate, I got a call that autumn from the office of Senator Patrick Leahy. My beloved mentor from DOJ, Eldie Acheson, had recommended me to lead the team Leahy needed on deck as the new chair of the Senate Judiciary Committee. The Judiciary Committee was charged with evaluating federal judicial nominees and determining whether to recommend them for confirmation, as part of the Constitution's "advice and consent" process. When I met with Senator Leahy's chief of staff, the dry-humored Luke Albee, and his chief counsel, the intense but witty Bruce Cohen, I made clear that I wanted to help keep unfair judicial candidates off the bench. I said I was not going to just process paper but wanted to be able to make the case for blocking the worst of Bush's nominees. We were on the same page. When I got the offer to become the chief counsel for nominations, I told my husband, Don, "It's more hours, more stress, and less pay—what do you think?" He replied, "When do you start?"

My first task after I arrived at my new office in the Dirksen Senate Office Building was to work closely with two women who were deeply devoted to our mission rather than to their own self-promotion. I feel so lucky that I got to work with the talented, kind, and passionate lawyers Kristine Lucius and Leesa Klepper, who would go on to become chief counsel to Senator Leahy and chief of staff to Representative Jamie Raskin (D-MD), respectively.

On becoming the chief counsel for nominations, I also inherited help from Andra Roy, a great law clerk who hailed from Louisiana, along with a few other part-time staffers.

My main task was to make a plan for the memos and draft statements we needed to get written or updated on whether a particular Bush nominee could be entrusted with a lifetime job as a federal judge whose rulings could have profound effects on people's lives. Those memos helped make the case about the nominees to the Democratic members of the committee and to the Democratic Caucus. As the leader of the team, I took up a new review of the background of John Roberts (forty-six years old) and Miguel Estrada (thirty-seven years old), another May 9 nominee to the DC Circuit, and we divided up the other three dozen pending judicial nominees.

By January 2002, when I wrapped up my transition from the judicial branch, the Senate had already confirmed twenty-eight of Bush's federal court nominees, including two uncontroversial May 9 candidates: Roger Gregory and Barrington Parker, the two Black men Bush nominated that day to the federal appellate courts. I knew Gregory's background from before, when President Clinton had nominated him in 2000. After the *Bush v. Gore* decision, we conferred with the White House Counsel's Office about whether Gregory would get a rare "recess appointment" (an appointment made when the Senate was not in session) to temporarily place him on the bench. In late December 2000, Clinton put Gregory on the US Court of Appeals for the Fourth Circuit in Richmond, Virginia, the former capital of the Confederacy. Gregory was the first Black person ever to sit as a judge on that court, which includes Virginia, North Carolina, South Carolina, West Virginia, and Maryland. All but West Virginia have large Black populations and are former slave states. The Mason–Dixon Line forms Maryland's northern border, and that is the very line that Harriet Tubman had to brave repeatedly to bring enslaved people to freedom. That history and those optics made it hard for Bush to displace Gregory.

Judge Parker had been appointed to the district court by Clinton, too, and the calculus seemed to be that Bush would never get "blue slips" for a hard-right nominee to a seat based in Connecticut on the Second Circuit. Not returning a blue slip allows a home-state senator to veto a nominee by withholding consent, which stalls their nomination. It is a controversial tradition that Democratic leaders follow, while Republicans disregard such rules when it suits them.

By putting forward two nominees backed by Democrats, Bush could sell the press on the May 9 slate as a bipartisan package. That gave cover for right-wing operatives like John Roberts and Miguel Estrada to be named to seats the GOP had been keeping open on the DC Circuit.

I knew these seats well, and one of my last acts at DOJ was to brief Attorney General John Ashcroft about the vacancies in the federal judiciary. As of May 1, 2001, the Bush administration had 100 seats available to fill: 31 in the circuit courts and 69 in the district courts. I will never forget preparing the binder to brief Ashcroft on the vacancies and on the Justice Department's institutional relationship with the federal judiciary as well as other matters like the US Marshal Service's role in providing security for Supreme Court justices. It had ten tabs with bullet points for each major issue, along with background information and any memoranda of understanding between the federal branches of government or executive branch components. When I had sent similar binders to Attorney General Janet Reno, she had asked well-informed questions about their contents. I had assumed Ashcroft would have a similar approach to materials needed to prepare for his first meeting with the Judicial Conference. I was surprised when the binder was returned to me, apparently unread, with the comment that it was "too long."

In contrast to my experience with Reno, I was directed to eliminate the attachments and reformat the material. As a result, the contents were reduced to about ten double-spaced paragraphs in eighteen-point Times New Roman font, which amounted to ten pieces of paper, plus the vacancy data. When I met with Ashcroft to brief him, I recall that he gestured toward the slender eighth-of-an-inch-thick set of stapled pages and drawled, "Do I get extra credit for readin' all of this?" Shocked, I swallowed hard and remember saying it was "the bare minimum" he needed to know "as the head" of a huge agency about its relationship with "another branch of government," as I thought to myself, "Holy cats, this guy cannot really be in charge of making decisions on complex issues like our national security." (This was just five months before 9/11.)

When we later met with the Judicial Conference, one of the chief judges who had been appointed by a Republican president practically bowed while telling Ashcroft he was so happy his cabinet nomination had been confirmed. Ashcroft—who, like Ken Starr, was the son of a Pentecostal preacher—leaned back in his chair and flashed a grin at me and the judges around his conference table. I remember him saying, "After I got confirmed, some Senators told me, 'John, you have a clean slate'—so whether it's the Senate [pause] or the Savior [pause] who wipes my slate clean is fiiiine byyyy meeee," to the laughter of some of the judges there. I noted to myself, with appreciation, that the savior never came up at any of Reno's Justice Department meetings.

Because I was the staff leader of Eldie's nominations team and regularly attended meetings in the White House Counsel's Office with her, I knew well how the Republicans had been trying to keep the DC Circuit seats open—for years—so they could be filled by up-and-comers devoted to the GOP's legal agenda. As a result, three vacancies on that court awaited Bush, including one that Republicans had blocked from being filled since 1996, throughout Clinton's entire second term.

So, when I got to the Senate Judiciary Committee, I focused on the two DC Circuit nominees, Roberts and Estrada, knowing that serving on that court was considered the most important Republican way station to being nominated to the US Supreme Court.

Clarence Thomas's path to becoming an associate justice established the playbook: Choose young men who had been installed to sit briefly on DC Circuit so they could look judicial while having little time to issue a ruling in a controversial case. By 2001, the front runners from 1992 were out of contention. Senator Orrin Hatch, at sixty-seven, was too old, and Ken Starr had sacrificed his shot when he took on trying to take down President Clinton. Although President Bush had plenty of sitting circuit court judges to choose from for a potential Supreme Court vacancy after twelve years of Reagan-Reagan-Bush appointments, most of them were too old to hit the sweet spot of the Republican strategy: Outlast Democratic appointees by selecting candidates for the Supreme Court who could hold power for four full decades or more—ten times the length of a presidential term. They were looking for people who could be stealth candidates, unlike Robert Bork, and partisan loyalists, unlike David Souter. By this measure, John G. Roberts Jr. was the perfect nominee.[1]

Working with Senator Leahy's longtime chief counsel, Bruce Cohen, the Judiciary Committee Democrats mapped out a strategy for blocking Bush's worst judicial candidates on the circuit courts while moving as many district court judges as possible to confirmation. It was challenging to let almost all of the trial-level judges go through no matter their backgrounds, like Terry McVerry, an antiabortion activist who handled the money for the political campaigns of Senator Rick Santorum (R-PA). However, our strategy was to focus on the biggest threats, which were the circuit court candidates who were potential Supreme Court nominees. For the circuit courts, we would pace the confirmations of the less controversial nominees to an average of about one confirmation a month, and we would hold the others off for as long as possible. As a practical matter that meant we were definitely not going to schedule a vote on

Roberts or Estrada in 2002. Meanwhile, we had to prepare memos documenting any concerns and help senators counter the pressure campaigns that the White House and its allies were orchestrating.

The pacing that Chairman Leahy set infuriated the Republicans. They did not want just some of their judicial nominees confirmed; they wanted them *all*—especially their top picks from May 2001. As the clock ticked toward a potential Supreme Court vacancy, with William Rehnquist in ill health and with their potential ringers stalled, the Bush team launched an intensive PR campaign to push for the confirmation of Roberts and the others, attacking us for delay. Even though the Democratic-controlled Senate had confirmed numerous Bush judicial nominees, it had not approved the nominees the Republicans wanted most. The White House pushed editorial board members—like Ben Wittes, whose op-eds read like White House stenography, in my opinion—along with reporters to assail Democrats and my boss for not giving Roberts and Estrada a vote. It was a near-constant refrain, but we were unmoved.

So, they tried to move us in a new way: by deploying a dark-money pressure group. They named it the Committee for Justice, and getting John Roberts confirmed was its top priority.

---

The Committee for Justice was launched by Clayland Boyden Gray, the former White House counsel for President George H. W. Bush. (He publicly went by C. Boyden Gray, but I will refer to him as "Boyden" below to make it easier to follow the twists ahead.) Boyden was most widely known for orchestrating the confirmation of Clarence Thomas to the Court. Bush and his closest advisors were counting on Democrats being fearful of being called racist if they opposed Thomas for his limited experience and his controversial record. Boyden helped get Thomas confirmed even after Anita Hill testified that Thomas had made repulsive sexual overtures toward her when he was her boss and mentor, which Thomas denied. With Senator Hatch and other Republicans attacking Hill's credibility, Boyden helped secure a winning 52–48 vote to confirm Thomas. His confirmation was also aided by a then-little-known group called Citizens United, which launched expensive media campaigns to push for Thomas's confirmation, before and after Hill testified.[2]

Boyden had been counsel to George H. W. Bush since Bush was Reagan's vice president. He became the White House counsel after the 1988 election. I first heard of Boyden around Thomas's nomination, but I first encountered his handiwork when he deployed Alex Acosta to attack Clinton's judicial nominees through the Ethics and Public Policy Center (EPPC).

In the late 1990s, Alex Acosta had become the director of EPPC's "Project on the Judiciary," which was steered by Boyden. Acosta had clerked for Judge Alito on the Third Circuit and helped on *Bush v. Gore*. He was rewarded with a post as deputy assistant attorney general for the Civil Rights Division in the George W. Bush administration, where he and his fellow political appointees undermined the enforcement of voting rights. Acosta's performance got him promoted to be assistant attorney general for the Civil Rights Division, even though he had little actual experience litigating any cases, let alone litigation to protect civil rights. He fell upward from there, becoming the US attorney for the Southern District of Florida, even though he had no actual prosecutorial experience. A few years into the job of top federal prosecutor for South Florida, Acosta cut a stunningly lenient plea deal with none other than Jeffrey Epstein, the sex trafficker who procured young girls and women to have sex with some of his famous friends.

From 1998 to 2000, while I was working with colleagues at the Justice Department and White House to get judicial candidates nominated and confirmed, Acosta was using his position at EPPC to praise Senate Republicans for blocking Clinton's judicial nominees. During that period, more than sixty judicial nominees never got a vote by the Republican-controlled Senate. That did not stop Republicans a few years later from making withering attacks on Democrats for not confirming all of Bush's nominees. Who penned op-eds and spoke out against "judicial activism" for EPPC's special project? It was Acosta's benefactor: C. Boyden Gray.[3]

Boyden died in 2023, at the age of eighty, having helped make the US Supreme Court much worse. He was one of the early white Southern Democrats to cross the line to become a Republican, joining the party of Lincoln that racist Southerners had previously disdained. His stated reason for leaving was his dislike for President Jimmy Carter's economic policies. Carter was a fiscal moderate and the last resistance before Ronald Reagan's reckless tax cuts, which did not actually "trickle-down," took hold. That made sense, because Boyden was very, very rich.

How rich? His grandfather's home, Graylin, was the second-largest house in North Carolina, right behind billionaire George Vanderbilt's Biltmore, the Gilded Age château-style mansion near Asheville, which has the honor of being the biggest. Boyden's grandfather, Bowman Gray, had been the president of R. J. Reynolds (RJR), America's biggest tobacco company, whose most famous cancer-causing product is Camel cigarettes and whose vape pens have kid-friendly flavors like "apple sour." Both his parents were born into RJR tobacco money.

Boyden's family history was surprising in ways that were not covered by numerous media stories mentioning him and his well-heeled roots. I was startled to discover that the big prenuptial party for his parents—Gordon Gray and Jane Henderson Boyden Craige—featured their hosts in Nazi uniforms greeting guests with "Heil Hitler" salutes, sporting Adolf Hitler mustaches, and wearing signs that read "I want to dictate to_______." The party's festive theme was "Come as your suppressed desire." In light of subsequent history, dressing as Nazis does not seem particularly festive, and it is difficult to believe that it was any more appropriate in the spring of 1938. The party for Boyden's parents-to-be came just weeks after Hitler had invaded Austria and as Nazi Germany had already adopted laws that required Jewish residents to register with the government. The story about that dance party for Gordon Gray and his betrothed, at the exclusive all-white country club—along with photos of the Nazi costumes and other attire—was featured contemporaneously in the *Winston-Salem Journal and Sentinel.* Who was the publisher and president of that paper? None other than Gordon Gray himself, so it was no accident that the Nazi-themed party for himself and his bride was consciously and shamelessly highlighted.[4]

After the United States entered the war to fight German fascism, Boyden's father volunteered for the US Army in 1942 and was quickly promoted to assistant secretary of the army. Whatever his deeply held views, he clearly wanted to be a member of the winning team. Gordon Gray still held that post in 1948 when President Harry S. Truman aligned with the National Association for the Advancement of Colored People (NAACP) and banned racial segregation in the military. President Truman attested, "My forebears were Confederates . . . but my very stomach turned over when I had learned that Negro soldiers, just back from overseas, were being dumped out of Army trucks in Mississippi and beaten." After the plain-spoken Missourian bested Southerner Strom Thurmond's segregationist "Dixiecrat" bid for the White House, Truman named Gordon Gray secretary of the army after Gray's predecessor slow-walked Truman's order to racially integrate the armed services—perhaps not grasping Gray's devotions.[5]

Gordon Gray's tenure, though short, was marked by his 1950 order to the US Military Academy at West Point to celebrate General Robert E. Lee, the commander of the Confederate army during the Civil War. Boyden's father dictated that West Point feature a portrait of Lee "wearing Confederate gray at the 'height of his fame' [which] reflected the secretary's resistance to Truman's desegregation order," according to historian Ty Seidule, a retired brigadier general. Gray asserted that featuring Lee's portrait would end "sectional" divides, but the symbolism was obviously the opposite: "Gray couldn't stop integration but he could highlight Lee" in the military's most hallowed halls, Seidule noted. As Brent Staples wrote in a piece about West Point finally removing Lee's portrait in 2023, "Men who nearly destroyed the country in defense of the right to own human beings are unworthy of federal veneration." The twenty-foot-tall portrait of Lee—replete with a Black man following Lee with his war horse, Traveller—had glowered over cadets for more than seventy years, directly as a result of Boyden's father.[6]

That was not Boyden's only forebear who venerated the Confederacy. One of his matrilineal forefathers, the towering former Representative Francis Burton Craige, whom Boyden resembled, was so central to defending Black slavery that he filed the insurrectionist ordinance to repeal North Carolina's ratification of the US Constitution. It was Craige's son and namesake who in 1910 would become counsel to Richard Joshua (R. J.) Reynolds, who used his part of his family's wealth—built on forcing enslaved Blacks to work in tobacco fields—to create a company in 1875 that made its first fortune with saccharine-infused chewing tobacco.

Another aspect of Gordon Gray's legacy was the use of the Gray Commission to revoke the security clearance of Robert Oppenheimer, the theoretical physicist who ran the Manhattan Project. The 1954 ruling of Gordon Gray's kangaroo court, which destroyed Oppenheimer's reputation, was finally vacated in 2022 due to its manifest "bias and unfairness." (Gray's poisonous star chamber was depicted in the Academy Award–winning 2023 film *Oppenheimer.*) In 1954, after the US Supreme Court's landmark unanimous decision in *Brown v. Board of Education of Topeka*, which ruled that public schools could not engage in racial segregation, Boyden's father publicly supported a completely private university system over a public one because, in his words, a private university would provide "a greater safeguard of the things for which we live." At the time, Gray was the president of the University of North Carolina (UNC).[7]

The year after *Brown*, federal courts ordered the admission of Black students to UNC and other public universities. That year, 1955, Gordon Gray left his post helming UNC and focused on his work at the Defense Department under Republican President Dwight D. Eisenhower. In January 1961, Eisenhower gave Gray, by then his national security advisor, the Presidential Medal of Freedom. That honorary medal cannot erase Gray's fuller history.

While the sins of the father are not the son's, Boyden's family background informed the path of the man who helped put regressive figures like Clarence Thomas into positions of power over others—people who have used their power to roll back the hard-won gains of the civil rights movement. Making John Roberts the chief justice of the United States, for example, put him in a position to undermine the enforcement of the landmark Voting Rights Act. In some ways, the insider press in Washington, DC, gave Boyden impunity by portraying the Republican strategist as a kind of local celebrity who hosted fabulous parties at his yellow mansion in Georgetown, where dirty jokes and juicy gossip were said to be traded. He was sometimes described as a wealthy heir devoted to public service, though the reporting rarely explained that his central devotion was to capturing the federal judiciary in order to overturn legal precedents that he and his regressive cadre disliked. Meanwhile, it was Boyden who worked with billionaire Charles Koch's political advocacy group, Americans for Prosperity, and its predecessor, Citizens for a Sound Economy, to oppose indoor-smoking rules and more—true to the source of some of his wealth. Boyden also nurtured Leonard Leo's quest for power: They were so close that when Leo seemingly became very rich while Brett Kavanaugh's nomination to the Supreme Court was pending, Leo bought a mansion in a tiny town in Maine—population

398—where he had vacationed with Boyden, whose family's summer "cottage" is nearby.

Boyden's wealth was truly generational. His patrilineal grandfather, Bowman Gray, had led Wachovia Bank—which Bowman's father, Alexander Gray, had helped create—before taking over R. J. Reynolds Tobacco and becoming the company's first leader who was not a Reynolds. After his sudden death in 1935, Bowman's brother James Alexander Gray took over RJR and led it into the 1960s as it fought the Food and Drug Administration's efforts to put health warnings on cigarette packaging. Meanwhile, Boyden's father, Gordon Gray, used a portion of that fortune to launch what became known as Summit Communications, a media empire said to be worth $500 million in 1989. When Boyden became White House counsel, he was compelled to disclose, for the first time, that aside from drawing a salary from taxpayers, he was a trustee of that company—and he refused to use blind trusts to avoid conflicts of interest.

The story of that recalcitrance came out just months before Boyden helped put the forty-one-year-old Clarence Thomas on the DC Circuit after Robert Bork resigned. That is the same seat to which John Roberts was first nominated after Boyden helped get Thomas confirmed to Thurgood Marshall's seat on the Supreme Court. It was a stroke of both luck and strategy for Boyden to find a Black man so willing to undo the gains that Marshall had fought for as the director of the NAACP's Legal Defense and Education Fund. In 1965, after signing the landmark Voting Rights Act into law in August, President Lyndon Baines Johnson had named Marshall the solicitor general of the United States and then, in 1967, appointed him to the Supreme Court. Marshall served there for twenty-four years, until 1991. Since then, Boyden's pick to replace him on the Supreme Court has spent more than three decades working to undo Marshall's legacy.

Boyden was lauded by the Right for Thomas's appointment in 1991, but he later came to regret accepting the advice of White House Chief of Staff John Sununu to support David Souter for the Supreme Court the year before, in 1990. Unlike Thomas, Souter did not deliver the political results against civil rights, abortion, and other matters that the right-wing wanted from the Supreme Court. Later, Boyden seemed determined to make up for the Souter appointment by helping to make sure Bush's son secured confirmation of judges hostile to voting rights, like Roberts, to the lower courts to get them in place for the Supreme Court vacancies that Republicans were eagerly awaiting. Boyden oversaw Roberts's unsuccessful nomination to Thomas's DC Circuit seat back in 1992, and he backed Roberts again when George W. Bush nominated him to the DC Circuit in 2001.

Boyden's generational wealth was vast, and the roots of his hostility toward civil rights and progressive ideas ran deep. However genteel and sociable Boyden may have been to his friends, he received astonishingly little critical coverage despite his enormous influence over the trajectory of our laws. He was an insider's insider, whose inherited wealth made his access to power seem natural or even inevitable while his ambitions for such influence were deeply reactionary. You actually see that a lot in Washington: well-dressed men in tailored suits and fine leather shoes who look almost like bankers, but their currency is power. The confirmations of John Roberts, Samuel Alito, and Clarence Thomas to the Supreme Court were big victories that demonstrated Boyden's power, although they constitute lasting losses for most Americans.

CHAPTER 5

# DIRTY TRICKS

I WAS NOT surprised when I learned Boyden Gray launched the Committee for Justice in 2002 to help John Roberts and other George W. Bush judicial nominees get confirmed. Boyden's presence helped give that new attack machine an aura of white-shoe sophistication. At the time, Boyden was a partner at Wilmer, Cutler & Pickering, where he represented corporate clients from 1993 through 2005, the year he helped get John Roberts appointed to the Supreme Court.

The Committee for Justice was housed within a for-profit lobbying operation called the BGR Group, which still exists. BGR had been launched a few years earlier by Haley Barbour (the former head of the Republican National Committee), Lanny Griffith (who worked on the George H. W. Bush–Dan Quayle 1988 campaign), and Ed Rogers. Rogers had worked on Bush's 1988 campaign as the senior deputy to campaign manager Lee Atwater, who orchestrated the racial dog whistle attacks in that campaign against Massachusetts Governor Michael Dukakis. Atwater's signature achievement was the infamous TV ad featuring a mugshot of Willie Horton, a Black man who committed violent crimes while on furlough from prison under a state prison-release program that had started before

Dukakis's governorship. Atwater bragged, "By the time we're finished, they're going to wonder whether Willie Horton is Dukakis's running mate."[1]

Atwater was a well-known proponent of the "Southern Strategy" deployed by the Richard Nixon campaign. Atwater would later become notorious for an interview he gave to a historian in 1981 about his strategy for how Republicans could win the votes of anti-Black racists, where he said the asterisked parts out loud:

> You start out in 1954 by saying, "N*****, n*****, n*****." By 1968 you can't say "n*****"—that hurts you, backfires. So you say stuff like, uh, forced busing, states' rights, and all that stuff, and you're getting so abstract. Now, you're talking about cutting taxes, and all these things you're talking about are totally economic things and a byproduct of them is, blacks get hurt worse than whites. . . . "We want to cut this," is much more abstract than even the busing thing, uh, and a hell of a lot more abstract than "N*****, n*****"[2] (my ellipses).

In 2002, Atwater's former deputy, Rogers, joined Boyden at the Committee for Justice operation.

The group was secretly launched in May 2002 around the first anniversary of President Bush's May 9 judicial nominations. The Department of Justice had marked that anniversary by issuing talking points that put Roberts at the top of its list of nominees who were being blocked. The first public notice of the existence of the Committee for Justice came in July 2002, when Boyden did a press tour, including an interview on FOX. He announced that the Committee for Justice was launching a TV ad campaign against Ron Kirk, the first Black mayor of Dallas, who was running for an open US Senate seat against the white Texas attorney general, John Cornyn III (R-TX). The committee's ad copy read,

> A new gang's riding into Texas gunning for our judge. President Bush wants Texas Supreme Court Justice Priscilla Owen on the federal bench. But liberal special interests are holding up her confirmation. Hillary Clinton, Tom Daschle, Pat Leahy, and groups like People for the American Way want to stop Judge Owen. Now they're being helped by one of Texas's own. At first, Ron Kirk said the Senate needed to confirm judicial nominees. Then he met the East Coast liberal gang, took their money, and changed his mind. Call Ron Kirk. It's time to confirm Justice Priscilla Owen.

The "call Ron Kirk" tagline was the standard lingo of an "issue ad," which had the effect of allowing campaign finance limits to be avoided, because the ad did not say to vote for or against a political candidate. We learned later that Boyden had raised money from rich Texans to assail Kirk. It turned out that Karl Rove—Bush's key political strategist since his days as Texas governor—had urged Boyden to start the group to run attack ads to get Republicans elected to the Senate and get Republicans confirmed as judges. Kirk failed in his bid to become the first Black US senator representing Texas in 2002. Those ads—made possible by Boyden, Rogers, Rove, and their funders—succeeded in helping Cornyn win that seat, a seat he still holds.

Meanwhile, the Senate Judiciary Committee had been blocking Priscilla Owen because she seemingly had sought to impose her religious beliefs on young women seeking abortions. Even Alberto Gonzales, who served with her on the Texas Supreme Court, criticized one of her judicial opinions by writing that to interpret the state Parental Notification Act as Owen did would be "an unconscionable act of judicial activism." In September 2002, the Judiciary Committee voted 10–9 against reporting Owen's nomination to the floor, which prevented it from being taken up for a vote by the full

Senate. Boyden responded by declaring, "If the Democrats seek a battle, let them know that the battle is now joined by the Committee for Justice which will redouble its efforts on behalf of the President's nominees." By then, the Committee for Justice's website was featuring its ads against Kirk alongside a gallery of Bush's judicial nominees it was backing, which listed John Roberts first—not alphabetically.[3]

It turns out Boyden's special project was receiving support from other major backers, too. One was the most powerful Republican in the Senate, Minority Leader Trent Lott (R-MS). He was upset Democrats would not allow the nomination of his friend from Mississippi, US District Court Judge Charles Pickering, out of the committee following a hearing in February 2002.

In looking into Pickering's decisions as a judge, Leahy's team saw that he had a history of giving stiff sentences to criminal defendants. But Judge Pickering had made one big "downward departure"—he reduced the seven-and-a-half-year sentence that prosecutors recommended for Daniel Swan, who was convicted of a federal hate crime for burning a cross on an interracial couple's lawn in 1994. In response to questions, Pickering told the Senate Judiciary Committee he objected to the sentence because the other two men involved accepted plea deals for testifying about the night that they terrorized a Mississippi family, and they received no jail time. Pickering's sympathy for the young man who was tried and convicted was repugnant, given the fear caused to the family in a state with a terrible history of grievous violence against Black people. The National Association for the Advancement of Colored People counted at least 581 lynchings of Black people in Mississippi between 1882 and 1968, the highest of any state—plus countless cross burnings, an abhorrent symbol of racial hatred and a threat of violence.[4]

Pickering made the jaw-dropping claim that he was clearly not a racist because when his son, Chip—who would grow up to become a congressman—sometimes brought home kids he played football with, including one Black child, his "wife would feed them steak." When asked why he had ruled against every racial discrimination claim ever filed in his court since 1990 (when Boyden, as White House counsel, helped him become a federal judge), Pickering asserted that the Equal Employment Opportunity Commission only issued "right-to-sue" letters when there was *no merit* to claims of discrimination, the opposite of how federal law actually works.[5]

Months later, in December 2002, I was invited to debate Boyden and Brett Kavanaugh alongside Nan Aron from the progressive Alliance for Justice at an event sponsored by the Washington Council of Lawyers. The title of the event was "Judicial Nominations in a Partisan Era." I remember Boyden and Kavanaugh condemning the Judiciary Committee's refusal to confirm Roberts, Miguel Estrada, and other Bush nominees like Pickering. I defended the Senate's actions because no one is entitled to a lifetime job as a judge, noting that the Senate has a vital role to play as a check on the appointment process under our Constitution.

Earlier that month, on December 5, I was up late researching nominees, preparing for the hearings the Republicans would hold once they held the gavels. I had C-SPAN on in the background, airing the hundredth birthday party of Senator Strom Thurmond, the senior senator from South Carolina, who had run against Harry Truman in 1948 as a Dixiecrat, on a platform of legally mandated racial segregation. I was stunned when I heard Mississippi's US Senator Trent Lott proudly state out loud, "I want to say this about my state. When Strom Thurmond ran for president, we voted for him. We were proud of it! And if the rest of the country had followed our lead we wouldn't have had all these problems over these years either."[6]

I immediately emailed a few of my friends on the Hill to tell them what Lott had said and to express the need to share his statement with the Congressional Black Caucus on the House side along with the press as soon as possible. After the story broke, Lott issued an apology, but it was not convincing—especially after Thomas B. Edsall and Brian Fahler reported in *The Washington Post* that this was not the first time Lott had said such a thing. Some have suggested that Karl Rove seized on the breaking news to push Lott out of leadership and get the Senate into the hands of the man he preferred, surgeon Bill Frist (R-TN). With Lott's diminished power and Judge Pickering's unpersuasive answers at his hearing, Senate Democrats held firm in blocking a vote on Pickering's nomination, but President Bush gave him a brief recess appointment anyway, in spite of the opposition of nearly every major civil rights advocacy group in the country.[7]

Meanwhile, in the winter of 2002, Ginni Thomas, the wife of Supreme Court Justice Clarence Thomas, was two years into her job as the Heritage Foundation's executive branch liaison, a high-paying role she was given after her husband cast the tie-breaking vote in *Bush v. Gore*. Following the 2002 midterm elections, she emailed Brett Kavanaugh (then the Bush White House's lead counsel on judicial nominations) to push Heritage's judicial agenda: "Congrats! Congratulations! President Bush was the difference last night and broke a historic trend of mid-term election losses for the President's party. Presidents have averaged a 26 seat House loss and a four seat Senate loss in midterm elections since WWII. President Bush's credibility continues to rise. Such a one[-]sided election could lead to quick compromises." That email message would not become public until Kavanaugh's nomination to the Supreme Court in 2018.[8]

But something else had shifted on judicial nominations besides Republican control of the Senate, although its significance was not apparent at the time. After Lott's resignation, Frist chose a middling Judiciary Committee staffer of Senator Orrin Hatch, Manuel "Manny" Miranda, to become the new majority leader's chief counsel on nominations, leapfrogging him over more experienced counsels on the incoming committee chairman's staff, such as Makan Delrahim. We learned ten months later that Miranda had been procuring internal memos written by me and other Democratic staffers about John Roberts and other nominees, along with our hearing schedules—and sharing these internal files with others.

At the time, however, Democratic members and staffers did not know about Miranda's conduct in taking my files and some memos belonging to other committee staff. We did know that once Senator Frist had the Senate's gavel and Senator Hatch had the reins of the Senate Judiciary Committee, the Republicans' highest priority was getting John Roberts confirmed. The first judicial nomination hearing of the new Congress, on January 29, 2003, featured Roberts, Jeff Sutton, and Deborah Cook, but it focused on Roberts. At that hearing, Roberts responded to a softball question from Senator Jeff Sessions (R-AL), who claimed to reject the notion that "all law is politics," to which Roberts replied, "If it all came down to just politics in the judicial branch, that would be very frustrating to lawyers who work very hard to try to advocate their position and present the precedents and present the arguments. They expect the judges to work justified [*sic*]. If a judge is going to rule one way or the other regardless of the arguments, well you could save everybody a lot of work but the rule of law would suffer."[9]

That reassurance now seems more like a prediction of what actually would come to pass under Roberts's rule. It is also odd that Roberts focused on a concern about wasting lawyers' time if rulings were preordained, which seems to miss the point, which is whether the rulings are fair. As a nominee, Roberts cast the courtroom as a contest among advocates to persuade a judge, but as a judge he has used the courtroom to move his advocacy—his political agenda—into law.

Shortly after that hearing, Chairman Hatch got Roberts's nomination out of committee on a 16–3 vote, with only Senators Chuck Schumer, Dick Durbin, and Ted Kennedy voting no.

As I've said, due to the Democratic support for Roberts, I asked for there not to be a recorded vote when his confirmation was considered on the floor by the full Senate. I was determined to preserve senators' ability to vote against him if—really when—Roberts was nominated to the Supreme Court. Senator Harry Reid, then the minority whip, agreed with and implemented this plan. On May 8, 2003, just a day less than two years after he was nominated to the DC Circuit, the Senate confirmed Roberts by unanimous consent, without a roll call vote.

However, it did not matter how many Bush nominees had been confirmed; as long as *any* were being blocked, the Republicans were still at war with us. I recall clearly that, at one point, Senator Leahy was slated to debate Senator McConnell in the Senate Radio-TV Gallery. Before the program was live, I heard McConnell thank my boss for the nearly 100 judicial nominees the Democrats had approved during the several months they'd controlled the Senate. That list included a Sixth Circuit nominee, University of Kentucky law professor John Rogers, who was confirmed even though he had urged federal judges to pre-reverse the US Supreme Court—the definition of "judicial activism." I remember that McConnell clearly and candidly said, "Thank you, Pat. We never would have done the same for you," and then—like an actor reciting lines he was paid to deliver—when the studio prompt light turned green, McConnell turned to his podium and adamantly claimed it was "unprecedented" for Democrats to block any of Bush's judicial nominees. I had never seen a politician lie so quickly and convincingly in my life. After the mic was off, McConnell thanked Leahy again and left the studio, where I sat stunned, having witnessed up close the lightning-fast switch between McConnell's Jekyll-Hyde personae.

---

After John Roberts was confirmed, Senator Hatch moved quickly to try to get Miguel Estrada confirmed to the DC Circuit, too. Senator Chuck Schumer, who would go on to become the majority leader, said Estrada was "like a Stealth missile . . . coming out of the right wing's deepest silo." Estrada had been hired at the Justice Department by Solicitor General Ken Starr and Starr's political deputy, John Roberts, for a career post in the Office of the Solicitor General. This had enabled Estrada to burrow deep into the Justice Department and later to be touted for serving in both the Republican and Democratic administrations. After he was nominated to the DC Circuit, the Democrats had been informed by Paul Bender (Estrada's later supervisor) that, contrary to his bipartisan work, Estrada was so "ideologically driven that he couldn't be trusted to state the law in a fair, neutral way." Estrada also "used to advise young lawyers coming out of the solicitor general's office, 'Go work for John G. Roberts. The "G" is for God.'" The Bush White House flatly refused to share memos Estrada wrote during his time at DOJ—despite numerous precedents for such sharing—which heightened the concerns of Democratic senators.

With the Republicans in charge of processing Bush's judicial nominees, Democrats had to decide whether to let all the bottled-up nominations roll through to confirmation or not. Meeting in the President's Room near the Senate chambers, Senator Reid and most of the Judiciary Committee Democrats conferred about whether to filibuster Miguel Estrada's nomination by refusing to allow "cloture" to be invoked to close the debate on his nomination. Senator Reid candidly shared his concerns about the right-wing effort to capture the judiciary, calling Republican senators "dirty rats," like the classic movie with the legendary James Cagney.

Senate Majority Leader Tom Daschle (D-SD), staffed by the brilliant and indefatigable Mark Childress and Jennifer Duck, soberly warned the Democratic Caucus that the Republicans could end up pushing for a vote nine or ten times, and so any senator who agreed to vote against ending the filibuster had to commit to sticking with that vote no matter the pressure. Daschle's insistence on that commitment led to forty-four of the Democrats in the Senate voting against ending the debate on Estrada's nomination, blocking a vote to confirm him in March 2003.

Ultimately, in September 2003, after six more cloture votes failed, Estrada withdrew his nomination. We heard that he had urged the Justice Department to release his memos that the White House had blocked from being shared, but they had refused. In hindsight, I suspect they were less concerned about weathering a storm over Estrada's memos on criminal procedure and more concerned about acknowledging the historical precedent for sharing Justice Department memos with the Judiciary Committee. I think that the Bush administration was more worried about keeping John Yoo's secret DOJ memos—which infirmly tried to redefine the illegal torture of "war on terror" prisoners as lawful "enhanced interrogation"—from being disclosed.

Estrada's defeat probably improved Roberts's chances for the Supreme Court. With a potential high court vacancy nearing, Republican objections to the Democrats' use of the filibuster intensified, and the Committee for Justice and the White House ramped up the pressure to break our will. In November 2003, Republicans informed us that they planned to hold a twenty-four-hour, round-the-clock debate on the nominations, a tactic that Boyden's Committee for Justice had been urging to aid the filibustered nominees. In preparation, I worked almost around the clock with the amazing counsels on Senator Leahy's nomination team, Kristine Lucius and Leesa Klepper, and our new clerk, Rachel Arfa (the first hearing-impaired clerk the committee ever had and now a fine lawyer) to prepare briefing books for Democratic senators to use in the debate. We also worked closely with several other superb Democratic counsels and communications teams from across the Senate to support all of our bosses.[10]

I had some very late shifts during the spectacle. Early on the first evening, after the Republican senators had filed into the chamber, timed to coincide with FOX's evening broadcast, Senator Frank

Lautenberg (D-NJ) and others spoke on the floor about an email sent by Manny Miranda from Senator Frist's office directing Republican senators to conclude all official Senate business early that day so they could march into the chambers on camera at the start of FOX's 6 p.m. show. We heard that a Republican senator, offended by Miranda's demand that the Senate's business yield to FOX's stage management, had shared the email with Democrats to use. Senator Durbin created a large poster of that email. We later learned that in response, a cache of internal memos written by Democratic staffers on the Judiciary Committee was provided to the editorial board of *The Wall Street Journal*. We awoke later that week to an editorial quoting from internal memos written by some of the counsels to Senators Durbin, Kennedy, and Biden. One of Senator Kennedy's longtime advisors, the amazing Brooklyn-born lawyer James Flug, responded by immediately calling the Capitol Police to report a crime. We knew none of us would ever have shared those sensitive files with the hostile *Journal* editorial writers.

The Capitol Police put crime scene tape on the door of the Senate Judiciary Committee's server room and seized the servers for forensic investigation. Within days we learned Manny Miranda had been taking our internal files without our permission for the prior two years. Senators Hatch and Leahy both condemned the breach and asked the Senate sergeant-at-arms to conduct a full investigation and determine if any criminal charges were warranted.

Miranda had initially been hired to serve as a counsel to Senator Hatch on the Senate Judiciary Committee, but following his secretive but brazen taking of our internal files he quickly assumed a post as Senator Frist's top advisor on judicial nominations. He served as the majority leader's liaison to the Bush White House Counsel's Office, where Brett Kavanaugh worked. From that leadership post, Miranda orchestrated attack campaigns, in conjunction with Boyden's Committee for Justice and Leonard Leo, to aid nominees like John Roberts and Miguel Estrada. Those attacks included calling Democratic senators "anti-Catholic," "anti-Hispanic," and "anti-woman," among other things, depending on the judicial nominee's demographic. At one point, in connection with the cross-burning sympathizer Charles Pickering, they called us "anti–white Southern male," which I joked was maybe the only semi-accurate epithet they ever threw at me—although, to be fair, I do have some white friends who are from the South.

Shortly after the *Journal*'s editorial, Miranda resigned. He admitted he had taken the internal memos and refused to tell the investigators whom he had given the memos to. Only years later, in 2018, were our suspicions confirmed: Future Associate Justice Brett Kavanaugh, then an associate White House counsel, had received internal files of mine and others that Miranda had taken without our permission. (One of the emails to Kavanaugh had the subject line "spying.") Back in May 2004, the politically independent Senate sergeant-at-arms, William Pickle, issued a report detailing his findings in what had become known as "Memogate." Among other things, the Senate report noted, "Sean Rushton, Executive Director for the Committee for Justice, who Mr. [Jason] Lundell believed to be the middleman between Mr. Miranda and the press, declined to be interviewed after investigators refused to give him a list of questions in advance. [Rushton] also returned investigators' call to interview C. Boyden Gray, Chairman of the Committee for Justice, reporting that Mr. Gray declined to be interviewed."[11]

That report indicated that Lundell, one of Miranda's fellow Hatch staffers, had cooperated with the investigation. Regarding the *Journal*'s editorial, the report noted, "Lundell stated that he specifically asked Mr. Miranda if he had leaked the documents to the press and that Mr. Miranda said 'No.' Mr. Lundell told investigators that he then asked Mr. Miranda whether he gave them to Sean Rushton who gave them to the press. Mr. Miranda's response, according to Mr. Lundell, was to nod his head affirmatively." A forensic review of Miranda's emails also revealed that months earlier, Miranda had asked Lundell to give a complete set of the files to Rushton to build up "his relationships with the press" for Boyden's Committee for Justice.[12]

The timing meant that Boyden's Committee for Justice had access to my memos about John Roberts and other internal matters. As the investigation concluded, we also learned that Senator Hatch's counsels, Rena Comisac and Alex Dahl, had seen the memos and argued against using them but never reported the breach to Hatch; they later got jobs in criminal justice in the Bush administration.

Pickle's report urged that the case against Miranda be referred for a criminal investigation into potential violations of 18 USC § 1001 (lying to federal law enforcement) and various potential computer crimes. Senator Hatch condemned Miranda's "improper, unethical, and simply unacceptable breach of confidential files," but the Bush administration, which benefited from Kavanaugh's access to our files, chose not to prosecute Miranda. After leaving the Senate staff, Miranda was given a slot writing op-eds for the *Journal*'s editorial page, the American Conservative Union gave him its Ronald Reagan Award at its Conservative Political Action Conference (CPAC), and the Bush administration even appointed him to be a "rule of law advisor" as the "Director of Legislative Statecraft" in Iraq. Since 2004, the Senate Judiciary Committee's servers have been divided, with separate email addresses for -dem and -rep staff.[13]

We did not let the news in November 2003 that our internal files had been taken weaken our resolve to continue to block Bush's controversial judicial nominees, who had no right to get jobs as federal judges. If anything, Memogate only served to strengthen our determination.

The following year, in 2004, as rumors swirled that a Supreme Court vacancy was coming soon, I helped write a major speech for Senator Leahy about the Court and also prepared a briefing book with the steps we would need to take in the event a vacancy was announced when the Court's term ended that summer. I was convinced that if any seat opened up it would go to John Roberts, so I kept an eye on the rulings he was issuing in his new post on the DC Circuit. That summer, we also prepared questions to grill Brett Kavanaugh, who had been nominated to the DC Circuit; we believed Miranda probably shared our internal memos with him because he was the key political operative working on nominations in the White House Counsel's Office. He denied receiving any of the memos, though years later the evidence showed that he had.

That fall, the 2004 election allowed Republicans to expand their margin in the Senate, and I decided to leave my Senate staff position. Senator Leahy implored me to stay on to help lead the response to the likely Supreme Court vacancies to come, but I knew it was time for me to push back on the Bush administration from a different vantage point. As I left my post in early 2005, a bipartisan group of senators was discussing an agreement to allow Bush's nominees to get a floor vote. Without Senator Daschle at the helm and with fewer Democrats in the Senate, there was no way Democrats would be able to sustain four more years of filibuster votes.

In 2005, the Committee for Justice continued to assail Democrats on nominations. That summer—after Justice Sandra Day O'Connor announced her resignation from the Court but before John Roberts was nominated—Boyden fired a shot across the bow. He threatened a wave of attack ads if anyone tried to block Bush's Supreme Court pick: "We will be watching Senate Democrats and intend to link moderate and red states senators to their liberal Senate colleagues and outside groups. If Sens. Kennedy, Schumer, Durbin, Leahy, and Boxer attack, it will be Ben Nelson (Neb), Mark Pryor and Blanche Lincoln (Ark) [and nine other named senators] who will be held accountable."[14]

When Bush formally announced that John Roberts would be the nominee, Boyden and the Committee for Justice enthusiastically endorsed him. Boyden also got a big reward. The week Roberts's nomination was reported out of the Judiciary Committee toward his confirmation as chief justice, Bush began the process of making Boyden an ambassador. Boyden also began transferring control of the Committee for Justice, with its initial mission accomplished, to Spencer Abraham, a founder of the Federalist Society, and Ron Cass, a later adjutant of Leonard Leo. Boyden's staffer, Sean Rushton, also later got a communications job in the Bush administration. Then, as Alito's nomination was speeding toward confirmation in January 2005, Bush named Boyden the US ambassador to the European Union, a cushy job known for luxurious parties.

## CHAPTER 6

# BIG MONEY

Before they received those rewards, in the summer of 2005 Boyden Gray and Sean Rushton appeared at a press conference alongside other right-wing groups planning to spend big on a Supreme Court vacancy. They described their role as "air traffic controller," directing the money flowing for their judicial agenda. By then, the Committee for Justice was no longer the biggest player at the table for the Right. Other big funders were joining the effort, a development that prefigured the next twenty years of right-wing efforts to rewrite the Constitution.

With a Supreme Court vacancy all but certain, a preexisting dark-money group shifted its focus from the presidential election toward the Court. In a kind of Orwellian turn, that group was called Progress for America (PFA), although it was created to aid "conservative" legal policy objectives and, specifically, to aid George W. Bush. PFA was launched as a nonprofit 501(c)(4) group in February 2001 by the political director of the Bush-Cheney 2000 campaign, Tony Feather, whose voter-contact programs were affiliated with DCI Group, a PR firm. Before the 2002 midterms, PFA raised tens of millions of dollars for ads and outreach targeting voters, including on Bush's judicial nominations. Some of its funding included $5 million from Dawn Arnell, whose fortune came from Ameriquest, the subprime mortgage giant that fueled the huge financial crisis to come later in the decade. As the presidential race cycle began in 2003, Feather formally stepped aside so it would not appear the campaign was coordinating with the group, and his partner, Tom Synhorst, took the helm. Boyden Gray was on PFA's board, and Ben Ginsberg was a key advisor to PFA while serving as the chief outside counsel for the Bush-Cheney 2004 campaign. Ginsberg was also a key fundraiser for PFA, which would later be deployed to help get Bush's nominee, John Roberts, confirmed to the US Supreme Court.[1]

In 2004, the Federal Election Commission stepped back from imposing new rules on the big money flowing into the presidential race outside the limits on direct donations to candidates and political parties. PFA stood up a new electioneering group, called Progress for America Voter Fund (PFAVF), to capitalize on these dark-money opportunities. PFAVF raised nearly $45 million and spent big on ads aiding Bush. In the last three weeks before the election, PFAVF spent "$16.8 million, more than all other Democratic groups combined," attacking John Kerry.[2]

PFAVF's attacks were complemented by another controversial group, called Swift Boat Veterans for Truth, which attacked Kerry's military service record. In August 2004, Ben Ginsberg resigned from Bush's presidential campaign after it was reported that he was also a key advisor to the Swift Boat group, which had raised millions to call Kerry "unfit to command." Uber-rich Swift Boat funders included T. Boone Pickens (oil and gas), Richard DeVos and Jay VanAndel (Amway), Alice Walton (Walmart), Paul Singer (hedge funder), Bob Perry (tract housing), and a then-lesser-known Texas real estate heir named Harlan Crow, who provided six-figure seed money to help Bush. (Crow had already begun, as early as 1995, providing luxury vacations and other gifts to Justice Clarence Thomas.) In all, Swift Boat spent more than $25 million to disparage Kerry, providing a counternarrative to Bush's spotty record in the National Guard. Swift Boat's PR firm was Creative Response Concepts (CRC), which would later buttress Leonard Leo's push to confirm John Roberts to the Supreme Court and then become such a key weapon in the court-capture arsenal that, in 2020, Leo joined that firm and rebranded it.[3]

In 2005, with the presidential election completed, PFA pledged to spend $20 million to aid Bush in getting his nominee(s) confirmed to the Supreme Court. PFA described its work as countering spending by People for the American Way, the Alliance for Justice, abortion rights groups, and others trying to prevent a confirmation to the Court that would augur the overturn of *Roe v. Wade* and other legal precedents. One of PFA's tactics was a website, JudgeRoberts.com, featuring Roberts in a judicial robe and a red tie, of course. It spent millions on TV ads on FOX, CNN, and other media outlets and deployed field campaigns in twenty states. It did a "rinse and repeat" to support Sam Alito's confirmation, too. To this day, the biggest donors to parts of that dark-money campaign that helped capture the US Supreme Court remain secret from the public.[4]

PFA and Boyden's Committee for Justice were not the only players backing Roberts. Others joining the effort included a little-known billionaire who was keenly focused on Supreme Court appointments. Only in 2023 did *ProPublica* uncover how extensively, in 2004 and beyond, a big donor named Robin (Rob) Arkley was also determined to help get Bush's judicial nominees confirmed.

In 2018, when I began to investigate the financial network around right-wing efforts to capture the Supreme Court, I ran into brief mentions of Arkley. I found that his family fortune was built on harvesting old-growth trees from national forests, and his family's company, Blue Lake Forest Products, had provoked many controversies, including unsuccessful efforts to block the Endangered Species Act protections for the northern spotted owl. Arkley used his family's wealth to enter another extractive industry, where he later became known as a "foreclosure king," profiting handsomely from kicking people out of their homes during the subprime mortgage crisis that began during Bush's second term. Arkley's holding company, Security National Master Holding Company, includes numerous real estate acquisition and management companies and reportedly has billions in assets. Although he has been described as a billionaire, Arkley does not appear on the *Forbes* annual list of billionaires.[5]

In 2023, *ProPublica*'s investigative reporting team that was focused on the Supreme Court—Justin Elliott, Joshua Kaplan, and Alex Mierjeski—reported that in 2005 Arkley took Justice Antonin Scalia on an exclusive salmon-fishing trip where, according to an eyewitness account, Arkley reportedly spoke with the justice about eliminating the Senate filibuster rules to prevent Democrats from blocking the confirmation of Bush's judicial nominees. According to that eyewitness account, Arkley talked with Justice Scalia about the prospect that Republicans would eliminate the power of Senate Democrats to filibuster judicial nominations. This was after the Senate had confirmed more than 98 percent of Bush's judicial nominees who had been reported out of the Senate Judiciary Committee; Democrats had filibustered only about a dozen nominees they considered too extreme to be awarded lifetime jobs as judges. Meanwhile, Scalia did not disclose that secret salmon-fishing trip—on a boat called the *Happy Hooker IV*—on his 2005 disclosure as required under the Ethics in Government Act. Scalia's trip with Arkley was so indulgent that it even included martinis chilled by ice chipped from an Alaskan glacier.[6]

Just months before that vacation underwritten by Arkley for Justice Scalia's pleasure, Arkley funded a "you're fired" TV ad campaign against Senator Tom Daschle in his 2004 Senate race against Republican John Thune, as of 2025 the Senate's majority leader. This was a political decapitation strategy targeting a small state where media buys were cheap, especially for an antiabortion plutocrat like Arkley. He was not the only political donor backing Republican efforts to punish the Senate's Democratic leader for trying to protect fair courts by blocking Bush judicial nominees but, with Arkley's spending, Daschle lost what had been thought to be a safe seat by 4,508 votes, or 1 percent of the votes cast. As *The Nation* noted at the time, Arkley's anti-Daschle ads mimicked *The Apprentice*, a show created in 2004 by right-wing TV producer Mark Burnett that portrayed Donald Trump as a successful business titan despite Trump's many business failures. Arkley's ads featured a Trump-like actor speaking to Daschle and asserting, "'We have one too many Democrats around here and that's not a good thing,' then punctuating his statement with the trademark 'You're fired.' Another Arkley ad charged that Daschle 'refused to protect marriage' and 'would let liberal, activist judges redefine it.'"[7]

Thune unseated Daschle, and George W. Bush won a second term and four more years to fill the courts with his nominees. A few weeks after that election, Arkley's money helped launch a new group to help capture the federal courts. The group was conceived at a 2004 dinner whose participants included Arkley, Justice Scalia, and Leonard Leo. According to investigative reporters Viveca Novak and Peter Stone in *The Daily Beast*, "'The big prize was to sit next to Scalia,' quipped one attendee at the soiree, adding that Arkley was one such lucky winner."[8]

That dinner led to the formation of the Judicial Confirmation Network (JCN) and the Judicial Education Project (JEP) to deploy secret funding to block Democratic filibusters and help Bush get judicial nominees confirmed. As *The Daily Beast* described their relationship, "Robin Arkley, the president and CEO of Security National Corp. who had tapped [Ann] Corkery to be his political liaison and senior advisor, became a key underwriter of JCN's operations, to the tune of the high six or low seven figures, sources say." Corkery's husband, Neil, became the treasurer of JCN, and she later launched a financial pass-through nonprofit called the Wellspring Committee, which became a major funder of JCN. Neil ultimately began handling the books for several of Leo's core operations. In the meantime, JCN, which changed its name to Judicial Crisis Network after Barack Obama was elected, grew bigger over subsequent years, from about $1.5 million in revenue in 2005–2006 to $52 million in 2022–2023.

From the beginning of the George W. Bush administration, Leo's power was on the rise. He was one of the "four horsemen" Boyden Gray assembled to prepare for a potential Supreme Court vacancy in Bush's first term. The group, nicknamed for the biblical apocalypse (with the horsemen representing conquest, war, famine, and death), included Boyden, Leo, Ed Meese (the former Ronald Reagan administration attorney general), and Jay Sekulow (an evangelical Christian broadcaster and tax attorney). As described in a news story for *The Wall Street Journal*, "Within weeks of Mr. Bush's second inauguration, Mr. Sekulow sat down for lunch at a *Morton's* Restaurant to plot a strategy for getting around the filibuster with the other horsemen. Mr. Sekulow was charged with educating conservative activists on Senate procedure, Mr. Leo assembled conservative legal scholars to counter Ivy League liberals, and Mr. Meese gathered the historical and legal underpinnings to justify the Republican position. The horsemen hold a conference call each Monday to plot priorities and tactics for the week."[9]

Leo's role in that period was more than just liaising with professors, however, as we later learned from some of the emails released during Brett Kavanaugh's nomination to the Supreme Court in 2018. During Bush's first term, Leo helmed what was known as "the umbrella group" that coordinated the activities of all the outside groups pushing for the confirmation of John Roberts to the DC Circuit and other nominees. That work included coordinating with Boyden's Committee for Justice and his point person, Sean Rushton. It also meant coordinating with Senator Bill Frist's counsel, Manny Miranda, until Miranda left the Senate in early 2004.

When Bush chose Roberts for the Supreme Court in 2005, Leo and Sekulow—both antiabortion and antigay activists—personally vouched for John Roberts. As David Kirkpatrick put it in *The New York Times*, "With a series of personal testimonials about Judge Roberts, his legal work, his Roman Catholic faith, and his wife's public opposition to abortion, two well-connected Christian conservative lawyers—Leonard Leo, chairman of Catholic outreach for the Republican Party, and Jay Sekulow, chief counsel of an evangelical Protestant legal center founded by Pat Robertson—gradually won over most social conservatives to nearly unanimous support, even convincing them that the lack of a paper trail was an asset that made Judge Roberts harder to attack." That behind-the-scenes campaign took shape to persuade others that Roberts would be a reliable vote for their agenda if he were appointed to the Supreme Court. So, while President Bush thought he was the driving force behind Roberts's ascent, Leo and Sekulow were working cleverly to maneuver Roberts onto the Court, with Brett Kavanaugh helping to seal the deal for his friend.[10]

Leo also reportedly talked up how he "had known Judge Roberts for nearly 15 years in legal and Catholic circles and at the opera." He also noted that Roberts's wife was active in a group called Feminists for Life. As David Kirkpatrick observed, John Roberts's "family life and religious convictions helped sell him to Christian conservatives as well."

After Roberts and Alito were confirmed to the Supreme Court, with no more vacancies likely in Bush's second term, Leo was tapped for an appointment that added to his credentials (like Boyden, Rushton, and Miranda). Bush named Leo to the United States Commission for International Religious Freedom in 2007. It was a part-time job, but it had prestige and made Leo into a kind of envoy to the Vatican and prominent religious figures. The appointment acted as an official ratification of Leo's role as one of the influential leaders of the religious right in America. Despite his controversial tenure, in the years to come, Leo would use that network, along with his Federalist Society contacts, to grow his base of operatives and funders seeking to overturn *Roe v. Wade* and more.

---

A lot of the money used to rewrite the Constitution through the capture of the Court came from a small number of people—mostly white men—wielding their wealth to limit other people's rights, especially women's rights and voting rights, but not just those. To be clear, the Roberts Court does not stand alone in the endeavor to limit these rights: It sits at the apex of a complex infrastructure of nonprofit groups and for-profit firms seeking to use the Court and protect it from critics. Leonard Leo's role in building this infrastructure cannot be overestimated. It would not be unreasonable to assert that he is the individual most singularly responsible for reversing Americans' reproductive freedoms and other rights through the Roberts Court. Of course, none of this would be possible without generous funding from billionaire zealots.

These vast resources were used to shape the composition of the Supreme Court and lower courts. Leo reached a pinnacle of power during the first Trump administration, when the selection of Supreme Court candidates and other judicial nominees was "insourced" to him. He was then the Federalist Society's executive vice president and top fundraiser. Leo now cochairs the group's board of directors.

The Federalist Society is the base of a sprawling personnel infrastructure for right-wing lawyers and judges.[11] The group began in 1982 as a right-wing pipeline to power in the federal courts and other key posts. Since then, its stated policy objective has been "reordering priorities within the legal system" to prioritize "traditional values" and "the rule of law," despite its relative silence in response to breaches of the rule of law by Trump. Although the group is often portrayed as a debating society at law schools or a lecture sponsor at law firms, it has the core substantive objective of reverting American law to the pre–New Deal era, when robber barons reigned. Its first national gathering was in the spring of 1982, where the featured headliners and its key advisors were newly appointed DC Circuit Judge Robert Bork and University of Chicago law professor Antonin Scalia, who would soon be named to the DC Circuit, too.[12]

In 1986, when Reagan chose to elevate Scalia to the Supreme Court, the Federalist Society backed his confirmation. That same year, Leonard Leo launched a chapter of the Federalist Society at Cornell Law School, where he was earning his JD. By 1986, the Federalist Society was boasting to *The New York Times* that "more than half the 153 Reagan-appointed Justice Department employees and all 12 assistant attorneys general are members or have spoken at Federalist Society events." Michael J. Horowitz—who had been the Reagan administration's counsel in the Office of Management and Budget—predicted, "Twenty years from now we will see our Cabinet secretaries and Federal Justices coming from the Federalist Society."[13]

Almost forty years later, *all* six of the Republican appointees to the US Supreme Court were either members of the Federalist Society or featured at its events, although in 2005 Roberts tried to distance himself from the group to protect his constructed image of neutrality.

By 2019, the Federalist Society's annual gala featured Senator Mitch McConnell bragging about capturing the Supreme Court and how "we have flipped the Second Circuit, the Third Circuit, and we will flip the Eleventh Circuit." He also crowed that blocking President Barack Obama's nominee to the US Supreme Court, Judge Merrick Garland, in the 2016 election year was the most important decision of his life. In a foreshadowing of his efforts to install Amy Coney Barrett on the Court as Americans were already voting Trump out of office in 2020, McConnell told the Federalist Society crowd—to great applause—that his new motto was "Leave no vacancy behind." Michael Horowitz's prediction about the reach of the Federalist Society from the 1980s had proven true.[14]

Of course, it helps that before joining the Reagan administration, Horowitz was advising rich right-wing funders, including Richard (Dick) Mellon Scaife, an heir to the mammoth Andrew Mellon banking and extraction fortune. Scaife's great-uncle Andrew Mellon was President Herbert Hoover's treasury secretary, until he resigned in response to impeachment articles alleging massive corruption. Andrew Mellon, an admirer of the Italian Fascist dictator Benito Mussolini, was one of the early proponents of the fantastical rich-man's tax policy that the humorist Will Rogers dubbed "trickle-down economics," a policy of tax cuts for the wealthy that later became known as Reaganomics. Decades later, with a massive fortune built on those tainted roots, Dick Scaife backed right-winger Barry Goldwater's failed presidential bid in 1964 and then gave $1 million to Richard Nixon's electoral goals. Years later, Scaife would fund *The American Spectator* magazine when David Brock was first deployed to target the Clintons.[15]

Dick Scaife's net worth was estimated to be between $500 million and $600 million in 1981. Back then there were only 13 billionaires in the entire United States (there are now at least 756, thanks in large part to trickle-down economics). As a demi-billionaire, Scaife was in a tiny but exceptionally rich club mostly made up of those who inherited their great wealth. He also controlled three nonprofits worth almost $100 million.[16]

In 1980, the year after John Roberts graduated from law school, Horowitz wrote a memo for the Scaife Foundation that was circulated to other right-wing elites. In it, he stated that "law schools and bar associations" needed to be their "critical focus." As David Daley noted in his book *Antidemocratic*, Horowitz argued that "'targets of opportunity abound' for the conservative movement . . . 'if such young attorneys can be recruited and, with proper training and leadership, can be given the chance to make their marks . . . to redefine what is moral in law.'" Horowitz's memo had a profound effect on helping to create generations of legally trained zealots devoted to a reactionary program to fundamentally change and regress American law.[17]

Of course Horowitz helped launch the Federalist Society, which was thus staked by the trusted advisor to one of the richest men in the nation. Back in 1986, when Horowitz was boasting of the Federalist Society's bright future, the group's annual budget was about $400,000. That ballooned by about $1 million a year on average during the George W. Bush administration when Leo began working on judicial appointments. Over the past two decades Leo has parlayed his access to the process for getting operatives appointed to the courts into increased funding for the Federalist Society and also into funding for his shadow empire of influence operations.

Leo has helped raise money for the Federalist Society from some of the richest interests in the world, like billionaire Charles Koch and his mega-corporation Koch Industries. He also raised money from billion-dollar nonprofits like the Bradley Foundation, formed with the wealth of antiunion industrialists in Milwaukee, Wisconsin. The Federalist Society also gets annual funding from big corporate law firms that pay for a table at its gala and the chance to rub elbows with some of the Republican-appointed Supreme Court justices who attend. Many of these law firms appear before the Court representing the financial interests of multinational businesses against governmental regulations, like assailing efforts to mitigate climate change.

But who is the Federalist Society's biggest funder? "Anonymous."

Leo talks a good game about anonymity. He has noted that there were anonymous funders of the civil rights movement, associating himself with the moral imperative of that valiant defense of human freedom. But, as much as Leo and his billionaire backers like Charles Koch try to liken themselves to the National Association for the Advancement of Colored People (NAACP), they are nothing like the thousands of Black workers who gave small sums to keep the NAACP afloat amid the deadly violence from the Ku Klux Klan and other racist vigilantes.

Although the Federalist Society's annual report lists names of lawyers at various giving levels, that disclosure does not add up to the bulk of its budget. Most of the Federalist Society's budget is from secret sources, and its largest known funders are "pass-throughs," otherwise known as donor-advised funds, that keep the identities of the true donors secret. Two other pass-throughs used by Leo groups, including DonorsTrust, threw in another $6.5 million to support the Federalist Society's activities in 2022–2023. In both of those years, the Federalist Society also spent about $1.5 million on a for-profit PR firm that Leo now helps lead: CRC Advisors.

It sounds like a complex set of arrangements because it is, and that is just the tip of the iceberg of the nonprofit empire Leonard Leo now helps stage manage. Leo is, by far, the biggest player in this enterprise, even though he is only recently a billionaire by proxy. Back in 2018, the year after Neil Gorsuch (a Donald Trump appointee) was confirmed to the US Supreme Court for the seat that Republicans blocked Barack Obama from filling for months, I began a research project with the industrious Evan Vorpahl. We looked into the money spent to steal that seat from the twice-elected Obama and to help install the arrogant son of Ann Gorsuch, one of the worst Environmental Protection Agency administrators in history, on the Supreme Court.

There are no limits on how much can be spent on advertising or grassroots lobbying around Supreme Court nominations or that major funders be disclosed. Internal Revenue Service rules also do not require that overall revenue and expenses be published by nonprofits until almost twelve months after a fiscal year concludes. So, when we began that research in mid-2018, I knew we would have a difficult time estimating how much in total was spent to block Merrick Garland's nomination in 2016 and to install Gorsuch on the Court in 2017. By mid-November 2018, we would know how much the main groups aiding Gorsuch had received and spent generally in 2017, in addition to their general finances in 2016. Those groups included the Judicial Crisis Network, Koch network groups, the National Rifle Association, and the Independent Women's Forum, in addition to mysterious new entities tied to Leo, like the BH Fund. In the summer of 2018, Vorpahl and I began tallying what I first called the "$50 million project," as in who spent $50 million to pack the Supreme Court with a ringer like Gorsuch? My related question was: Shouldn't the American people know who spent so big to install someone on the Court in order to repeal our rights?

As we began to unpack the filings of the core groups in Leo's court-capture operation, it became clear the network was much larger than anyone realized and its spending was much wider than known. It also looked as though most of its funders were anonymous. We suspected that the bulk of the funding came from just one or two superrich people tied to Leo. We looked for clues in the acronyms he used and other breadcrumbs, and we came to suspect that two right-wing billionaires, Barre Seid and Charles Koch, were the anchors. We kept digging.

By the fall, Evan and I had tallied more than $100 million for reshaping the law, including through Supreme Court appointments, that had been raised by Leo-tied groups before any 2018 amounts were known. The staggering figure kept growing as we dug. I was standing in the cold on the back porch of an Airbnb in Chicago when I called the legendary investigative reporter Jane Mayer to talk with her about our research. I had met her a few years earlier after reading her masterpiece on Charles and David Koch, called *Dark Money*. I had started digging into Koch front groups tied to the emerging Tea Party when I became the executive director of the Center for Media and Democracy in the summer of 2009.

Jane said she was intrigued but was tied up on a different investigation. My dear friend Kert Davies—who had led Greenpeace's excellent research team—urged me to reach out to *The Washington Post* to discuss Leo. I had admired the investigative reporting of the great Robert O'Harrow, and I was thrilled that he took my call. He had a reputation for incisive reporting on complex issues like national security surveillance and was such a compelling writer. He and his intrepid colleague Shawn Boburg looked into my tip and took a deep dive into the data, including IRS Form 990s that had finally become available. After wading through the financials and other information they gathered about Leo's network, they tallied that Leo-tied groups had secured more than $250 million from 2014 through 2017. That did not include the money those groups had received or spent around the nomination and confirmation of Brett Kavanaugh to the Court in late 2018—we would not see those filings for that year until 2019.[18]

That is not all. O'Harrow and Boburg's shoe-leather investigation revealed that, despite claims of how separate the Federalist Society and the Judicial Crisis Network were on paper, in reality Carrie Severino's JCN office was literally just steps away from Leo's office at the Federalist Society. Moreover, O'Harrow and Boburg reported that in the summer of 2018, as Justice Anthony Kennedy had announced his retirement and Brett Kavanaugh was slated to replace him, Leo paid off the thirty-year mortgage on his home near DC, twenty-two years early. They also reported that, on the eve of the vote to confirm Kavanaugh, Leo closed on a seaside mansion in Maine, paying $1 million cash down with a $2.2 million mortgage the same day senators voted on "cloture," the Senate procedure to end a debate. That mansion, named Edgecove, had been built as a summer cottage for W. R. Grace, a wealthy industrialist and the first Catholic mayor of New York. It was also in the same town as Boyden's family cottage.[19]

Because he was not an employee of the White House, Leo did not have to file financial disclosures revealing his sources of income from 2016 to 2018. Did he inherit new wealth or have another job? There was no legal requirement that he disclose how he seemed to have millions in cash available as he was helping to replace the Supreme Court's swing vote on abortion, gay marriage, and other issues. After *The Washington Post*'s blockbuster investigation was published in May 2019, Leo paid off the $2 million mortgage on the Maine mansion.[20]

Back in 2017, Ginni Thomas had introduced Leo at a gala by saying, "Leonard Leo has single-handedly changed the face of the judiciary under the auspices of Ed Meese and many of the people who started the Federalist Society." She added, in that obscure video I first uncovered in 2018, "He has many hats. That isn't even all he does. He doesn't really tell all that he does." Investigative reporter Jane Mayer further described these made-up awards in *The New Yorker*:

> Ginni Thomas inaugurated the Impact Awards—an annual ceremony to honor "courageous cultural warriors." . . . She presented the awards at luncheons paid for by United in Purpose, a nonprofit that mobilizes conservative evangelical voters. Many of the recipients . . . have had business in front of the Supreme Court, either filing amicus briefs or submitting petitions asking that the Justices hear cases. [In 2019, Ginni] Thomas also gave a prize to Mark Meadows, then a hard-line Republican in Congress, [who] said, "Ginni was talking about how we 'team up,' and we actually *have* teamed up. And I'm going to give you something you won't hear anywhere else—we worked through the first

> five days of the impeachment hearings [the first Trump impeachment effort]."

Leo's many hats, which Ginni extolled, have seemingly made him a very wealthy man.[21]

When *The Washington Post*'s documentary film crew met with Leo for an interview in 2019, he welcomed them into his office at the Federalist Society. Earlier that year, a different reporter from the paper had published a magazine piece that read like a victory lap for Leo on his role getting Gorsuch and Kavanaugh on the Court. I had been disappointed by that piece, but it could not have provided a better setup for what came next. Given that laudatory coverage, Leo appeared surprised when the documentary crew asked him about all the money he had raised to capture the Supreme Court. Leo responded, clearly uncomfortable, that *The Washington Post* was free to write stories "about money in politics but I don't engage in that conversation because, one, I'm not particularly knowledgeable about a lot of it, but secondly because it's just not what I do."[22]

The *Post*'s documentary filmmakers, Dalton Bennett and Jorge Ribas, juxtaposed that astonishing assertion with the paper's investigative reporters describing how Leo had created three new stealthy nonprofits in 2016, the same year he became an advisor to then–presidential candidate Donald Trump on nominees. In June 2016, Trump told Breitbart News, "We're going to have great judges, conservative, all picked by the Federalist Society." As the *Post*'s documentary noted, "Neil Gorsuch and Brett Kavanaugh were chosen by Trump from a list provided by Leo. They took their place on the Supreme Court alongside justices Clarence Thomas, John Roberts, and Samuel Alito, all current or former members of the Federalist Society. Most of President Trump's circuit court nominees (who will handle thousands of cases each year) are also connected to the group."[23]

Those three new Leo nonprofits—BH Fund, America Engaged, and the Freedom and Opportunity Fund—would set the new pattern for Leo's dark-money empire. As Shawn Boburg pointed out, they were established by the same law firm (Holtzman Vogel), and "they have no employees; they have no office space; no website; and virtually no public profile." But they had a lot of money coursing through them. When the *Post* asked Leo about the BH Fund, he said it had a charitable purpose. Its mission was described as "to promote the rule of law and limited, constitutional government." As Boburg noted, the BH Fund received $24 million from a single anonymous donor in 2017. Leo responded to the *Post*'s documentary team in 2019, "I have a very simple rule, which is I'm engaged in the battle of ideas and I care very deeply about the Constitution and the role of courts in our society and I don't waste my time on stories that involve money in politics because what I care about is ideas." Yet, a few months before this interview, Leo had told a closed-door session of the Council on National Policy, "We're going to have to understand that judicial confirmations these days are more like political campaigns." Just a few months before that speech, Leo had purchased that posh seaside mansion in Maine.[24]

---

After the publication of these blockbuster investigations, some in the Federalist Society's inner circles began to share concerns about Leo's luxury lifestyle of silk ties and fine wine. The exposure seemingly prompted Leo to announce in 2020 that he was leaving his day job with the Federalist Society for a new venture called CRC Advisors. He had been working with this for-profit PR firm since 2005, when it was called Creative Response Concepts, or CRC. It helped John Roberts get confirmed. CRC was led by a friend of Leo's, a fellow right-wing Catholic named Greg Mueller, who cut his teeth in politics trying to get Pat Buchanan elected president.

In January 2020, Leo announced that CRC Advisors would provide communications advice to its clients—both for-profit and nonprofit—and also advise donors on which groups to fund. Along with that announcement came the news that the Judicial Crisis Network (which had spent seven figures on ads backing Trump's Supreme Court nominees and had millions in earned media with the help of CRC) would also be known as the Concord Fund, presumably named after the first battle of the American Revolutionary War. Another name change was that the Judicial Education Project would morph into The 85 Fund, which grew from zero in revenue in 2005–2006 to more than $143 million in 2023, the most recent year for which data is available. Both groups would also acquire other legal aliases, such as the Honest Elections Project and the Honest Elections Action Fund, which helped reinforce Donald Trump's stolen-election claims by pushing for voting and election law changes Trump mentioned in his January 6, 2021, speech.

Those groups, and others Leo helped fuel, sprang into action when Ruth Bader Ginsburg died in September 2020 and Trump nominated Amy Coney Barrett to fill her seat. With the help of the Judicial Crisis Network, which was still using its long-standing brand name—and the machinations of Senator McConnell—Republicans moved rapidly on her hearing and confirmation. They pushed her onto the Court even as Americans were voting and even though McConnell had blocked Garland for almost eight months before the 2016 election, claiming that the American people had a right to vote on the presidency before that vacancy could be filled.

All of that was happening on the surface in 2020. Behind the scenes, Leo was in private talks with Barre Seid, who was selling one of his businesses to fund Leo's project to transform America's courts and our society. Seid had made his fortune selling power strips for consumers and hospitals. He had also been backing anti-abortion candidates and operatives since the 1990s.

In the summer of 2022, I got a call from a reporter with *ProPublica* about my research on the Court, and I urged him to take a closer look at Seid. In the midst of that investigation, *ProPublica* reported that in September 2020 Seid sold of one of his companies and created a massive trust with Leo as trustee. When the transaction details were settled, Leo stood at the helm of a $1.6 billion trust, one of the biggest gifts of its kind in US history.

Leo is the key managing trustee of that billion-dollar trust, and he is paid over $350,000 a year. As his successor trustee, Leo named Jonathan Bunch, who had first started working with Leo two decades earlier on efforts to destroy the merit selection process for state supreme court judges in Missouri. When Leo left the Federalist Society's employment, Bunch left too, to join Leo in leading CRC Advisors—in addition to their other financial arrangements. Bunch's wealth has grown alongside Leo's. Bunch, too, bought a second home by the sea—not in Maine, but on the Chesapeake Bay, where Bunch joined the yacht club attended by CRC's Greg Mueller.

Since 2020, Leo appears to have purchased a second mansion in Maine, in addition to buying a Catholic church near his home, which also sits across from a yacht club. Apparently taking away Americans' right to abortion access and other freedoms can be very lucrative.

Accountable.us and other groups tallied that Leo's CRC Advisors and its predecessor company received more than $100 million in consulting fees from nonprofits Leo has supported. The four owners of CRC Advisors are Leo, Mueller, Bunch, and Neil Corkery. In early 2024, DC Attorney General Brian Schwalb opened an investigation into the matter of potential self-dealing, which Leo has denied. In response, some Republican state attorneys general have assailed Schwalb. Leo refused to cooperate with that investigation, whose status is unknown. (Leo-linked groups are the biggest funders of the Republican Attorneys General Association, which aids their electoral campaigns.) The amount or percentage that Leo receives from the profits of CRC Advisors is not publicly known, and he is not required to disclose it. How flush with money is CRC Advisors? That is not public. However, through my research I discovered one outward indication of the scale of its financial success: In 2021, Leo's CRC Advisors hired a sommelier who had worked at the resort where Clarence Thomas has often hosted retreats for his former law clerks along with his "honorary" law clerk, Leonard Leo. That is not illegal. It is just unusual for a company to hire a professional wine steward. It raises questions, like how much fine wine has been used to toast the successes of Leo and his fellow operatives bent on destroying access to abortion?

Of course, there are also groups on the other side, spending money to alert people that Gorsuch, Kavanaugh, and Barrett would overturn *Roe* despite ad campaigns by Leo and Koch groups claiming they would be "rule of law" judges. But the groups investing in opposing those nominees were telling the truth about the rulings to come; their defenders were peddling spin.

With John Roberts as captain, the Supreme Court has been on a spree of destruction, upending precedent after precedent to side with a far-right agenda, just as leading progressive groups predicted. The Roberts Court seems drunk on power and eager to hamstring Democratic-led Congresses enacting progressive reforms and Democratic presidents deploying agencies to ameliorate harms. The Court has been stacked with handpicked justices who are wielding the judicial power to behave like partisan political operatives in robes. In my view, the key to understanding Roberts's intransigence in the face of the corruption scandals that have engulfed the Supreme Court is to recognize that he *needs* the other Republican appointees. Their votes are essential to accomplishing the ambitious goals of the Right—the regression of a century of legal rules, the restriction of our rights, and the shrinking of government agencies—no matter how corrupted or compromised any of them may be. Plus, sometimes, Roberts's own ambitions eclipse other values.

PART III

# DISTORTION

## CHAPTER 7

# CORRUPTION

THE ROOTS OF John Roberts's willingness to wrestle for power—his arrogance and ambition—were there from the outset. However, in the midst of his instant celebrity in 2005 with flashing cameras capturing his seemingly modest smile, it was a little hard to see.

In December 2004, Roberts was assigned to a three-judge appellate panel to hear a case called *Hamdan v. Rumsfeld.* On April 1, 2005, just thirty days after he joined an order scheduling oral arguments in that case, Roberts was interviewed by President George W. Bush's second attorney general, Alberto Gonzales, for a vacancy that Bush was anticipating on the US Supreme Court. On April 7, Judge Roberts heard oral arguments from Gonzales's Department of Justice on the question of whether Salim Ahmed Hamdan—a driver for Osama bin Laden, the al Qaeda leader who orchestrated the 9/11 attacks on the US—was a "prisoner of war" under the Geneva Conventions. If the DC Circuit found that Hamdan was a prisoner of war, then he would be subject to court-martial under the Uniform Code of Military Justice; if he was not, then the administration was set on trying him before a military commission convened under special orders issued by President Bush. In other words, US Circuit Court Judge John Roberts was secretly interviewing with a litigant in a very important case he was presiding over.

Even though he had just interviewed for a Supreme Court appointment, which the president held the sole power to offer him or not, Roberts did not recuse himself before the oral argument in *Hamdan*. On May 3, as he and two of his fellow judges were considering the case, Roberts interviewed again with the head of the Justice Department, along with Vice President Dick Cheney, President Bush's chief of staff (Andrew Card), the White House counsel (Harriet Miers), President Bush's deputy chief of staff (Karl Rove), and the vice president's chief of staff (Lewis Libby). Of particular note was Dick Cheney, who played a central role in the response to 9/11 and who actively worked with then–White House Counsel Gonzales to declare people like Hamdan "enemy combatants," precisely so they could not invoke the rights secured by the Geneva Conventions. Those highest officials in the Bush administration knew Roberts was sitting on the three-judge panel considering their legal arguments for overturning a lower court's ruling against the Bush-Cheney-Gonzales scheme. Roberts knew that they knew that too.

Three prominent legal ethics professors later concluded that this arrangement was illegal under federal law, which "requires judges to step aside if their 'impartiality might reasonably be questioned,'" even in instances where the judges are actually impartial. On May 23, 2005, Roberts had yet another interview with Bush's proxies, in this instance with Miers. Then on July 1, while the *Hamdan* case was still pending before John Roberts, Justice Sandra Day O'Connor announced her retirement. A week later, on July 8, Roberts had another interview with Miers, along with Deputy White House Counsel William Kelley, by phone. That would have been when the draft ruling in *Hamdan* was circulating, as is customary the week before a ruling is issued.[1]

At no time after any of these four sets of interviews did Roberts recuse himself from the case or tell Hamdan's lawyers that he was seeking a big promotion—the biggest—from Bush.

On July 15, the very day that the DC Circuit issued its order, which was joined by Roberts and which sided with the Bush administration, Roberts was interviewed by President George W. Bush himself. That's where Roberts tried out his good-judges-are-like-baseball-umpires line for the Texas Rangers' superfan at the White House. Four days later, Bush announced he was nominating John Roberts to the Supreme Court. Most reporters neglected to cover this as the enormous conflict of interest that it was. Instead, much of the coverage recited Roberts's self-serving version of the timeline that focused on his scramble to return from London, where he was supposed to teach a class, for the meeting with Bush, after which he would be nominated in the wake of O'Connor's sudden retirement a few weeks earlier. In reality, Roberts's interview process with a party to a major case he was presiding over was much longer than that—more than one hundred days long, in fact.

It strains credulity to believe that Bush would have chosen Roberts if Roberts had ruled against him in his administration's then most important case involving the war on terror. Had he wished to put integrity over ambition, Roberts could have withdrawn from participating in the case, but doing so might have hurt his chances of getting the most powerful role in the American court system. Roberts's ruling—along with the cleverly crafted baseball umpire image—surely helped him clinch the seat over the other finalist, Judge Michael Luttig, a true-blue conservative who had come up with Roberts in the Ronald Reagan and George H. W. Bush administrations.

Because Roberts failed to reveal this profound conflict of interest, neither Hamdan's attorney nor the attorneys who filed amicus briefs had any opportunity to ask him to recuse himself under 28 USC § 455. That statute commands that a judge "shall disqualify himself in any proceeding in which his impartiality might reasonably be questioned." How could Roberts be impartial if ruling for or against the very administration appearing before him could affect whether he got the job he was secretly being interviewed for, a job he intensely wanted? The conflict of interest existed even if his interviewers were not foolish enough to ask him how he would rule. The outcome was implied.

Senator Chuck Schumer and Senator Russ Feingold (D-WI) did ask Roberts about the case, although this line of inquiry at the nomination hearing received relatively little press attention. When Senator Feingold asked Roberts whether he'd considered recusing himself, Roberts refused to answer and even asserted that the Code of Conduct for US Judges barred him from answering because Hamdan had filed an appeal asking the US Supreme Court to hear the case. Roberts claimed that Canon 3A-(6) forbade him from commenting on a case while it was pending appeal, but the senators were not asking him to comment on the merits of the case—which were obvious in the written decision he joined. Instead, they were rightly asking him to answer for his own conduct in failing to recuse himself from participating in a case while seeking a huge promotion from a party to the case. If it had been a law firm on one side of the litigation that he was interviewing with, such a breach would have been obvious and intolerable, too. A master of oral advocacy, Roberts literally used the ethics code to sidestep questions about his own ethics, even though the top line of Canon 3 of the code requires a judge to "perform the duties of the office fairly, impartially and diligently." Roberts failed in those duties completely.

Republicans recruited a GOP-aligned law professor to run interference against the trio of more widely well-regarded ethics professors who agreed that Roberts's secret job interviews created, at a minimum, the appearance of impropriety. The trio noted that Roberts had cast a decisive vote against the Geneva Conventions and for President Bush. As they explained, even vaunted conservative Judge Richard Posner observed in a similar scenario that "the dignity and independence of the judiciary are diminished when the judge comes before lawyers in the case in the role of a supplicant for employment." I don't think any reasonable person who was not a partisan for Roberts would believe that he was acting impartially in continuing to participate in that case and ruling in favor of the Bush administration, with a seat on the Supreme Court on the line. His participation was part of his audition: Would he follow the long-standing law on prisoners of war, or would he side with the controversial procedures dictated by a president embroiled in a rolling scandal over leaked evidence of torture and abuse in violation of long-standing provisions of the Geneva Conventions? We all know how that turned out.[2]

After Roberts was pushed through to confirmation, however, he did then recuse himself from the case when it was before the Supreme Court—because he had participated in the earlier ruling. But his compliance with that ethical standard then does not negate his failure to do so when it benefited him immensely to rule for Bush. While he may well have sided with Bush without the promotion on the line, that does not undo his conflict of interest in ruling for the man who had the power to decide whether to select him for a seat on the nation's highest court. When the eight other members of the Court considered the case, they reversed the opinion Roberts had joined while interviewing with the Bush administration, something a keen judicial observer like Roberts probably anticipated when he made his ruling. The fact that the ruling was overturned only underscores John Roberts's calculated ambition in ruling for his patron and in hiding behind ethics rules to avoid questions about his deliberate and repeated ethical failures in doing so.

Most alarmingly, he got away with it.

How could he be expected to uphold ethical rules for other justices, even with evidence of egregious violations and self-enrichment by Thomas, when he failed to apply them to himself?

That's not all. During the hearings on Roberts's nomination to the Supreme Court, Senator Patrick Leahy asked him about a leaked memo by the Bush administration's Department of Justice that asserted, he paraphrased, that "Congress lacks authority to set the terms and conditions under which a President may exercise his authority as Commander in Chief." Leahy observed that such an interpretation creates "a sweeping assertion of Executive power which puts a President above the law." Roberts replied, under oath, "No one is above the law under our system, and that includes the President. The President is fully bound by the law, the Constitution and statutes."

Roberts's assurance became the headline for *The New York Times* story covering the hearing that day: "No one is above the law." But Roberts broke that promise when it mattered most, when he used his judicial office during the 2024 presidential election to intervene in special counsel Jack Smith's prosecution of Donald Trump for federal crimes related to Trump's efforts to overturn the legitimate results of the 2020 election and to incite an insurrection on January 6, 2021.

In 2005, to get the Senate's consent to his appointment to the most powerful court in the country, Roberts smoothly promised the American people that he would follow that core tenet of our Constitution, which is that the president is not above the law. On July 1, 2024, on the eve of the anniversary of America's literal declaration of independence from tyranny, Roberts delivered an anticonstitutional victory for Republican presidential candidate Trump by impeding his prosecution, just sixteen weeks before Election Day. As *The New York Times* later reported based on multiple sources inside the Court, John Roberts himself was unswervingly determined to overturn the well-reasoned ruling of the DC Circuit that rightly rejected Trump's unmoored claims of criminal immunity. Roberts prejudged the case and was seemingly prejudiced against the prosecution of Trump. It was Roberts who drove the appalling and unprecedented result to immunize Trump, showing his deep partisanship—and his arrogant recklessness.

---

John Roberts took it upon himself to essentially rewrite the Constitution and the rules that always governed presidential power in order to wipe away the stain and legal consequences of Trump's actions. The main case is called *Trump v. United States*, and that title is unusually appropriate in this instance where Roberts manufactured a victory for Trump over the United States literally and figuratively. Roberts's 6–3 partisan edict that Trump is immune from criminal prosecution for so-called official acts is sheer invention by Roberts, in defiance of the Constitution's twice-expressed command that the duty of the president is to "faithfully execute" the laws—which is, in fact, the opposite of breaking the law and engaging in criminal acts. That language in our governing document forms the very oath of office a president swears to follow upon becoming our chief executive. "Immunity" for a president appears nowhere in the Constitution because it is antithetical to the form of government that our founding document establishes, one in which—as John Roberts once attested in order to get his hands on the levers of power he so deeply desired—no one is above the law. Indeed, as Alexander Hamilton wrote in Federalist No. 77, the president is "at all times liable to impeachment, trial, dismission [an archaic word for dismissal] from office, incapacity to serve in any other, and to the forfeiture of life and estate by subsequent prosecution in the common course of law." To issue this edict by a majority of the Court—a ruling that should be considered a judicial coup to aid Trump—Roberts needed the votes of two judges who never should have been allowed to participate due to their appearance of bias that Roberts was well aware of: Sam Alito and Clarence Thomas.[3]

Roberts manipulated the case from the beginning so that he could achieve his desired outcome. First, the Supreme Court declined a request in 2023 by the special prosecutor to dismiss Trump's extreme claims of immunity. Then the Roberts Court waited until almost the last day of February 2024 to intervene, making it the last case the Court chose to hear that term. The Court then scheduled oral argument for almost two months later, in sharp contrast to the expedited approach Roberts took to ensuring that Trump was on the ballot in Colorado by March 5. At the time, commentators noted that setting the oral argument so late that spring made it almost impossible for the US District Court in DC to handle the trial of the January 6 criminal case against Trump before the 2024 election. However, few then recognized that Roberts's real ambitions were even bigger and more destructive than simply delaying the trial until after the election.[4] His objective was to prevent any trial on those criminal charges against Trump.

That April, the Supreme Court also heard oral argument in the case of Joseph Fischer, a Pennsylvania town police officer who had stormed the Capitol on January 6, knocking over other police. Fischer had texted, "Take [the] democratic congress to the gallows. . . . Can't vote if they can't breathe . . . lol" and "drag all the democrates [*sic*] into the street and have a mob trial." Roberts assigned the opinion in *Fischer v. United States* to Alito, but then *The New York Times* reported that an upside-down US flag, a symbol of the violent January 6 insurrection incited by Trump, had been flown over Alito's home days after that deadly assault on the US Capitol. So, Roberts exercised his privilege of assigning opinions as chief justice and reassigned the opinion to himself. Thumbing his nose at ethical standards, he allowed Alito to participate in the *Fischer* case, as well as the case involving immunity. Roberts seemingly wanted Alito's vote, along with the vote of Thomas, in order for his reactionary and revolutionary ruling to reflect the entire Republican majority on that Court and not risk Amy Coney Barrett defecting in whole or in part as she did in the Colorado case and in *Fischer*. As Representatives Jamie Raskin and Alexandria Ocasio-Cortez (D-NY) wrote to Chief Justice John Roberts,

> You took the "highly unusual" step of replacing Justice Alito as the author of the Supreme Court's opinion in *Fischer v. United States*, a case involving the January 6 insurrection, just days after the public learned that Justice Alito and his spouse repeatedly flew flags and banners supportive of the insurrectionists and the "Stop the Steal" movement. Your decision suggests that you recognized that Justice Alito's partisan ideological activity called into question his impartiality with regard to the Fischer matter. Yet, Justice Alito, like Justice Clarence Thomas, whose own ties to the "Stop the Steal" movement are well established, was allowed to participate in the Fischer case, in violation of . . . the principle that a Justice must "disqualify himself or herself in a proceeding in which the Justice's impartiality might reasonably be questioned." (internal citations omitted)

Samuel Alito's claims about the timing of when a flag tied to the insurrection was hoisted by his wife, Martha-Ann Alito, have been refuted by his neighbors and a police report from February 2021—a story that *The Washington Post* killed despite its obvious newsworthiness. Shortly after that flag had been raised, Alito dissented in a case pivotal to Trump's 2020 election litigation where the Court declined to hear a challenge to a Pennsylvania court ruling to protect the constitutional right to vote in the midst of the deadly COVID-19 pandemic. Alito's upside-down American flag was also captured on film on January 17, three days before Joe Biden's inauguration. Alito later claimed he stayed away from that outdoor ceremony on January 20, 2021, due to concerns about COVID. Two years later, another banner carried during the insurrection, called the "Appeal to Heaven" flag, was flown over Alito's waterside summer home in New Jersey, as reported by *The New York Times* in May 2024.[5]

While the *Fischer* and *Trump* cases were still pending before the Court that June, as the controversy over the flags raged, the Alitos attended a gala for the Supreme Court Historical Society. At that event, undercover investigative reporter Lauren Windsor asked Mrs. Alito about the flags, and she responded by saying how much she hated the rainbow pride flag that other Americans—whose spouses were not justices on the Supreme Court—flew across the lagoon from her summer house. Mrs. Alito also described how she fantasized about flying a "sacred heart of Jesus flag" and also envisioned making a white flag with flames surrounding the Italian word for shame, "V-E-R-G-O-N-A," or as she said, "Shame, shame, shame on you." She also talked about getting revenge on her enemies. Windsor also asked Justice Alito about political polarization and repairing that rift or whether the Right just had to win, and he replied, "One side or the other is going to win. . . . There can be a way of working, a way of living together peacefully but it's difficult, you know, because there are differences on fundamental things that really can't be compromised. So it's not like you are going to split the difference."

In 2023, as part of its series investigating ethical crises at the US Supreme Court, *ProPublica* documented how Alito took a private jet from Washington, DC, to Alaska for a luxurious salmon-fishing trip with billionaire hedge funder Paul Singer. The secret trip in July 2008 had been arranged by Leonard Leo, who had helped Alito get confirmed to the Court two years earlier. Alito's $1,000-per-night luxury lodgings were underwritten by Rob Arkley, who bankrolled the Judicial Crisis Network group that had helped get Alito installed on the Court. It was Arkley's attack ads that had helped oust Senator Tom Daschle for filibustering some of Bush's judicial nominees and secure a Republican majority ready to confirm Bush's nominee to any vacancy that arose on the Supreme Court. Leo, Judge Raymond Randolph (who was on the three-judge panel with John Roberts that issued the *Hamdan* decision when Roberts was vying for a seat on the Supreme Court), and *Wall Street Journal* editorial board member John Fund joined Alito on the luxe vacation, which included sightseeing plane rides to a waterfall, salmon fishing with expert guides, and expensive "multicourse meals of Alaskan king crab legs or Kobe filet." As *ProPublica* noted, on the last evening of the luxurious vacation, "a member of Alito's group bragged that the wine they were drinking cost $1,000 a bottle," which Alito later disputed.

As Justin Elliott, Joshua Kaplan, and Alex Mierjeski reported, one of Alito's main companions on that vacation, Singer, had spent years trying to get the Supreme Court to take a case involving his acquisition of Argentinian debt. A few years later, in 2014, Singer finally won that case—in which the Judicial Crisis Network submitted its first and only amicus brief in its own name. Alito did not recuse himself from that Supreme Court decision and joined that ruling favoring Singer's substantial financial interests.

In 2023, when *ProPublica* published its investigation of the conflicts of interest and posted a photo of Alito and Singer each holding a three-foot-long salmon, I and some others quipped, "Guess which one is the trophy." Even though federal law has long barred public officials from flying on private jets without disclosure, Justice Alito flew on Singer's private jet and did not disclose that gift. When confronted about this breach in 2023, Alito had the audacity to claim in a *Wall Street Journal* editorial page "interview" that Singer just happened to have a spare seat going to the destination—where they planned to vacation together—so the gift of private jet travel with a six-figure value supposedly did not count for disclosure requirements. Surely, Paul Singer offers seats on his private jet to anyone hanging out at a private jet terminal who is looking to hitch a ride heading in his direction. Sure.

In order for Roberts to effectuate his radical campaign to grant Trump immunity from criminal prosecution and aid him more broadly, Roberts also needed Clarence Thomas, who was compromised from the start. At his nomination hearing in 1991, after Professor Anita Hill testified under oath that Thomas—her supervisor and mentor when they worked together in the Reagan administration—had made repulsive sexual overtures toward her, Thomas had responded by claiming he was the victim. He exclaimed that he was being subjected to a "high-tech lynching," a line intended to invoke the scourge of racial terror lynchings that killed more than 4,400 Black Americans. Thomas also condemned the Senate Judiciary Committee for allowing Professor Hill to testify at all. The Senate ultimately confirmed Thomas to a lifetime appointment to the Court in a very close 52–48 vote.[6]

Although it may be difficult to fathom, Clarence Thomas is even more compromised now than he was then. For example, it is crystal clear that the actions of his spouse, Ginni Thomas, unequivocally compromised his appearance of impartiality—and actual impartiality—in cases the Court was considering related to the events of January 6.

Ginni had "unfettered access" to Trump's chief of staff, Mark Meadows, including text exchanges late on the night of November 24, 2020. That night, for example, she exchanged ten text messages with him, including one saying "It is so evil" that some Republicans had congratulated Joe Biden for winning the election. Meadows responded, "This is a fight of good versus evil." She thanked him for his encouragement and mentioned that her "best friend" was helping her to "keep holding on" in her support for "DJT" (Donald J. Trump). During her January 6 Committee interview, she admitted she was referring to her best friend Clarence Thomas, but she also repeatedly claimed that she'd forgotten what they had talked about. As *The Washington Post* put it, "The messages . . . show for the first time how Ginni Thomas used her access to Trump's inner circle to promote and seek to guide the president's strategy to overturn the election results—and how receptive and grateful Meadows said he was to receive her advice."[7]

Those messages were available to the January 6 Committee only because the Supreme Court had rejected Trump's request to overturn a lower-court ruling and block access to them. Clarence Thomas participated in that case—even though he had been helping Ginni "keep holding on" in trying to get the election overturned. Justice Thomas cast the only vote against allowing congressional investigators access to administration communications in January 2022, a breathtaking act of corruption and brazen bias. As David Brock discovered when he interviewed former Representative Denver Riggleman, the head of data for the January 6 Committee, there is even more to this story. One of the texts Ginni forwarded to Meadows was from the chief of staff of Representative Louie Gohmert (R-TX), who sought a pardon from Trump after January 6. That text, sent at 5 a.m. on November 14, read, "The most important thing you can realize right now is that there are no rules in war. . . . You must destroy your enemy's ability to fight." As Riggleman told Brock, "I thought it was the biggest thing we could have found . . . that we have a Supreme Court Justice's wife saying she is talking directly to the Executive Branch, coordinating with the Legislative Branch and directly hooked to the Judicial Branch who is pushing this kind of stuff [the rhetoric used by Gohmert] out."[8]

Ginni Thomas also appears to have been in close contact with John Eastman, a lawyer who had clerked for Clarence Thomas and had become a prominent figure in the Thomases' inner circle. Eastman had "spent the final weeks of Trump's presidency driving a strategy to pressure then–Vice President Mike Pence to stop Congress from certifying Joe Biden's victory, a plan that relied on legal theories so extreme the Jan. 6 select committee says they could amount to criminal conspiracy and fraud."[9]

One detail of Eastman's campaign stands out as particularly chilling: "The select committee has evidence that when a top Pence aide challenged Eastman's plan on Jan. 4, 2021, Eastman initially told him he believed two Supreme Court justices would back him up. One of them was Ginni Thomas' husband, Justice Clarence Thomas." Presumably the other vote Eastman was counting on was Alito's. With pushback from Vice President Mike Pence's legal counsel, Greg Jacobs, Eastman did not pursue litigation asking the courts to rule that Pence had the power to set aside the votes of swing states that voted against Trump. "They're going to be really disappointed," Eastman told Jacobs, without saying who "they" were.[10]

Trump pursued a pressure campaign to get Pence to follow Eastman's plan. That's why Trump called for the "it will be wild" gathering on January 6, the day Pence was slated under the Constitution to preside over the counting of the votes. This is also the reason why at 1 a.m. on January 6, Trump tweeted the claim that "if Vice President @Mike_Pence comes through for us, we will win the Presidency. Many States want to decertify the mistake they made in certifying incorrect & even fraudulent numbers in a process NOT approved by their State Legislatures (which it must be). Mike can send it back!"[11]

That morning, Ginni Thomas also used social media to say that she loved "MAGA people!!!!" and "GOD BLESS EACH OF YOU STANDING UP," and then she headed to the Stop the Steal event where Eastman, Rudy Giuliani, and Trump called out Pence from the stage. Eastman's extreme legal theories undergirded Trump's efforts to menace Pence, inciting the restive crowd against him and instilling in them the belief that he was ultimately responsible for preventing Trump from serving another term as president. Senators Ted Cruz and Josh Hawley also objected to Pence certifying the votes in order to allow time for Eastman's scheme to unfold. At 8 a.m. Trump tweeted, "All Mike Pence has to do is send them back to the States, AND WE WIN. Do it Mike, this is a time for extreme courage!" That's why, for hours, Trump refused to call off the marauding crowd that left the Stop the Steal rally to smash through police barricades and halt Congress's efforts to certify the election.[12]

Although Ginni later claimed she had departed the Ellipse before the riot because she "got cold," she did not leave behind her conviction that Pence was to blame for the failure of the attempt to subvert the count. Just four days after the violence on January 6, she told Meadows, "Most of us are disgusted with the VP and are in listening mode to see where to fight with our teams. Those who attacked the Capitol are not representative of our great teams of patriots for DJT!!" The Supreme Court justice's wife also asserted, "We are living through what feels like the end of America [and] The end of Liberty."

Clarence Thomas plainly knew his wife was engaging numerous efforts to overturn the 2020 presidential election. By any ethical standard, Ginni Thomas's intimate involvement and support of Trump's efforts to illegally maintain power would mean that her husband, Associate Justice Clarence Thomas, would need to recuse himself from any case involving Trump's election-related activities or alleged criminal conduct. Thomas did not recuse himself from any such case and has in fact been Trump's most aggressive defender on the Supreme Court. Likewise, John Roberts still allowed Thomas to participate in the trio of cases the Court had taken up about those events, despite the obvious bias at play and the appearance of bias.

---

I had an unexpected hand in Pence's ascent in 2016. A few years earlier, *The New York Times*'s Eric Lipton published an investigation into the Republican Attorneys General Association (RAGA), a group I had first encountered when a whistleblower reached out to the Senate Judiciary Committee while I was the chief counsel for nominations. After Lipton's story, I renewed my focus on RAGA, a pay-to-play group getting big sums for access to state attorneys general, like Oklahoma Attorney General Scott Pruitt, at conferences where efforts to aid corporate interests, like assailing the Clean Power Plan, were discussed. My team at the Center for Media and Democracy pursued scores of public records requests and other leads. In early 2016, a source flagged material from an event where Pruitt spoke, and we gave that tip to *ProPublica*'s Robert Faturechi for a potential story about RAGA. At that time, Donald Trump had not yet clinched the nomination of the Republican Party and was being strongly criticized by some Republicans, like former Speaker of the House Newt Gingrich, as it turns out.

That summer, I was driving my little black Beetle to Saint Louis, Missouri, for a Netroots Nation meeting. While I was navigating the rain-slick roads of rural Illinois, Nick Surgey, a researcher I had hired in 2013, got a call from Faturechi asking if they could use the part of the material where Gingrich called Trump "stupid" and told people not to fund him. Gingrich also described Trump as "some weird combination of the Kardashians" and politics, referring to the Bravo TV reality show that popularized Kim Kardashian and her family. He also called Trump "the grizzly bear in the room. He's not normal [and] not a conservative."

On speaker, we told the reporter we needed to confer about his request and would call him back. I pulled over near a farm field, and we sat in my car in the pouring rain discussing it. The news could affect whom Trump chose. At that point, the VP slot was down to Gingrich and Pence because there was no way Trump's son-in-law, Jared Kushner, would agree to let Chris Christie on the ticket after he had prosecuted Kushner's dad. Pence and Gingrich were more right-wing than Christie, but their temperaments diverged. The theatrical, thrice-married Gingrich had far more in common with the thrice-married Trump than the prudish Pence.

Gingrich was considered the front-runner, and on July 11, Trump's close friend Sean Hannity was telegraphing that Trump's pick would be Gingrich, calling him the best choice. The next day, July 12, Trump tweeted that the big announcement would come at 11 a.m. on Friday, July 15, in Manhattan. Meanwhile, on that rain-drenched Wednesday, July 13, Nick and I agreed the public had a right to know what Gingrich told the crowd about Trump. He dialed Faturechi, and we said yes, telling him we would post the audio on ExposedbyCMD.org, by the morning. Faturechi called the Trump campaign for comment and published the story around 11 p.m. By the next morning the Trump campaign was downplaying Gingrich's criticism of the thin-skinned Trump as a nonissue and getting word out ahead of schedule that Trump had chosen Pence, news that reportedly surprised Gingrich. Trump apparently preferred Gingrich but would look weak if he changed his mind. Ultimately, Trump announced Pence, who then was elected vice president.

I thought about this occasionally in the ensuing years, when there was reporting about Pence, but I mostly I did not think about him at all because he was part of the background in Trump's circus. Despite reporting of weird practices like refusing to be alone in a room with a woman, Pence was still a better man than Gingrich, who was so eager to move on with his paramour that he sought to discuss the terms of the divorce he wanted from his first wife while she was still in the hospital after having a tumor removed, having survived cancer years earlier.

On January 6, 2021, however, the significance of Pence being the VP was impossible to overstate. After my husband walked into my home office alarmed that Trump had unleashed a mob attacking the Capitol in his quest to overturn Americans' votes in the 2020 election, like millions of people around the world I watched in disbelief as the destructiveness of Trump's followers unfolded.

That night, when a visibly shaken but determined Vice President Pence returned to the chamber with House Speaker Nancy Pelosi and presided over the counting of the Electoral College votes, I was intensely grateful for how events played out. Had Gingrich become vice president, I do not think our Republic would have survived his unholy alliance with Trump, with the enormous power of the presidency on the line. I do not think Gingrich would have certified the 2020 election results. I think he would have gone along with the coup, aggressively and self-righteously preserving Trump's power and his own—democracy be damned. I think we helped prevent a real constitutional disaster, with the ace reporting of *ProPublica.* Trump and his superfans tried almost everything they could to stop the count, but Vice President Pence's principles foiled them.

---

Clarence Thomas's refusals to recuse himself from January 6 cases based on Ginni's activities to recruit alternate (fake) electors and more were merely the latest ethical breaches in his long history of unethical conduct throughout his entire tenure. Since he joined the high court, as a public interest group called Fix the Court has detailed, Thomas has accepted more than $4 million worth of secret gifts from billionaire benefactors who befriended him *after* he became a justice on the Supreme Court. As *ProPublica* documented, that pattern accelerated after Thomas made known in 2000, while Bill Clinton was president, that his judicial salary did not allow him the lifestyle he desired, sparking a flurry of efforts to raise judicial pay. Thomas did not wait for such a congressional increase in his remuneration and instead accepted a secret loan to purchase a Prevost Le Mirage XL Marathon motor home for $267,230—dubbed by aficionados the "Rolls Royce of RVs"—a loan he kept hidden and never fully repaid before it was "forgiven."[13]

Leonard Leo stepped in too, helping to arrange trips for Thomas, including to an event to promote Thomas's book with key funders of billionaire Charles Koch's political network. Thomas also took gifted trips to the exclusive all-male Bohemian Grove gatherings with Harlan Crow, the billionaire Nazi-memorabilia collector. Crow also made his private jet available to Thomas, who did not disclose those gifts of luxury travel to Crow's homes, including his Camp Topridge resort in the Adirondacks. Crow also took Thomas and his wife on trips to foreign countries, including Russia, and arranged trips to Greece and New Zealand on his superyacht. Crow even secretly paid the tuition for the Thomases' legal ward, Thomas's nephew. Crow also bought Thomas's mother's home and then allowed her to continue to live there rent-free. These and other perks were uncovered by the Supreme Court investigative team at *ProPublica* after they reached out to me and I urged them to look into Clarence Thomas's life of luxury, based in part on a photo of a painting we found in 2022 of Thomas with Crow and Leo at Camp Topridge.[14]

As George Conway put it to *ProPublica*, "'There was always a concern that Scalia or Thomas would say, 'Fuck it,' and quit the job and go make way more money at Jones Day or somewhere else,' Conway said, referring to the powerful conservative law firm. 'Part of what Leonard does is he tries to keep them happy so they stay on the job.'" The gifts kept Thomas from leaving the Court to cash out in private practice while letting him live the lifestyle of a big firm partner and continue to cast judicial votes to accomplish Leo and his benefactors' agenda.[15]

We can also see this dynamic at work in what happened with *Citizens United v. FEC*, another ruling Thomas should have recused himself from. After John Roberts orchestrated an unusual second oral argument in a challenge to the 2002 Bipartisan Campaign Reform Act (BCRA), Ginni began working with right-wing lawyer Cleta Mitchell to form a 501(c)(4) nonprofit group called Liberty Central to take advantage of the ruling to come. The case was initiated because BCRA had been cited in an effort to require a group named Citizens United to disclose the donors who underwrote a film-length attack ad called "Hillary the Movie," which had been slated to run when Hillary Clinton was considered the Democratic front-runner in the 2008 presidential election. Because Barack Obama won the primary and then the presidency, ostensibly the case was moot. In the summer of 2009, the Roberts Court ordered an unusual pre-October oral argument—the second oral argument in that case—and changed the question the Court wanted the parties to consider, a prelude to ruling that BCRA supposedly violated the First Amendment. A few years earlier, before Roberts and Alito were confirmed, the Supreme Court had found BCRA constitutional over the objections of Senator Mitch McConnell and his partner against campaign finance laws, the American Civil Liberties Union. But, now with Obama's first midterm elections for control of Congress looming, the Roberts Court was preparing to undermine BCRA and unleash massive spending by billionaires to use their enormous wealth to influence elections.

Had Thomas recused himself from the case, the Court would have tied 4–4, and the lower-court ruling upholding BCRA would have stood, which would have prevented the surge in dark money in that 2010 election season and the ensuing ones. The campaign donations from corporations and wealthy billionaires that BCRA attempted to regulate significantly benefited Republican candidates more than Democrats, since it was the Democrats who generally sought to regulate and tax the corporations that have fueled the riches of billionaires. Thomas is so unabashed that although he surely knew Crow had just bankrolled his wife's new advocacy group by staking it with a half-million dollar gift, Thomas issued a concurring opinion asserting that the disclosure of donors would also be unconstitutional—by purportedly chilling the expression of speech in the form of spending cold, hard cash.[16]

---

These ethical failures by Justices Alito and Thomas also represent an ethical failure by the chief justice who enabled them. But Roberts needed his cronies on the Court, however compromised they might be, to continue advancing the right-wing program through the Court. In *Trump v. Anderson*, Donald Trump asked the Supreme Court to overrule the Colorado Supreme Court's decision that he had engaged in insurrection in connection with his actions around the January 6 attack on Congress and that Colorado could therefore invoke Section 3 of the Fourteenth Amendment to disqualify him from appearing on the ballot as a candidate for president. In this case, Roberts ignored the plain language of the Constitution, which states that the only way to remove the bar on holding office for insurrectionists is for a supermajority of Congress to vote to lift that disqualification. To aid Trump's bid for a second term, Roberts concocted an interpretation that the Fourteenth Amendment's bar could not be applied to Trump without new implementing legislation, an interpretation rejected in the well-reasoned decision of the Colorado Supreme Court and an approach belied by the history of how the ban was effectuated after the Civil War. On the surface, the ruling was unsigned, but subsequent reporting ascribed it to Roberts, who cravenly withheld his authorship of the opinion from the public.

Plus, even though the ruling was characterized as unanimous, it appears that the four women on the Court only went along with the five men in the majority to try to mitigate the ruling, objecting to the inconsistency of one state following the ban but not all states. The concurring opinions did not agree with the portion of Roberts's ruling requiring new legislation to implement the Constitution's bar on insurrectionists holding office. Clarence Thomas and Samuel Alito provided critical support for Roberts's rewrite of the Fourteenth Amendment to negate the post–Civil War bar on insurrectionists holding office. If they had properly recused themselves due to their obvious conflict of interest, this case might have been decided very differently, 4–3, with Roberts, Brett Kavanaugh, and Neil Gorsuch in the minority.

This situation—where ethically compromised justices were making critical decisions about the election of the president—harkens back to *Bush v. Gore*. In 2000, Clarence Thomas refused to recuse himself from the *Bush v. Gore* case despite a very serious conflict of interest involving, once again, his spouse. Rather than recusing himself, Thomas proceeded to cast the decisive vote in the Court's 5–4 decision to stop the recount in Florida, thereby making George W. Bush president. As part of her job at the Heritage Foundation, Ginni Thomas helped lead the screening and recruiting of appointees for a future Bush administration. At the time, the Heritage Foundation was working on its sixth edition of its "Mandate for Leadership," which provided the blueprint that funders and operatives wanted the Bush administration to implement. Given how rapidly the *Bush v. Gore* ruling for Bush unfolded, there was little reporting on Ginni's role and not enough time for Al Gore's team or outside groups to file papers demanding that Thomas recuse himself due to the appearance of impropriety that her role posed or based on the ways in which she—and they—could benefit financially from George W. Bush becoming president.

After Clarence Thomas failed to recuse himself, the Heritage Foundation promoted Ginni to director of executive branch relations, working directly with the Bush administration. In that role, liaising with the administration for which her husband's vote had secured the presidency, the Thomases were rewarded: She received nearly $1 million in compensation over the next seven years. Ginni became one of Heritage's highest-paid nonboard employees, and her husband basked in her top role there: He was photographed at Heritage events that were opportunities for Heritage's big funders to meet very important officials.[17]

In response to mounting public criticism of the ethical breaches at the Supreme Court, in 2024 Chief Justice John Roberts, through his spokesman, asserted that the Judicial Conference has no power in recusal matters and that only justices can decide for themselves whether to recuse, with no oversight. As Representatives Raskin and Ocasio-Cortez noted, however, "The notion that individual Justices can decide for themselves whether their own conduct violates the Constitution, federal law, or the Court's Code of Conduct is untenable in our Republic and clearly violates the fundamental and original principle of due process that 'no man can be a judge in his own case.'" In the face of revelations of Alito and Thomas's corruption and bias, why didn't Roberts stand up to protect the integrity of the Court by agreeing to commonsense and enforceable ethics rules? In my view, the compelling explanation for why the self-described institutionalist facilitated Thomas and Alito's unethical participation is that Roberts needed their votes to accomplish his agenda of aggrandizing presidential power to try to save Trump—as no one on the Court had dared to do for Richard Nixon—and to expand the power of the Court to have the final say over almost every issue. That's because Roberts, too, has been corrupted. As the saying goes, "A fish rots from the head down."[18]

John Roberts is presiding over the most corrupt Supreme Court in American history, and he is doing so in order to use the judiciary to entrench Republican power and roll back legal precedents that secured rights that he dislikes. Despite his superficial geniality, Roberts may go down as the worst chief justice in US history, presiding over the destruction of the law and the decimation of the Constitution. In many ways Roberts is a radical dressed in conservative clothes, hiding behind his black robes to accomplish a political agenda that no legitimate and fair court would ever undertake. In his supreme arrogance, John Roberts believes this is his right, but he is profoundly wrong.

CHAPTER 8

# MANIPULATION

THE COURT-CAPTURE MACHINE that Leonard Leo built with his billionaire contacts from the Federalist Society has played an instrumental role in giving John Roberts the supermajority on the Court he needed to accomplish the broader program Leo has been driving to reverse much of the legal progress of the twentieth century. No Supreme Court majority in American history has ever been constructed the way the Roberts Court has—with the help of big, dark secret money.

The health of our democratic republic depends on a fair judiciary that ensures that the promises of our Constitution are faithfully kept. We cannot let our constitutional freedoms become mere aspirational statements that amount to little more than propaganda in print. The sad truth for America is that only in the mid-twentieth century did the US Supreme Court begin actually enforcing the rights guaranteed to ordinary people. For most of our history, the Supreme Court failed to play that role, despite what we were taught about checks and balances.

After the bloody assassination of President Abraham Lincoln—and despite the actions of the post–Civil War Congress to secure key rights by amending the Constitution to override a judicial blockade of civil rights statutes—the US Supreme Court grievously failed the newly freed people who had been enslaved. It converted the Constitution's new amendments into rights for corporations rather than for human beings, and it failed subsequent generations of Black Americans who were born free but whose freedoms were enchained by laws that gave free rein to white racist discrimination—especially when it came to voting rights. For nearly a century after the Civil War, the Supreme Court blessed a despicable Jim Crow regime. Similarly, the Court nearly always sanctioned the breaking of promises made to Indigenous tribes whenever white people decided to appropriate their lands and the riches their property held. For decades, the Court also stood in the way of women's equality, invented so-called doctrines to block legal protections for millions of workers of all races and ethnicities, and allowed the jailing of brave conscientious objectors to the obvious involuntary servitude that a military draft constitutes.

The Supreme Court sanctioned constitutionalized fear in order to allow more than 120,000 Japanese Americans, like Fred Korematsu, to be imprisoned during World War II, even though they had done nothing wrong. Justice Frank Murphy's dissent in *Korematsu v. United States* marked the first ever use of the word "racism" in a US Supreme Court decision. He warned that the internment of men, women, and children of Japanese descent "falls into the ugly abyss of racism" and resembles "the abhorrent and despicable treatment of minority groups by the dictatorial tyrannies which this nation is now pledged to destroy." It took nearly forty-five years for Congress to begin to right the grave wrongs that Justice Hugo Black's majority opinion for the Court had blessed in that case. Not until 1988 did President Ronald Reagan sign the Japanese Internment Compensation Bill into law.

A few years after World War II, the US Supreme Court finally—miraculously, almost—had a majority of justices with the courage to read the Constitution to protect real freedom for all Americans and not just primarily to guard liberty for the most powerful people and companies.

That miracle was due in part to President Franklin Delano Roosevelt's public condemnation of the justices who were abusing the power of the Court to enshrine their personal economic agenda in law. Although FDR's proposed reforms of the Court—namely, expanding the size of the Court beyond nine members, an arbitrary number set by Congress and not by the Constitution—were not enacted, the chokehold of the arrogant judges of that era abated, and the Court stopped blocking key legislation of the New Deal. In FDR's four terms as president, he appointed nine men to the Court, and his successor, Harry S. Truman, appointed four more.

As chief justice, John Roberts has gone out of his way to praise the most widely known justice of the regressive era before FDR's New Deal: Chief Justice William Howard Taft. He was a Republican appointee and former Republican president who used his powerful post at the helm of the Court to entrench the growing power of corporations. In 2021, Roberts used his annual year-end letter to praise Taft for his supposed "independence" from "political influence." Roberts wrote that he was lauding Taft for creating the Judicial Conference, a leadership body within the federal judiciary that was actually created by an act of Congress, though Taft endorsed it. Roberts leads the Judicial Conference, but that is a misnomer in the sense that he has presided over its repeated responses to ethical breaches by Clarence Thomas by sweeping them under the rug.

What is Roberts's hero, Chief Justice Taft, really known for? He helped expand racial segregation in schools. The Taft Court also made the—absurd even at the time—ruling that phones could be tapped without warrants because the Fourth Amendment did not mention that technology. It was the Taft Court that ruled against widely popular legislation that set a minimum wage for workers. It also blocked federal legislative penalties for child labor. It upheld coercive "yellow dog" contracts that barred workers from organizing unions. The Taft Court even issued rulings that allowed robber barons to hire children to work dangerous jobs without penalty and forced other workers to toil for seven days a week without state or federal regulation of hours or safety. Such rulings by Taft and his predecessors on thc Supreme Court bolstered the wealthiest while risking and wrecking other people's lives, contributing to numerous industrial tragedies, like the Triangle Shirtwaist Factory blaze that killed 146 textile workers.

The Supreme Court's evolution from applying the law to protect the interests of the economically and politically powerful to interpreting it in light of the ideals enshrined in the Constitution began to pick up steam when Republican Dwight D. Eisenhower named the former governor of California, Earl Warren, to be chief justice. By putting his Republican political rival on the nation's highest court, Ike cleared the way for his own reelection while unintentionally transforming the Court. Despite his roots as a tough prosecutor and his role as the governor who presided over California's part in interning Japanese Americans, Warren took seriously his oath to administer justice equally to the rich and the poor and to impartially discharge his duties as a judge.

As chief justice, Earl Warren had the courage to help the Court unanimously insist that the equal protection of the laws in our Constitution protected Black schoolchildren eager to learn in desegregated public schools in Topeka, Kansas, and everywhere else. The Warren Court also ruled that the vaunted freedom of speech applied equally to white kids passionate for peace in Des Moines, Iowa. It recognized that American women could not fully share in the liberty guaranteed by our Constitution if a state interfered with their private medical decisions by blocking access to contraceptives. Among its other rulings, it implemented the long-dormant rights of the accused that the generation that ratified the Constitution insisted be included (like the right against self-incrimination). It read the Constitution's promise of a right to counsel to mean exactly what it said for the impoverished Clarence Gideon and others, and so much more.

The backlash against those landmark rulings—especially *Brown v. Board of Education of Topeka*—that finally upheld the human rights of ordinary Americans, as promised by our Constitution, was swift. That reactionary force has endured in some ways to this day, amplified by unparalleled amounts of money injected into the judicial appointment process over the past two decades in aid of Leonard Leo's court-packing agenda. Now the grievances of billionaires who oppose unions and environmental regulation, among other things that might impinge on their ability to amass more money, have taken center stage, with John Roberts at the helm.

The sustained backlash provoked by the Warren Court's landmark decisions birthed the false doctrine of "originalism," as a supposedly neutral basis for rejecting *Brown*'s order of racial integration because the public schools in Washington, DC, were segregated when the Fourteenth Amendment was adopted. Originalism purports to constrain judges to apply the "original intent" of those who long ago wrote or amended the Constitution or other laws, as if a slaveholder's narrow understanding of "liberty" forever enchains us and the meaning of that word to the limitations of his mind and his inhumanity toward others. Originalism and its kin are a rhetorical device to justify dragging the law backward in time. That method of interpreting the law has been used selectively in ways that are highly political but well correlated with the Right. Over the years, originalism and its relatives have been deployed to rationalize efforts to claw back gains of the civil rights movement, overturn *Roe v. Wade*, constrain our ability to regulate corporations, increase access to deadly weapons, and judicially rewrite the Constitution and statutes to limit our freedoms and expand the power of the powerful in myriad other ways.

In his first decade as chief justice, Roberts moved the Right's regressive agenda while cultivating a facade of moderation—hiding behind the larger-than-life and more out-of-the-closet right-wing characters of Antonin Scalia, Clarence Thomas, and Samuel Alito. They served as colorful front men in the scheme to rip away our rights. Roberts also had to contend with Justices David Souter and John Paul Stevens, as well as with Justice Anthony Kennedy, who had become a powerful swing vote open to constitutional protections for gay rights. Roberts seemed skilled at unleashing Kennedy to advance some of the core elements of the right-wing agenda, as with his opinion in the 5–4 *Citizens United v. FEC* case, but failed with others. However, as Roberts began his second decade at the helm of the Supreme Court, that was all about to change.

Justice Scalia died unexpectedly on February 13, 2016, on a luxury trip. The festivities had been underwritten by a secret funder as part of an all-male hunting society, the International Order of St. Hubertus, which had been created by Spanish royalty. Scalia was staying at the ultra-expensive Cibolo Creek Ranch in Texas, owned by multimillionaire John Poindexter, who also just happened to have business before the US Supreme Court.[1]

On March 16, 2016, President Barack Obama nominated Merrick Garland to the vacancy created by Scalia's death. Garland had been the chief judge of the US Court of Appeals for the DC Circuit and had been appointed to that court by President Bill Clinton in 1997. In his ensuing twenty years on the bench, Garland earned a reputation for fairness—Roberts had even praised him in 2005, saying, "Anytime Judge Garland disagrees, you know you're in a difficult area." Before becoming a judge, Garland had spent his legal career not in politics but as a federal prosecutor. He was best known for the successful prosecution of Timothy McVeigh and Terry Nichols, whose grotesque act of domestic terrorism at a federal office building in Oklahoma City murdered 168 Americans and injured hundreds more. As such, Garland was perceived as a moderate candidate for the Court. As a sixty-three-year-old white guy—older than Roberts, who had been confirmed a decade earlier—he was a Stephen Breyer–style nominee who fit Senator Orrin Hatch's strategy for gaining Republican approval. But Senator Mitch McConnell made sure Garland's nomination to the Supreme Court was dead on arrival.

A week after Garland was nominated, Donald Trump became the presumptive Republican nominee for president. Trump met with his campaign lawyer, Don McGahn (whom McConnell had previously tapped for the Federal Election Commission to make it harder to enforce election laws), and with the Federalist Society's Leonard Leo at the posh law offices of Jones Day. After that meeting, Trump announced he was developing a list of Supreme Court candidates for Scalia's seat and crowed, "We're going to have great judges, conservative, all picked by the Federalist Society." In May, Trump announced Leo's initial list of candidates and pledged he would choose from among them if elected.[2]

In the ensuing months, Republicans ignored entreaties by the Obama White House to hold a hearing for Garland. Leo-tied groups and his PR machine were fully deployed to defend against holding any hearing on the Democratic president's nominee. Their strategy was to claim, as Senator McConnell asserted, that no one should be confirmed to the Supreme Court in a presidential election year until the people had their say. Even though Garland was nominated early in 2016, McConnell tried to brand the blockade as the "Biden strategy," because when Joe Biden led the Judiciary Committee in 1992, the Senate slowed on judicial nominees near the election (this was actually known as the "Thurmond rule," named for Senator Strom Thurmond). Senator McConnell would later gloat, "One of my proudest moments was when I looked Barack Obama in the eye and I said, 'Mr. President, you will not fill the Supreme Court vacancy.'"[3]

Leonard Leo and Senator McConnell worked in tandem to keep the vacancy unfilled for months so that if a Republican became president, the seat would be his to fill. In September 2016, just weeks before the election, Leo's list for Trump was expanded to include Neil Gorsuch and a few others. Just days after his inauguration in 2017, Trump nominated Gorsuch to Scalia's seat. His confirmation was backed by the National Rifle Association with a $1 million ad campaign; that year, its advocacy arm received $950,000 from a Leonard Leo group called America Engaged. In 2016, after Scalia died, a dark-money group called the Wellspring Committee—led by Ann Corkery, a longtime ally of Leo's—also received more than $28 million from a single secret donor. In 2016–2017, Wellspring gave the Leo-tied Judicial Crisis Network $38 million, as it blocked Garland and backed the forty-nine year old Gorsuch.[4]

Although he still had his day job as executive vice president of the Federalist Society, Leo seemed to be working full-time to coordinate the effort to get Gorsuch onto the Court. The billionaire Charles Koch's Freedom Partners Chamber of Commerce (now called Stand Together Chamber of Commerce) also fueled campaigns backing Gorsuch. Koch's trade group even received $700,000 from Leo's America Engaged. Koch's network later took credit for pressuring Senators Joe Manchin (D-WV), Heidi Heitkamp (D-SD), and Joe Donnelly (D-IN) to vote for Gorsuch. The Koch operation "contacted nearly 400,000" people, using a front group called Concerned Veterans of America to claim that Gorsuch "respects the rule of law and won't legislate from the bench." But once on the Court, Gorsuch has shown this pitch, at best, to be a cynical deception: Among his "accomplishments," Gorsuch voted to overturn *Roe*. And, in a case called *West Virginia v. EPA*, he voted to impose a new and totally invented "major questions" theory to thwart administrative regulations—a theory fueled by Koch's desire to limit the Environmental Protection Agency's power to mitigate climate changes and protect our planet from the burning of carbon, the main driver of his vast wealth.[5]

During the consideration of his Supreme Court nomination, when Gorsuch was asked how he came to Trump's attention, he wrote that he was "contacted by Leonard Leo." Gorsuch has long been a controversial figure. In 1988, he had chosen as his motto for graduating from Columbia University a quote by Henry Kissinger, Nixon's morally bankrupt foreign policy advisor: "The illegal we do immediately, the unconstitutional takes a little longer." Even as a primary school student, Gorsuch was known for his brash opinions, fueled by right-wing talk shows like the McLaughlin Group and his mother's growing political career in the Republican Party.

Once elected to Congress, Ann Gorsuch became a member of a proto–Freedom Caucus, informally called the "House Crazies" by their colleagues due to their opposition to mainstream environmental protections. Meanwhile, Neil transferred to Georgetown Prep, where he was two years behind Brett Kavanaugh. At that elite DC-area boarding school, Gorsuch led a group that actually called itself "Fascism Forever" and agitated against teachers they considered "liberal." He was the president of that group for all four years of high school. One of his yearbook photos shows him posing with William F. Buckley's 1959 book *Up from Liberalism*, a thoroughly regressive piece of work that assails *Brown v. Board of Education* and defends the indefensible with pronouncements like "The white South perceives, for the time being at least, qualitative differences between the level of its culture and the Negroes', and intends to live by its own."[6]

Gorsuch chose to pursue a career in law, attending Harvard Law School and clerking for Justice Byron White and then in the chambers of Justice Anthony Kennedy, where he worked alongside his former schoolmate, Kavanaugh. Gorsuch then worked at a boutique law firm, before briefly joining the Justice Department during George W. Bush's second term.

One of Gorsuch's rich benefactors is Philip Anschutz, a billionaire backer of Republican politicians. Colorado's richest man, Anschutz urged President Bush to name Gorsuch to the US Court of Appeals for the Tenth Circuit, and Bush did. As noted by Accountable.us, Gorsuch previously served as outside legal counsel to Anschutz's business empire. While he was serving as a federal judge, their association "deepened": "Gorsuch became a semi-regular speaker at annual dove-hunting retreats on Anschutz's sprawling Eagles Nest Ranch in eastern Colorado. Years before he was nominated to the Supreme Court, Gorsuch also purchased a mountain property along with a director at Anschutz Exploration and another Anschutz associate. The trio jointly owned the 40-acre property on the Colorado River for several years" and had been trying to sell it for some time. On his disclosure forms for his Supreme Court nomination, Gorsuch valued his share in the getaway at between $250,000 and $500,000. Right after he was confirmed to the Court in 2017, the trio sold the property for $1.85 million. Only in 2023 did the public learn who the buyer was: Bryan Duffy, the chief executive officer of Greenberg Traurig, a law firm with a lot of cases before the Supreme Court and corporate clients affected by Court rulings. Gorsuch has not recused himself from any of the cases involving that law firm.[7]

Gorsuch was confirmed in a 54–45 vote on April 7, 2017, 400 days after Scalia's seat had become vacant. Afterward, the law school at George Mason University—which had been renamed the Antonin Scalia Law School thanks to $30 million in gifts procured by Leonard Leo from Charles Koch and Barre Seid—arranged a lovely summer teaching post with housing in Italy for the Court's newest justice.

---

In 2018, when Anthony Kennedy decided to retire from the Supreme Court and Donald Trump nominated Brett Kavanaugh to the seat, the first major questions about Kavanaugh's nomination was how his replacement of Kennedy would affect abortion rights and gay rights. However, once the process was underway, the highest-profile objection came from the compelling testimony of

Dr. Christine Blasey Ford, which went to the heart of his character, temperament, and trustworthiness. Ford claimed that Kavanaugh had sexually assaulted her when they were seniors in high school. She testified that she will never forget his efforts to hold her down and try to force her to have sex with him at a party near their homes in Chevy Chase, Maryland. Over the years, as Kavanaugh's name appeared in news stories, she had repeatedly disclosed what had happened to close friends, but she never imagined that he would be nominated to the highest court in the country.

After her powerful testimony to the Senate Judiciary Committee, Kavanaugh responded aggressively, verbally attacking Democrats who had dared to seek out or believe her testimony. He was surly and uninhibited in his answers—at one point angrily saying, "I like beer!"—displaying behavior so intemperate for a judge that Justice Stevens withdrew his support for him. But Republicans were determined to get Kavanaugh on the Supreme Court, no matter what.

The White House Counsel's Office—then led by Don McGahn, a close friend of Leo's—directed the FBI to "reopen" the background investigation process to examine evidence from other potential witnesses about Kavanaugh's treatment of women. But that investigation was later proven to be a total sham. The FBI, led by Trump appointee Chris Wray, did not interview other people Democrats flagged, like his Yale classmate Deborah Ramirez, who said that Kavanaugh had displayed his penis to her and put it on her head, without her consent. She was not alone in making such an allegation. But the FBI did nothing with the tips it received. It merely forwarded them to McGahn, who took no action on them. Only in 2024, six years after the fact, did the Senate obtain key information showing that the FBI conducted no investigation whatsoever, leading to calls by Senator Sheldon Whitehouse and other members—along with more than fifty civil rights and watchdog groups—to demand reforms. Kavanaugh should never have been confirmed with such serious allegations pending against him in the first place.

Those allegations and related news accounts helped spark an expanded "#MeToo" movement, with thousands of women showing up at the Capitol in protest along with protests across the country. Some right-wing groups that had received funding from Leonard Leo, like the Independent Women's Forum (IWF), unleashed scathing attacks on Dr. Ford. (Leo's Freedom and Opportunity Fund had given IWF $4 million as the group sought to keep Scalia's vacancy open and then supported Gorsuch.) Outlets like FOX and its commentariat repeatedly asserted that Kavanaugh was "wrongly accused," even though the reality of sexual assault is that most survivors do not file charges. In my view, the most common phenomenon is "false denials." In almost all rape and attempted sexual assault cases, if accountability is pursued, the aggressor falsely denies the charge even when the evidence against him is compelling.

Following the playbook established in the Clarence Thomas nomination, Leonard Leo and Boyden Gray were not going to let anything stand in the way of getting a sure vote for their political agenda, even if that meant putting another accused sexual predator on the nation's highest court. With Senator McConnell in charge of the Senate, Republicans would allow nothing to stop Kavanaugh's appointment. And Trump—who has been accused of sexual assault repeatedly, which he has denied, and was found by a civil jury to have sexually abused E. Jean Caroll and then repeatedly defamed her—stood by Kavanaugh as the right man for the Court.

Before Dr. Christine Blasey Ford's story broke, I had been at the center of an effort to block Kavanaugh for thrice lying under oath to the Senate about internal memos that were taken from me and other Judiciary Committee staffers. In 2004, shortly after the sergeant-at-arms investigated Manny Miranda for taking our internal files without our permission, Kavanaugh appeared before the committee on his nomination to become a judge on the DC Circuit. He was asked by Senator Hatch if he had ever received any of our confidential memos, letters, or files; and he lied, saying he had not. His nomination failed to get out of committee that year, even with Republicans in charge. The following year, Senator Ted Kennedy asked Kavanaugh if he had received any of the files that had been taken, and he again lied under oath when he said that he had not. Then in 2018, Senator Patrick Leahy asked him about the files after records revealed that he had received some of them, and Kavanaugh dissembled again by claiming that it was normal for him to receive Democratic memos about matters being deliberated, which was a bold-faced lie when it came to nominations. I wrote a piece for *Slate* detailing that Kavanaugh had received my internal files and calling for him to be impeached, not elevated—the first person to do so. Other Democratic staffers who had served on the committee also spoke out against Kavanaugh's claims, and fact-checkers concurred that he had lied to the Senate. Senator Leahy also wrote an op-ed detailing how Kavanaugh had deliberately misled Congress, which was disqualifying for any nominee, especially a person nominated to the highest court.

Serious concerns were also raised about financial ambiguities, including how Kavanaugh had paid off up to $200,000 in debt before he was nominated, how he had accessed money for the downpayment on his home, and how he had come up with the initiation fee of nearly $90,000 for his new membership at the tony Chevy Chase Country Club. Though the money could have come from his father, a former cosmetics industry lobbyist, Kavanaugh refused to say. He also indicated that he had incurred substantial debt in part by charging season tickets and playoff tickets for a block of seats at games of the Washington Nationals to his personal credit card and then having his friends pay him back in cash. Using credit cards in trade for cash is not illegal; it is also something that some people with high personal debt engage in to increase their cash flow.

Meanwhile, Kavanaugh's confirmation was backed by the usual crew with ties to his friend Leonard Leo's court-capture machine—including the Judicial Crisis Network and the National Rifle Association. Ed Whelan, who led the Ethics and Public Policy Center (EPPC), even asserted that Kavanaugh's accuser was confused about the identity of her assailant and the house where she was assaulted, based on Whelan's analysis of locations on Zillow maps. He later apologized by tweet and took a brief leave from EPPC, a group that has had long ties to Boyden Gray and Leo.

Kavanaugh's nomination and confirmation also coincided with a seemingly dramatic increase in Leonard Leo's personal wealth. That year, Leo had the resources to pay off his home mortgage decades early and to close on a $3 million mansion in Maine on the eve of Kavanaugh's confirmation, which was made possible in part by Senator Susan Collins (R-ME). The following year, in 2019, Leo hosted a fundraiser for her reelection at his mansion on the coast of Maine, with big name funders, like Boyden Gray. The "stench," as David Brock put it, surrounding Kavanaugh's confirmation to the Supreme Court is overwhelming.

For Leo, the confirmation of Kavanaugh and Gorsuch gave him the numbers to help speed up the revolution in the law that John Roberts was methodically unfolding. At a closed-door meeting of the Council on National Policy in February 2019, Leo proudly proclaimed to the crowd of donors and operatives, "I think we stand at the threshold of an exciting moment in our republic. The revival of our structural constitution by the US Supreme Court, a revival in those very important principles of limited, constitutional government. . . . And this is really, I think in recent memory, a newfound embrace of limited constitutional government in our country. I don't think this has really happened since probably before the New Deal, which means no one in this room has probably experienced the kind of transformation that I think we are beginning to see."

---

The death of Ruth Bader Ginsburg on September 18, 2020, opened another seat on the Court. Ginsburg was a Democratic appointee, an icon of the women's movement, and a reliable vote for upholding the rights of ordinary Americans. Although Election Day was just weeks away, Leo and McConnell jumped at the opportunity to solidify and expand the right-wing majority on the Court by getting Amy Coney Barrett nominated to Ginsburg's seat. In 2020, Senator McConnell moved rapidly to get Trump's nominee confirmed even as Americans were already voting in that year's presidential election—despite McConnell's previous claim that no one nominated to the Court should get a vote in an election year until after the people had voted. Leo basically prenominated Barrett to the Supreme Court and maneuvered her into position.

According to a book coauthored by the Judicial Crisis Network's Carrie Severino, Leo met with then–White House Counsel Don McGahn in April 2017 to discuss expanding Trump's Supreme Court list to include Barrett. At that time, Barrett had been a law professor for fifteen years and had no judicial experience, but Leo and the White House Counsel's Office were going to remedy that by getting her some time sitting on a federal circuit court. The very next month, in May 2017, Trump nominated Barrett to a vacancy on the Seventh Circuit created by Senator McConnell's refusal to allow President Obama's nominee, Myra S. Powell (the first Black woman appointed to the Indiana Supreme Court), a hearing and a vote for nearly a year.

According to a book Severino coauthored, Leo then met for dinner with Trump in June and again in September to discuss putting Barrett on Trump's list for the next vacancy on the Court, which was thought to be the seat held by the aging Ginsburg. Barrett was confirmed to the Seventh Circuit on Halloween of 2017. On November 17, McGahn announced that Trump had added Barrett to his short list for the Court, news announced at the Federalist

Society's national convention, where Barrett spoke about Justice Antonin Scalia for whom she had clerked.

After becoming a federal judge, Barrett appeared to have a lot more time to speak at Federalist Society events than when she was teaching a few classes a semester as a law professor. Like Scalia, Barrett became a frequent flier to Federalist Society events. In the nearly three years she was paid to be a federal circuit court judge, she addressed Federalist Society meetings almost two dozen times—more than any other forum. After Ruth Bader Ginsburg died on September 18, 2020, Leo's empire of nonprofit groups and Republican allies acted quickly to support President Trump's selection of Barrett for the Supreme Court. Barrett's confirmation in 2020 was backed by a well-heeled who's who of professional anti-abortion activists. The Rose Garden announcement of her nomination was practically a coronation and a precelebration of the anticipated end of *Roe v. Wade*. And, on October 26, less than two weeks before Election Day, the forty-eight-year-old was confirmed to the Supreme Court in a 52–48 vote. Since then, Barrett has largely voted in lockstep with her fellow Republican appointees, with a few surprising exceptions. She could end up serving on the Supreme Court for more than four decades.

---

When viewed as a whole, the Roberts faction dominating the Supreme Court is quite the cast of characters. Each of them was carefully selected not because they were thought to be fair but because they were believed to be dependable votes for a revolution in the law—one Leo and his cohorts knew could be accomplished only by keeping Americans in the dark about their views. Unlike Robert Bork, each of them claimed to have no agenda to erode reproductive rights or overturn *Roe*, even though they were chosen to do so. The illusionary nature of the theater that the confirmation process has become facilitated how the Roberts Court was constituted.

The core of corruption is dishonesty, no matter how the term may be redefined by the Roberts Court. In a recent stunning—and damning—partisan ruling, the Republican appointees on the Supreme Court revealed how deeply out of touch they really are, and it was not even in a case about access to abortion. It came in a ruling on public corruption. In the midst of the higher-profile edicts issued in the summer of 2024, this case received relatively little attention, but it is very revealing in showing the amorality of the Court's right-wing faction. In *Snyder v. United States*, John Roberts and his fellow GOP judges struck down decades of legal precedent on the meaning of bribery and corruption in federal criminal law. In that case, they declared that a public official *can* accept big money, dubbed a "gratuity," as a so-called reward for an official public action. In their view, the timing of the payment magically converts what most would consider unlawful corruption into a lawful "tip" to a public official for a job well done.

This is not about cupcakes for a teacher. The case involved John Snyder, the mayor of Portage, Indiana, a city about twenty minutes down the road from where John Roberts grew up. A jury of Snyder's peers convicted him of "steer[ing] more than $1 million in city contracts to a local truck dealership, which turned around and cut him a $13,000 check." He was sentenced to twenty-one months in jail, and he appealed his conviction all the way to the Supreme Court.[8]

The majority's opinion was penned by Donald Trump–appointee and Leonard Leo–selectee Brett Kavanaugh. Kavanaugh tried hard to make it appear as if the Court was on the side of the little guy by asking what if "police officers" or "prison guards" accept "gifts," and they are faced "with the threat of up to 10 years in federal prison if they happen to guess wrong" about whether they can legally accept such gifts. What if? Seriously? The $13,000 kickback to Snyder was no small thing: It is about 25 percent of the median pretax wages of an American worker. If a hardworking waitress at a diner got a tip like that, it would be viral news, but it is less a gift than a grift when such a sum is secretly solicited by an elected official. It is morally wrong.[9]

If the gift had been just a "You're #1" coffee mug, of course, Snyder would never have been charged, and a jury of his peers would never have convicted him. But the ethically challenged Kavanaugh tried to equate the blatant corruption charged in the case with trifling gifts via rhetorical questions like "Is a $100 Dunkin' Donuts gift card for a trash collector wrongful?" Chief Justice Roberts assigned the opinion to Kavanaugh, which was practically an act of trolling. During the oral argument, Roberts even tried to get the advocates to agree that they were really arguing that a "gratuity" is "bribery" *without* a "quid pro quo" (and thus is not corrupt). But the $13,000 Snyder solicited *was* a favor for a favor, the very definition of that Latin phrase. It was a kickback that he solicited and received because he used his government position to arrange contracts with terms only that particular dealership could meet. The brothers who owned the business testified under oath that Snyder shook them down for cash he said he needed to pay off his debts. The testimony and evidence show the $13,000 was no "tip," and that is why the jury found Snyder guilty as charged. But that evidence was not relevant to Roberts and his gang.

Justice Ketanji Brown Jackson, in her dissent, which was joined by Justices Sonia Sotomayor and Elena Kagan, had the proven facts on her side. She also had the superior argument. Jackson noted, "Officials who use their public positions for private gain threaten the integrity of our most important institutions. Greed makes governments—at every level—less responsive, less efficient, and less trustworthy from the perspective of the communities they serve. . . . [Snyder] says . . . bribes require an upfront agreement to take official actions for payment, and he never agreed beforehand to be paid the $13,000 from the dealership. Snyder's absurd and atextual reading of the statute is one only today's Court could love." Indeed.[10]

Under John Roberts, an "absurd and atextual reading of the law" has become a cornerstone of the Court's jurisprudence. Only the corrupted Roberts Court would try to launder a straightforward case of corruption as lawful. Could the $4 million in secret gifts Clarence Thomas has taken over the years just be considered tips for a job well done? Are Thomas's luxury gifts just the nine-figure version of the mayor's five-figure reward for making a richer person happy?

John Roberts and his confederates chose to rewrite federal corruption laws even as the Court was facing the biggest corruption scandals any Supreme Court has seen in US history. Scandal after scandal has been revealed as investigative reporters have finally been assigned to the Supreme Court beat. The nation's highest Court has been engulfed by revelations of jaw-dropping avarice; and yet Roberts repeatedly sought to thwart reasonable efforts to investigate the ongoing crisis. The demonstrable corruption and his obstinate inaction—along with reckless rulings—have decimated public confidence in the integrity of the Supreme Court.

Roberts tried to derail congressional subpoenas and undermine their investigations. He even refused to testify before the Senate Judiciary Committee, claiming disingenuously that the "separation of powers" prohibits it. Some senators who mistook his formal politeness for integrity seemed mystified that Roberts rebuffed them as he worked to place himself and the Court he leads beyond checks and balances. Their misapprehension is a testament to the lasting effects of Roberts's soft-spoken salesmanship and the devilishly misleading analogy he deployed to get the best job on the Supreme Court: the claim that he was not going to be a player for any team and would be just an umpire calling balls and strikes.

PART IV

# CONTROL

# CHAPTER 9

# GUNS

THE MAJORITY OF Americans want stricter gun laws, but John Roberts has used his judicial office to reverse decades—one might argue, centuries—of legal precedent, contorting the Constitution in order to make it easier to buy, stockpile, carry, conceal, and use deadly weapons. The Roberts Court's unilateral revision of our laws has unjustly limited the power of states and Congress to enact and enforce commonsense gun legislation that is profoundly needed to stanch the gun violence that plagues America. The Roberts Court even blocked a rare Republican-led effort to limit access to "bump stocks," accessories that enable assault-style rifles to more easily fire hundreds of high-velocity rounds per minute, with high-caliber bullets that cause "an explosion inside the body." So much for Roberts and the other Republican justices being "pro-life."[1]

Working in conjunction with his accomplices on the Court—and backed by a phalanx of powerful lobbyists, lawyers, and donors—Chief Justice Roberts has helped make our country far more dangerous, ushering in a savage chapter of American history. Obviously, John Roberts did not commit the wicked rash of crimes himself, but the changes to US law that he has supported have helped fuel a disastrous epidemic of deaths from guns. Mass shootings in the United States are so common now that they barely stay in the news for more than a day or two before they are replaced by the next mass killing. That's the real "American carnage," not the fraudulent specter Donald Trump tried to conjure in his first inaugural address, after an election victory in 2016 that the gun industry spent tens of millions to bring about.[2]

The murderers using these incredibly deadly weapons against schoolchildren, grocery shoppers, concertgoers, and faithful worshippers are certainly to blame, of course, but the "guns don't kill people, people kill people" crowd ignore the reality that it is people with guns who kill a lot of people, a blood-drenched act no blunt instrument or knife could as easily accomplish. The weapons manufacturers who design these guns to kill as many people as possible almost as quickly as a fully automated machine gun—and the wholesalers and retailers of such weapons, ammunition, speedloaders, bump stocks, and other force-multiplying accessories—also have blood on their hands. That industry has largely been protected from any legal liability, and thus any real financial responsibility, through legislation pushed by Republican legislators.

Each year, "the gun industry rakes in approximately $9 billion while gun violence kills more than 40,000 people in America and wounds twice as many," according to Every Town for Gun Safety's figures. Behind those revenues are the sales of millions of guns per year. US corporations manufacture more than 7 million guns annually, not counting the guns they make for the military produced on contracts with the Pentagon. These companies export about 5 percent of the guns produced here, but each year we import another 7 million firearms from other countries, including more than 4 million handguns. Experts estimate that there are more guns (nearly 400 million) than people (335 million) in the United States, along with exponentially more bullets. While about 60 percent of Americans do not have a gun in their home, most of those who do have multiple firearms, sometimes dozens. No responsible hunter needs a military-style assault rifle to hunt a deer, let alone a wild turkey or a tiny quail. But the industry has aggressively marketed weapons for recreation that are modeled on those designed for war, promoting a sense of power or thrill from firing a gun, the bigger and faster the better.[3]

Until 1977, the NRA was predominately a "sportsmen's" group. But then it went through an internal hostile takeover by a Second Amendment absolutist contingent that backed the NRA's lobbyist, Harlon Carter, to be its new leader. Carter had been convicted of murder. As a seventeen-year-old he had shot and killed a fifteen-year-old neighbor named Ramón Casiano whom he accused of stealing. Carter got off on a technicality on appeal, and instead of serving a prison sentence, he went on to college and law school before following in his father's footsteps and joining the Border Patrol. It was Carter who led the Border Patrol in 1954 when it launched a repressive mass deportation project, offensively named "Operation Wetback," that conducted more than 200,000 "sweeps" of immigrants and purportedly caused more than a million people to flee across the southern border. It was Carter who changed the direction of the NRA toward absolutism. He also hired Wayne LaPierre to be the NRA's lobbyist in the 1980s. LaPierre ultimately became the group's leader and continues to help steer it to this day, despite scandals over using NRA donations to pay for hairstylists and other perks.[4]

Over the past four decades, the NRA has ballooned in revenue and political power, while promoting a "guns everywhere" agenda, such as pushing for permitless carrying of firearms and concealed-carry reciprocity between states. It has opposed almost every effort to better regulate firearms in response to mass shootings and the ubiquity of guns in crimes. The NRA is notorious for claiming that the solution to gun violence is more guns. It has routinely asserted that Democrats are trying to take people's guns away, repeatedly fearmongering by invoking the specter of Adolf

Hitler and authoritarian regimes. The NRA is so shameless that even though firearms are now the leading cause of death for American teens and children, its website specifically objects to restrictions on marketing "firearms, parts and accessories" to those under eighteen. The age verification pop-up on its website claims that limiting its ability to peddle its agenda to kids violates its rights.[5]

The National Sports Shooting Foundation (NSSF) is a lesser-known but powerful counterpart of the NRA that acts as the voice of the gun industry. The NSSF is the firearm industry's trade association, "with a membership of thousands of manufacturers, distributors, firearm retailers, shooting ranges, sportsmen's organizations and publishers nationwide." While the NRA says it represents "shooters," the NSSF is officially the powerful lobby for the profit-hungry companies that shower civilian shooters with guns, ammunition, accessories, and services and also equip police forces and militaries worldwide. The NSSF operates the gun industry's biggest trade convention, the Shooting, Hunting, Outdoor Trade Show, branded as the "SHOT Show." In litigation, the NSSF assumes many of the same positions as the NRA. Both spend millions each year to influence federal and state law, and in recent years the NSSF has outspent the NRA on lobbying. The NSSF was also listed in Cambridge Analytica documents as being part of efforts to aid Trump's 2016 election by providing "data from gun brokers" to help his campaign.[6]

The gun industry is fully devoted to selling more guns for profit no matter the consequences in lives lost, people maimed, or families ruined. A portion of these massive profits is then driven into political influence operations, to run or threaten to run attack ads against elected officials who might dare to vote *for* what most of their constituents want and *against* what the gun industry demands. The gun lobby also serially funds the electoral campaigns of their human accessories in state legislatures, governors' mansions, Congress, and the White House. The gun profiteers also make their views and their demands known by filing amicus briefs on firearms and regulatory cases that come before the US Supreme Court.[7]

The NRA and the NSSF have actively backed the confirmation of Republican nominees to the nation's highest court. For example, the NRA spent millions to help get the Donald Trump / Leonard Leo nominees—Neil Gorsuch, Brett Kavanaugh, and Amy Coney Barrett—confirmed. The NSSF endorsed all three, calling them, respectively, "a worthy successor to Scalia," "on target," and "in the mold of Scalia."[8]

Perhaps nowhere has the gun lobby's influence been more corrupt, obvious, and egregious than in the Roberts Court's Second Amendment rulings, starting with *District of Columbia v. Heller*. In that case, Antonin Scalia wrote the majority opinion, disregarding long-settled law and marking a new era of extreme judicial activism.

---

The *Heller* case was one of the first major cases decided by the Supreme Court in the early years after John Roberts was confirmed as chief justice. The case acts like a proof of concept of how a court-capture machine decades in the making could warp the Constitution to serve a right-wing agenda, based on a change in personnel at the Court. The justices who made it possible were the two new George W. Bush appointees, John Roberts and Samuel Alito, who both had stamps of approval from the NRA, the Federalist Society, and the up-and-coming Leonard Leo, who led the Catholic outreach campaign for Bush's 2004 run.

In *Heller*, the Roberts Court declared it was unconstitutional for Washington, DC, to limit the ownership of handguns and require that licensed firearms be stored unloaded or equipped with a trigger lock to prevent unauthorized use. At the core of the majority opinion is the Supreme Court's redefinition of the right to bear arms as an individual right rather than a collective right under the aegis of a militia. The ruling, made possible by Sandra Day O'Connor's retirement and William Rehnquist's death, upended more than a century of legal precedent. The 5–4 decision set aside the "consistent agreement among courts, and really scholars . . . that the Second Amendment did not confer an individual right" but rather protected a collective right that allowed guns to be regulated to promote public safety. In *Heller*, the Roberts Court threw open the door to claims that an array of gun laws were unconstitutional.[9]

To make such a dramatic change in the nation's laws, Scalia and four of his brethren blotted out the first half of the Second Amendment, which reads, "A well regulated Militia being necessary to the security of a free State. . ." As Justice John Paul Stevens noted in his *Heller* dissent, which was joined by Justices David Souter, Ruth Bader Ginsburg, and Stephen Breyer,

> The Second Amendment was adopted to protect the right of the people of each of the several States to maintain a well-regulated militia. It was a response to concerns raised during the ratification of the Constitution that the power of Congress to disarm the state militias and create a national standing army posed an intolerable threat to the sovereignty of the several States. Neither the text of the Amendment nor the arguments advanced by its proponents evidenced the slightest interest in limiting any legislature's authority to regulate private civilian uses of firearms. Specifically, there is no indication that the Framers of the Amendment intended to enshrine the common-law right of self-defense in the Constitution.[10]

The 5–4 *Heller* decision that John Roberts joined in full was issued in June 2008, but that is only part of the story. The year before, on March 9, 2007, the US Court of Appeals for the DC

Circuit issued its ruling in that case, in an opinion written by Scalia's gun club buddy, Judge Laurence Silberman. On that very day in 2007, Scalia was in Nuremberg, Germany, with Alan Gottlieb, creator of a nonprofit group called the Second Amendment Foundation (SAF). Gottlieb later told Armed American Radio that being with Scalia at the International Weapons Exhibition that day was "like watching a kid in a candy store"—Scalia was obsessed with finding the most "expensive highly engraved shotguns by various manufacturers." He was in Germany to give the keynote address to the World Forum on Shooting Activities (WFSA). The NRA and NSSF were, and still are, funders of the WFSA.[11]

That day, the WFSA gave Scalia its highest award, the Shooting Ambassador Award, which comes with a silver replica of a sixteenth-century gun. Gottlieb published a photo with Scalia at the International Weapons Exhibition in his group's subscription newspaper, *The New Gun Week*. He later told NRA Radio he learned from Scalia that day that the DC Circuit had just ruled that the Second Amendment protects an individual right to bear arms and not just a collective right. In those conversations, Scalia told him, "You know, Alan, it takes four votes on the Supreme Court to hear a case, and it takes five to win it. If I don't think we have the five to win it, there won't be four to hear it." Gottlieb's reaction to Scalia's assurance was "That just made me feel like I knew at that point in time that if the Supreme Court took the *Heller* case, that we were going to win it." The Roberts Court agreed to take up the *Heller* case later that year.[12]

During the March 2007 exhibition in Nuremberg, Justice Scalia also held a private "real roundtable discussion" with "half a dozen" gun rights lawyers where they discussed the notion that "the only really solid Second Amendment in the world is in the United States." At the time of these remarks, SAF and the NRA had submitted amicus briefs in the *Heller* case at the DC Circuit level. The outcome had been pursued by a wealthy lawyer named Bob Levy, who worked at Charles Koch's Cato Institute. Levy recruited the plaintiffs and paid for their lawyers.[13]

Just a few days after issuing the *Heller* ruling in 2008, Justice Scalia had dinner with veteran Supreme Court reporter Nina Totenberg. I will let the astounding story she told in her memoir about her friendship with "Nino" Scalia speak for itself:

> There were eight of us, and David [her husband], who has operated on hundreds of gunshot victims in the course of his career, brought eight plastic squirt guns and put them in the empty soup bowls, so when everyone sat down, that was what they would immediately see. When we got to the table, everyone burst out laughing, including Nino. That's not the end of the story, however. Scalia's opinion in the *Heller* case contained a much-quoted line saying one of the advantages of a handgun is "it can be pointed at a burglar with one hand while the other hand dials the police." So, after soup, David reached under his chair and pulled out a massive Super Soaker, pointed it at Scalia, and asked "Shall I call 911 with the other hand?" That brought down the house.

There is no indication that in 2008 any of the traditional gaggle of Supreme Court reporters knew that Justice Scalia had recently been named the "Shooting Ambassador" by an international gun rights group funded by the NRA and SAF, which had submitted amicus briefs urging the Court to reverse long-standing legal precedents. Scalia did not reveal that fact to any of the opposing parties involved in the *Heller* case. Under the federal recusal statute that expressly applies to "justices and judges," justices are required to recuse themselves from a case when their impartiality might reasonably be questioned. A fair reader would reasonably question whether the new "Shooting Ambassador" could be impartial in a case asserting gun rights. But Scalia did not recuse himself. Instead, he cast the decisive vote in the 5–4 Roberts Court decision, and then he wrote a judicial opinion that basically declared open season on long-standing gun regulations.

The day after the Court issued the *Heller* decision, Gottlieb's SAF filed suit challenging Chicago's handgun ban. Scalia did not recuse himself from that case either. The 5–4 *McDonald v. Chicago* ruling extended *Heller* to the states, invalidating handgun bans across the country.

Less than three months after the Supreme Court issued the *Heller* decision, the Italian gun manufacturer Beretta got more involved in US gun regulations when Ugo Gussalli Beretta, then Beretta's worldwide CEO, announced a $1 million donation to the NRA. The NRA said the gift would benefit the NRA's "litigation activities to further expand the scope of Second Amendment protections in the wake of the recent United States Supreme Court ruling in *District of Columbia v. Heller*." WFSA had named Ugo Beretta its Shooting Ambassador the year before it gave Scalia that title. A few years later, in 2012, Scalia gleefully discussed the Second Amendment with Chris Wallace on FOX, saying that under his interpretation of the US Constitution, he ruled out a right to own "cannons" because those very heavy weapons "cannot be hand-carried," but he would not rule out a right to own "handheld rocket launchers that can bring down airplanes."[14]

There were some important precursors to the Roberts Court's dramatic revision of the meaning of the Second Amendment, which I witnessed firsthand from my position in the Justice Department. Back in January 2001, I was serving as deputy assistant attorney general, and part of my portfolio at the Justice Department was firearms policy. I closely watched the hearings on John Ashcroft's nomination to become attorney general—and my new boss—paying particularly close attention to his views on gun policy. His testimony, which could be convoluted at times, was fairly summarized in *The Baltimore Sun*, which reported that if Ashcroft became attorney general, "he would put his personal views on such issues as . . . gun rights behind him and just carry out the laws on the books. As Mr. Ashcroft put it then, he recognized he would be moving from the 'enactment-oriented role' of a legislator to a 'law-oriented role' as head of the Justice Department and the nation's chief law-enforcement officer. In that capacity, he suggested in his eagerness to be confirmed, he wouldn't ever try to persuade President Bush to make changes to support those personal views." That is, Ashcroft had assured the Senate Judiciary Committee that the Second Amendment would remain, as it had been interpreted for decades, a collective right and not an individual right to bear arms.[15]

When the Bush political appointees arrived at the department, they invited me to the newly reconstituted gun group, which consisted of twelve white guys and me. After Ashcroft was confirmed, I would hear reports that the NRA's representatives were in the building. By the time I left the department in May 2001, twenty men and I were attending those meetings—except for one they secretly held at the NRA's shooting range in Northern Virginia to which the political appointees at the Justice Department did not invite me, even though my aim is true.

Shortly before I left the Justice Department to join the judicial branch, Ashcroft did an extraordinary thing that signaled big changes to come. He wrote a public letter to the NRA, as attorney general, stating that in his opinion the Second Amendment reflects an individual right to bear arms, not a collective one. This reversal from his promises to the Senate provoked outcry from Democrats, who had sought his assurances on exactly this issue. As *The Baltimore Sun* then reported, Ashcroft "remains the same defender of the right of almost every Tom, Dick and Harry to carry a gun who has marched lockstep with the National Rifle Association throughout his political career and is now moving to make it federal policy."[16]

In 2002, after I left the department, Solicitor General Ted Olson informed the courts that the Justice Department had changed its long-standing position and would no longer defend the precedent that the Second Amendment protects a collective right and instead would argue that it protects an individual right to bear arms. That became the US government's position in the *Heller* case. Then, in 2008, the Roberts Court ratified Ashcroft's NRA-centric hostility toward public safety firearms regulations. To this day, America is still suffering from the horrendous consequences of this extraordinary shift by the Roberts Court in rewriting our Constitution.

---

In 2022, the day before the Roberts Court overturned *Roe v. Wade*, it issued a thoroughly radical and regressive ruling in a firearms case called *New York State Rifle & Pistol Association, Inc. v. Bruen*. The ruling in this case expanded on *Heller* and made it even more difficult for federal, state, and local governments to regulate deadly firearms. Gun rights and abortion rights might seem worlds apart, but in fact the Court employed a similarly regressive interpretation of the law in order to get its desired results in both cases. As Natalie Nassi, director of the Hunter Legal Center for Victims of Crimes Against Women, astutely observed, after *Bruen* we now have to "look back to the 1700s, to the 1800s, to see if something passes constitutional muster. You are just by definition going to take women's lives back to a time when they had fewer rights, when they were less safe, where they had less autonomy. And again, I don't think . . . that it's an accident . . . that all these things are happening at the same time." *Bruen* was about shifting the playing field itself, changing the rules of the game, and altering the way the Supreme Court commands that the Constitution be interpreted—a radical shift pushed by right-wing partisans whose claims get cited in Supreme Court opinions.[17]

John Roberts assigned the majority opinion in the *Bruen* case to Clarence Thomas. Through that ruling, they overturned a century-old law and concocted a new and extreme way of assessing whether a firearms law is constitutional. *Slate* called the *Bruen* opinion "one of the most intellectually dishonest and poorly argued decisions in American judicial history," noting,

> Indeed, with little sense of irony, Thomas even quotes Chief Justice Roger B. Taney's infamous opinion in *Dred Scott* [*v. Sandford*] approvingly, not only treating it as good legal authority but suggesting that the author of the worst decision in American law understood the Second Amendment better than any other judicial figure in American history. Turning to Taney for judicial inspiration would have once ended a judge's career, but the court's new originalist majority appears most of the time to be making history by inventing it, instead of by interpreting the law.[18]

John Roberts—the amateur collegiate historian and so-called judicial umpire—signed onto an opinion that credited Taney's analysis from his most discredited ruling, the decision that hastened a deadly Civil War and is larded with rank bigotry, immorality, and arrogance.

If that were not astonishing enough, the pretext of the ruling is that for more than 112 years the State of New York had acted contrary to a purportedly more "deeply rooted" right from the century before to carry a concealed weapon. In fact, Georgia, Indiana, and Arkansas had laws on the books against concealed carry as of 1837, 1819, and 1837, respectively. The Republican justices—the supposed "rule of law conservatives" that Leonard Leo and Charles Koch helped install on the Court—audaciously dispensed with long-respected constitutional standards of review for assessing whether a government has a compelling or important interest in a regulation and whether the law at issue is tailored to achieve that interest. Instead, the Roberts Court's political activists in judicial robes invented a new approach to the Second Amendment and decreed that the government cannot adopt any gun restrictions that are not "relevantly similar" to the laws on the books in 1791, when the Constitution was ratified, or 1868, when the Fourteenth Amendment was adopted and incorporated the Bill of Rights to apply to the states.[19]

The Roberts majority used this "deeply rooted" test to strike down the New York statute requiring residents to apply for permits to carry a concealed firearm. The *Bruen* ruling comes from the same troupe of berobed politicians who would later strike down *Roe* based on Samuel Alito's discredited assertion that access to abortion in the early stages of pregnancy is not "deeply rooted" in history, despite history to the contrary. As Jacob Charles has noted, "One of the most remarkable features of Justice Stephen Breyer's trenchant dissent in *Bruen* is his frank assessment of the appalling quality of the history being peddled by his colleagues. Calling out the justices for engaging in 'law office history,' a degraded form of legal analysis that warps history to fit the desired ends favored by a judge or justice.... *Bruen* is an opinion filled with legal and historical errors that all cut in the same direction, expanding gun rights by rewriting the American past."[20]

The reality is that American states and cities had been imposing restrictions on the types of weapons people could carry, where people could and could not carry weapons, and who could carry weapons—including racially discriminatory laws barring Black Americans and Native Americans from owning guns—for a long time. Even Tombstone, Arizona, of Wild West lore, banned the carrying of deadly weapons within city limits in 1881. As historians have documented, such restrictions date back centuries to England in the year 1328: "Although it's unpopular to quote the Statute of Northampton, this is a 14th-century statute in England against people carrying weapons as they travel to the 'terror of the people.' This law was in fact still active in the US in the early years of the Republic and a famous case in North Carolina in 1843 argued that even the Statute of Northampton was only codifying a long standing principle of common law, which is that you don't travel armed. . . . [I]t's a kind of highly fictionalized jurisprudence that suggests that everyone was armed."[21] To be clear, I am not suggesting that the scope of US rights be governed by feudal England. I am saying that when the Roberts Court recites "history," it is describing the past in a distorted way that would not pass muster in academia where peer review of claims and disclosure of conflicts are used to ward off quacks and hacks.[22]

I vividly recall from my time working on gun policy that the Justice Department's Office of Legal Counsel had a practice of answering legal questions from the public on an array of issues, including the Second Amendment. In reviewing those answers, I saw that a recurring question asked by the mid-century public was whether the Second Amendment protected the right to bear arms equivalent to those used by the military, if the purpose of the amendment is self-defense against the government? In other words, what qualifies as a constitutional "arm"? Does a grenade? A howitzer? A tank? One letter asked whether the Second Amendment protected a right to own a neutron bomb if the government had that weapon too. If the purpose of the Second Amendment was to defend against the government, what would prevent someone from claiming a right to own a fighter jet, acquire grenade launchers, or stockpile bombs? Of course, doing so is not reasonable—despite Scalia's later off-the-cuff assertion of a supposed constitutional right to own rocket launchers. Yet, compared to a musket or even Civil War–era repeating rifle, an AR-15, with its velocity and rapid fire, might as well be a bomb; it is almost 1,000 times more deadly than firearms were when the Constitution was ratified.

The 6–3 partisan ruling by the Roberts Court in *Bruen* provided yet another vehicle to dismantle commonsense gun laws and other protections disliked by John Roberts's political party and its financial benefactors. The ruling led to a free-for-all of Trump appointees striking down an array of long-settled and reasonable gun regulations for not being equivalent to rules purported to govern in a long-ago period of American history, as cherry-picked by Republican appointees to the Supreme Court. This onslaught led the Supreme Court to take up a case called *Rahimi v. United States.*[23]

In 2020, a state court judge issued a restraining order against a Texan named Zackey Rahimi on behalf of his ex-girlfriend after he threw her onto the pavement, dragged her into his car, and then shot at a bystander. Despite this order, which barred him from possessing firearms, Rahimi carried out five different shootings around Arlington, Texas. When someone "started talking trash" about Rahimi online, he drove to that man's house and shot at it with an AR-15 assault rifle. After that, he got into an accident with another car and shot at the driver. A few days after that, he fired a gun into the air in a residential neighborhood. After that, he shot at a driver during a road rage incident. Finally, when a friend's credit card was declined at a Whataburger, Rahimi responded to the situation by firing into the air outside that fast-food restaurant. When the police later searched his home, they found guns and ammunition in breach of the agreement Rahimi made not to possess such weapons. They pressed charges, and Rahimi was convicted. It was an open-and-shut case—until it wasn't. A Trump-appointed judge named James Ho asserted that the Framers of the Constitution who wrote the Second Amendment would not have taken a man's gun away under a restraining order—not even in the case of an obviously dangerous man like the defendant.

How did we even get here? How can any fair judge rule that an unstable domestic abuser with a history of shooting at strangers has a right to own guns? The most cogent answer to that question is that Jim Ho is not a fair judge.

The law at issue in *Rahimi*, 18 USC § 922(g)(8), had been adopted in 1998 as an amendment to the 1968 Gun Control Act. It barred people subject to restraining orders from possessing firearms and disqualified them from passing a background check for buying a gun. This is the result of what is known as the Lautenberg Amendment, named for US Senator Frank Lautenberg. Over the past twenty-five years, that law has blocked the purchases of more than 80,000 firearms by people who should not have them. That did not matter to Trump-appointee Ho. He claimed that historical laws that banned firearms possession by categories of people who were understood to be dangerous were in place to preserve *societal* order, but the Lautenberg Amendment was about protecting an *individual* person, not society, and so he declared that rule unconstitutional under *Bruen*.

Although Ho's ruling in *Rahimi* was outrageous, it was facially consistent with the extremism of the Roberts Court's ruling in *Bruen*. Indeed, it was precisely the type of injudicious ruling that *Bruen* invited. As one scholar described the chaos the Roberts Court has provoked, "Courts have said things like, 'Even if this kind of law existed in close to half the states that were then in the Union, that is not enough.' Other courts, by contrast, have said, 'We expressly disagree with a majority-of-the-states approach.' Instead, one court said, 'I need to see three laws that are analogous, and that's going to be enough to constitute a tradition.' We've seen still other courts say, 'Oh, well, Bruen called three laws an outlier at one point in the opinion, so that can't be enough. It's got to be more than three laws.'" The reality of John Roberts's tenure on the high court is chaos and disruption, not impartial decisions that promote stability and consistency.[24]

Ultimately, however, Roberts wrote the opinion overturning Ho's morally repugnant ruling in *Rahimi*. With the chance to get a Republican back in the White House, the politician in judicial robes at the helm of the Court could not afford, so close to the presidential election, to inflame women voters by following *Bruen* to its intended conclusion and striking down domestic violence restraining orders that take away an abuser's guns. Consequently, Roberts issued a decision only someone as morally monstrous as Clarence Thomas would dissent from. Though the Court issued a resounding rebuke in its 8–1 ruling overturning Judge Ho and his cohorts, the decision did not touch *Bruen*, which will continue to limit gun regulations for years to come.

---

In 2024, the Roberts Court also gave the gun industry another big win that will help it fight future gun regulation. In *Garland v. Cargill*, Justice Clarence Thomas, with the support of John Roberts and the other Republican justices, invalidated a federal regulation limiting access to "bump stocks." That regulation was issued by the Trump administration, with bipartisan support, after a violent massacre at the Route 91 Harvest Music festival in Las Vegas. The murderer had fitted more than a dozen AR-15 assault rifles with "bump stocks," an accessory that allows a shooting rate of ninety rounds in ten seconds, enabling him to rapidly fire a hail of .223-caliber bullets into the crowd. In about ten minutes, that evil man fired 1,049 bullets from his AR-15s, murdering 60 people, wounding more than 400 others, and harming another 400 who were injured in the process of trying to escape his storm of bullets. Under long-standing federal law banning machine guns, the Bureau of Alcohol, Tobacco, Firearms, and Explosives (ATF) responded by issuing a regulation extending that ban to bump stocks that allow semiautomatic firearms to fire almost as continuously as machine guns. Fancying himself a firearms engineering expert, Justice Clarence Thomas strained to argue that a weapon fitted with a bump stock was somehow not "automatic" enough to qualify as a gun subject to the machine gun ban, despite the patently obvious similarity.[25]

Roberts and his fellow Republican appointees went along with this depraved charade and struck down the regulation, which Merrick Garland and the Biden administration had defended. Justices Sonia Sotomayor, Elena Kagan, and Ketanji Brown Jackson dissented, noting,

> Today, the Court puts bump stocks back in civilian hands. To do so, it casts aside Congress's definition of "machine gun" and seizes upon one that is inconsistent with the ordinary meaning of the statutory text and unsupported by context or purpose. When I see a bird that walks like a duck, swims like a duck, and quacks like a duck, I call that bird a duck. A bump-stock-equipped semiautomatic rifle fires "automatically more than one shot, without manual reloading, by a single function of the trigger." §5845(b). Because I, like Congress, call that a machine gun, I respectfully dissent.

Again, the Roberts Court ignored the plain meaning of the law, distorted the facts, and made it harder for the political branches to regulate deadly weapons to protect public safety.

While Justice Sam Alito added a concurrence noting that Congress could amend the federal machine gun ban to include bump stocks, he knows that his political party uses its legislative power to support the gun industry at nearly every opportunity and that the chance of banning bump stocks through legislation is remote. In the Roberts Court's 6–3 decision, the Republican appointees sided with the amicus briefs submitted by the NRA and the NSSF. Other right-wing groups funded by Leonard Leo and Charles Koch also urged the Court to strike down the bump stock ban. Koch has long fueled groups with extreme agendas against commonsense gun regulation. In the mid-1970s, Koch and his family were the biggest underwriters of the Libertarian Party, at a time when its political platform stated, "We oppose all laws at any level of government restricting the ownership, manufacture, transfer or sale of firearms or ammunition."

Another big decision in 2024 also has implications for the sustainability of federal gun regulations as well as other federal regulations. In a case called *Loper Bright Enterprises v. Raimundo*, John Roberts wrote the Court's opinion reversing the forty-year-old *Chevron v. NRDC* "deference" precedent. The NSSF filed an amicus brief in *Loper Bright* that assailed ATF regulations and singled out the bump stock regulation in particular. So, Roberts's ruling will not only help carbon kingpins like Koch but also aid the gun industry, too.[26]

As of this writing, another wave of gun cases is headed to the Roberts Court. Making their way through the lower courts are challenges to state laws banning assault rifles and high-capacity magazines, defining sensitive places where guns can be prohibited, and forbidding people under twenty-one from carrying weapons. With their 6–3 majority, John Roberts and his judicial clique will continue to explore the destructive possibilities of using *Bruen* to undo or block commonsense gun limits, no matter how desperate the American people are to curb mass shootings and other gun violence. Meanwhile, early in 2025, the second Trump administration announced plans to drive cases assailing gun restrictions, too. As of this writing, under one of Trump's former personal attorneys, Harmeet Dhillon, the Civil Rights Division will for the first time in history be deployed on "Second Amendment rights litigation," no doubt aiding the NRA.

## CHAPTER 10

# ABORTION

One of the first major decisions of the Supreme Court under John Roberts's rule was in the 2007 *Gonzales v. Carhart* case discussed earlier, but Roberts had been on the (undisclosed) record as critical of *Roe v. Wade* since at least 1981. That year, when he was working as an advisor to the attorney general and shaping legal policy at the very top of the Justice Department, he wrote favorably that the leading voices on the Right "recognized a serious problem in the current exercise of judicial power," which he said was illustrated "by what is broadly perceived to be the unprincipled jurisprudence of *Roe v. Wade*." But, in 2005, when John Roberts took the oath to testify truthfully in the Senate hearing on his nomination to the Supreme Court, he had to get around the fact that the majority of the American people, and probably the majority of senators, supported *Roe*. To overcome this problem, Roberts offered obfuscating testimony. Despite his oath to tell "the truth, the whole truth, and nothing but the truth" at his confirmation hearing, it was not until 2022 that Roberts chose to fully reveal his views on *Roe*, when he joined the majority of justices in *Dobbs v. Jackson Women's Health Organization* in upholding Mississippi's fifteen-week abortion ban, in direct contravention of *Roe*.[1]

One persistent piece of spin by Roberts was to say that the antiabortion briefs he signed on to or supervised when he was the political deputy in the Solicitor General's Office of the George H. W. Bush administration were just "the position of the administration" and thus did not reflect his own views. These positions included supporting a state law requiring women to notify their husbands before they could obtain an abortion and defending a gag rule barring family planning clinics that received federal money from discussing abortion.

Roberts also omitted *Bray v. Alexandria Women's Health Clinic* from a list of his most significant cases that he provided to the Senate Judiciary Committee. In that litigation, Roberts took the same side as antiabortion extremists against a women's health center that had sued under federal civil rights laws to stop those extremists from blockading abortion clinics. The petitioners included Randall Terry, who relaunched "Operation Rescue" in 1986 (after it was initially launched in 1970 by the radical Catholic antiabortion activist L. Brent Bozell Jr., William F. Buckley Jr.'s brother-in-law). Its slogan was "If you believe abortion is murder, act like it's murder." Other petitioners were Michael and Jayne Bray. Michael Bray was a member of a violent domestic terrorist group called the Army of God, which called for a biblically based government in America. He had been convicted a few years earlier, in 1985, of bombing abortion clinics and women's health advocacy centers. After serving a four-year sentence, Bray returned to civilian life and to protesting abortion clinics in the Washington, DC, area. The Brays and Terry were represented by Jay Sekulow, who later helped launch the Judicial Crisis Network, which helped get John Roberts and Samuel Alito confirmed to the Supreme Court. (Sekulow also later represent Donald Trump in his first impeachment trial.) On the other side of the *Bray* case was the National Abortion Federation, the NAACP Legal Defense Fund, the American Civil Liberties

Union, and more than two dozen other groups committed to women's health and equality.[2]

Roberts sought to distance himself from the violent extremists on his side of the case by suggesting they could be charged instead with trespassing, while he argued that the people Terry and the Brays were targeting at clinics did not deserve federal civil rights protections. As principal deputy solicitor general for the United States, John Roberts argued that antiabortion protesters who obstructed access to clinics had not violated federal civil rights laws that banned conspiracies to deprive other groups of their rights. Roberts specifically argued that the Ku Klux Klan Act of 1871 should be construed to apply only to discrimination based on race, not gender, even though the Congress that adopted that statute stated that it expected the protections of that act to extend to "all the thirty-eight millions of the citizens of this nation." The statute did not limit its protections to Blacks but applied to any "class of persons" deprived of their rights.[3]

Roberts also argued that federal civil rights law should not apply because the blockaders were also obstructing men accompanying women, too, and not just women. That is like saying the Black civil rights activists in the South could not be protected from conspiracies to deprive them of their rights because some whites joined them in the cause. But the Supreme Court adopted Roberts's approach and gave antiabortion groups a major victory. Justice Antonin Scalia wrote the majority opinion, asserting, "The characteristic that formed the basis of the targeting here was not womanhood, but the seeking of abortion."

Justices John Paul Stevens and Harry Blackmun dissented, noting, "Congress enacted legislation imposing on the Federal Judiciary the responsibility to remedy both abuses of power by persons acting under color of state law and lawless conduct that state courts are neither fully competent, nor always certain, to prevent. The Ku

Klux Klan Act . . . was a response to the massive, organized lawlessness that infected our Southern States during the post–Civil War era." The dissent noted that the lower courts agreed that the statute "provides a federal remedy for petitioners' violent concerted activities on the public streets and private property of law-abiding citizens." They also recognized the detailed factual findings of the lower courts that Operation Rescue's swarming activities could cause women seeking an abortion or continuing an abortion procedure "serious physical and psychological injuries." Justice Sandra Day O'Connor also dissented, crediting the reality of the "threats of mob violence" faced by patients and staff. The risk of violence was real. In 1994, the year after the Court's ruling in favor of Roberts's argument, Michael Bray wrote a book, *A Time to Kill*, arguing that people were justified in using "godly force" to murder abortion doctors.[4]

As Justices Stevens and Blackmun wrote in a critique that really applied to both Scalia's opinion and Roberts's contentions, "It is unfortunate that the Court has analyzed this case as though it presented an abstract question of logical deduction rather than a question concerning the exercise and allocation of power in our federal system of government. The Court ignores the obvious (and entirely constitutional) congressional intent behind [that law] to protect this Nation's citizens from what amounts to the theft of their constitutional rights by organized and violent mobs across the country."

After the Supreme Court adopted John Roberts's analysis, Congress sought to pass a new federal law to redress the harmful consequences. In 1994, after Dr. David Gunn was assassinated by an antiabortion extremist, Congress adopted the Freedom of Access to Clinic Entrances (FACE) Act to make sure federal law protects against "the use of physical force, threat of physical force, or physical obstruction to intentionally injure, intimidate, interfere with or attempt to injure, intimidate or interfere with any person who is obtaining an abortion" and "intentional damage or destruction of a reproductive health care facility." According to one study, in the fifteen years before FACE was adopted, there had been "at least 9 murders, 17 attempted murders, 406 death threats, 179 incidents of assault or battery, and 5 kidnappings committed against abortion providers [plus] 41 bombings, 175 arsons, 96 attempted bombings or arsons, 692 bomb threats, 1993 incidents of trespassing, 1400 incidents of vandalism," and other extremely disruptive tactics deployed by antiabortion extremists. The FACE Act, however, did not bar protesters from carrying signs or distributing literature.[5]

That new federal law helped reduce the violence of antiabortionists at clinics, and other states adopted analogous laws. Massachusetts, for example, passed the Reproductive Health Care Facilities Act, which initially prevented interfering with driveways and entrances, after the Supreme Court ruled in 1999 that a Colorado law requiring consent to approach people within 100 feet of abortion facilities was constitutional. That ruling was in *Hill v. Colorado*, a 6–3 decision written by Justice Stevens. However, a few years after John Roberts became chief justice and Alito was confirmed, Roberts wrote the Supreme Court's opinion in *McCullen v. Coakley*, which struck down the Massachusetts "buffer zone" law that barred people from occupying roads and sidewalks within thirty-five feet of a reproductive health care facility. Citing the First Amendment, Roberts allowed aggressive and obstructive "sidewalk counseling" by antiabortion activists urging women not to have abortions. That case did not present the question of whether to uphold *Roe v. Wade*, but it was one in a line of cases that chipped away at women's health care rights, impeding their ability to freely exercise their rights under *Roe*.[6]

After Donald Trump became president in 2017, a group called the Alliance Defending Freedom (ADF) launched a new strategy for overturning *Roe*. ADF, which the Southern Poverty Law Center has designated a "hate group" for its attacks on gay rights, was launched in 1993 by a group of antiabortion/antigay televangelists and spearheaded by James Dobson (founder of the Family Research Council). By 2017, ADF's budget from secretive sources was about $50 million. That summer, at a "summit" at the luxurious Ritz-Carlton resort overlooking the beach in Laguna Niguel, California, ADF lawyers and other right-wing operatives discussed pursuing a fifteen-week abortion ban. That marker was chosen as a way to challenge *Roe*'s constitutional protection of access to abortion prior to "viability"—the capacity of a fetus to survive outside the womb—which is generally marked at about twenty-three weeks of gestation. ADF then wrote the "model" bill that became the Mississippi law at issue in the *Dobbs* case. Mississippi was chosen not because abortions were especially common there but because its government was politically amenable to advancing such an overtly unconstitutional law.[7]

Mississippi Governor Phil Bryant signed the Gestational Age Act into law in March 2018. It provided no exception for rape or incest and specified a ten-year prison sentence for doctors who provide an abortion after fifteen weeks. The Jackson Women's Health Organization, the only abortion provider in Mississippi, challenged the law as facially invalid under *Roe*. US District Court Judge Carlton Reeves granted summary judgment and issued a permanent injunction against the fifteen-week ban. The following year, in December 2019, the US Court of Appeals for the Fifth Circuit affirmed that decision in a 3–0 ruling, noting, "In an unbroken line dating to *Roe v. Wade*, the Supreme Court's abortion cases have established (and affirmed, and re-affirmed) a woman's right to choose an abortion before viability. States may regulate abortion procedures prior to viability so long as they do not impose an undue burden on the woman's right, but they may not ban abortions."

In March 2020, Lynn Fitch, the state's new attorney general, sought review by the US Supreme Court. Her campaign had been funded in part by Neil Corkery, the person Leonard Leo trusts to keep the financial records of his core nonprofit arms. (Fitch's election was also aided by the Republican Attorneys General Association, whose largest funders have been Leo-tied groups.)

While the petition to hear the case was pending, on September 18, 2020, Justice Ruth Bader Ginsburg died. Senator Mitch McConnell orchestrated Amy Coney Barrett's confirmation, in a party-line vote, just seven days before Election Day, and that change in personnel gave Chief Justice John Roberts a new 6–3 Republican "supermajority." For seven months afterward, the Roberts Court held off on agreeing to hear the *Dobbs* case, putting distance between Ginsburg's passing and Barrett's confirmation before taking up the case. In May 2021, the Roberts Court allowed the case to move forward. Dozens of groups submitted amicus briefs on both sides, including several with ties to Leo—such as the Ethics and Public Policy Center, the Becket Fund, Students for Life, and CatholicVote.org—all of which attacked *Roe*. The brief on behalf of the Family Research Council was submitted by the law firm of Consovoy McCarthy, where the administrative trustee of Leo's billion-dollar trust fund is a partner. Also attacking *Roe* in an amicus brief to the Court was Trump's January 6–tied lawyer John Eastman.

US Senator Josh Hawley (R-MO) also submitted an amicus brief, alongside Senators Ted Cruz (R-TX) and Mike Lee (R-UT). They called *Roe v. Wade* and *Planned Parenthood v. Casey* "unworkable"—invoking one of the prongs for the reversal of a precedent that John Roberts had emphasized during the Senate hearings on his nomination to the Court. They urged that those precedents protecting the constitutional right to access abortion be overturned. Leo and Corkery had also helped launch Josh Hawley's political career when he ran for attorney general of Missouri over a decade before. Unbeknownst to the public, Senator Hawley's wife, Erin Hawley, was helping to manage the *Dobbs* litigation for ADF, which had orchestrated the legislation and the ensuing court case. Her activities included helping Mississippi with its briefs and coordinating amicus briefs from so-called third parties. One reason why Erin's work was kept from the public is that backers of the litigation found it useful to present the Mississippi law as written by a state legislator, Becky Currie, who previously worked as a nurse. After the case was won, however, right-wing media boasted that ADF's "relative anonymity was not an oversight and instead was part of a deliberate strategy" to avoid public focus on its role. Notably, Hawley clerked for John Roberts, and she has deep ties to the Leo-backed antiabortion agenda.[8]

The Court held oral arguments in the case on December 1, 2021, with Julie Rikelman from the Center for Reproductive Rights and US Solicitor General Elizabeth Prelogar arguing that the Mississippi law violated the constitutional rights enshrined in *Roe v. Wade*. Mississippi Solicitor General Scott Stewart, who had clerked for Clarence Thomas in 2015–2016, urged the Court to reverse *Roe* as "egregiously wrong." After the argument, Stewart, Fitch, and Hawley together addressed an exclusive group of ADF allies. Fitch reportedly said, "First of all, to God be the glory. . . . We all prayed, worked so hard for this day. It all came together because everyone here . . . we're believers, and we knew this day would come. . . . God selected this case. He was ready. The justices were ready to hear what we were all going to be talking about."[9]

Five months later, with no ruling on the case yet issued, *The Wall Street Journal*'s editorial page warned that John Roberts "may be trying to turn another Justice" to uphold the Mississippi law without outright reversing *Roe*. The *Journal*'s tactic appeared to be bullying Roberts to solidify the willingness of Brett Kavanaugh and Amy Coney Barrett to expressly reverse *Roe*, despite the seeming assurances they gave in public and private around their confirmation hearings, during which they acknowledged that *Roe* was an important precedent that, implicitly, they would not reverse. Just a day or two after the *Journal*'s extraordinary warning, a copy of the draft majority opinion in the *Dobbs* case was leaked to *Politico*.

It was published in a piece bylined by *Politico*'s Supreme Court reporter Josh Gerstein and, curiously, a national security reporter named Alexander Ward. Although some on the right vociferously blamed Democratic appointees to the Court or their staff for the leak, it is not clear that they had even seen Alito's draft at that point. The leak helped lock in Alito's majority for outright reversal, which the *Journal* had been aiming for, because right-wing intelligentsia would see flip-flopping as discrediting. Roberts was apparently outraged by the leak and launched a one of a kind investigation. That probe required nearly everyone working for the Court—except the justices themselves and their spouses—to answer questions under penalty of perjury. Ultimately, the investigation could not determine the source of the leak.[10]

On June 24, 2024, the Supreme Court announced its decision in *Dobbs* in an official opinion that was substantially identical to the leaked draft. Five of the Republican justices—Alito, Kavanaugh, Barrett, Thomas, and Neil Gorsuch—struck down *Roe* and *Casey* and upheld Mississippi's law. Roberts concurred in the result of allowing the previability abortion ban to go into effect but said it was not necessary to overturn precedents explicitly to do so, even though the statute was plainly unconstitutional under those precedents, as the lower courts had found.

With Barrett confirmed to the Court in place of Ginsburg, Alito did not have to tolerate Roberts's artifice of gradualism to get a fifth vote to destroy the protections for accessing abortion guaranteed by *Roe* and *Casey*. Alito's ruling characterized *Roe* as an illegitimate expression of "liberty" by asserting that only "deeply rooted" rights could be recognized and access to abortion was not one of them. Alito went so far as to cite archaic pronouncements of men like Sir Matthew Hale, "a 17th-century [English] jurist who conceived the notion that husbands can't be prosecuted for raping their wives, who sentenced women to death as 'witches,' and whose misogyny stood out even in his time."[11] Hale sowed into English history the notion that juries should be skeptical of women's claims of rape—even though the documented evidence over centuries shows that the real problem is not false accusations by women but false denials by the men who raped them. It is also repugnant for the US Supreme Court of the twenty-first century to suggest that the rights of American women should be informed by the views of a Puritan witch hunter born in 1609; yet Alito and his fellow Republicans had no compunction about citing such a monstrous man as Hale in a ruling by America's highest court.[12]

Alito also cited another man, who lived in medieval Europe, to claim that abortion had been a "crime" since the thirteenth century. He copied that claim from the brief of a close ally of Leonard Leo named Robbie George, who runs the Witherspoon Institute, an Opus Dei–linked outpost at Princeton. The Organization of American Historians and the American Historical Association rebuked the Roberts Court for Alito's assertions, noting, "The court's majority opinion refers to 'history' 67 times, claiming that 'an unbroken tradition of prohibiting abortion on pain of criminal punishment persisted from the earliest days of the common law until 1973.' Our brief shows plentiful evidence, however, of the long legal tradition, extending from the common law to the mid-1800s (and far longer in some American states, including Mississippi), of tolerating termination of pregnancy before occurrence of 'quickening,' the time when a woman first felt fetal movement."[13]

Alito's opinion—inlaid with bombastic, religiously inflected rhetoric—reads like a partisan editorial. It's almost as though the supremely arrogant editorial board of *The Wall Street Journal* were operating from within the nation's most ornate courthouse. Unlike the *Journal*'s rants, however, Alito's screed carries the force of law and is forcing Americans into crises that threaten their lives, their health, and their future ability to start a family if and when they choose.

In his concurring opinion, John Roberts voted to uphold Mississippi's abortion ban after fifteen weeks of pregnancy, when a fetus is definitely not viable outside the womb, but he did not join Alito's opinion striking down *Roe* and *Casey* outright. He also chose not to join the dissenters—Justices Stephen Breyer, Sonia Sotomayor, and Elena Kagan—defending those legal precedents. Instead, Roberts wrote that he would have preferred to wait for a case that litigated an abortion ban from an earlier point in pregnancy, in order to consider overturning *Roe* entirely. Roberts apparently preferred to divest *Roe* of meaning, quietly extinguishing its protections, while leaving a neutered husk behind.

Roberts's concurring opinion echoed the public claims made by his former two-time law clerk, Erin Hawley. Where Hawley claimed, "We are only one of seven countries that allow abortion until viability and that puts us in the company of China and North Korea," Roberts wrote, "Only a handful of countries, among them China and North Korea, permit elective abortions after twenty weeks; the rest have coalesced around a 12-week line." Strikingly, Hawley and Roberts also home in on the exact same countries, China and North Korea, out of the seven possible examples to list, thereby implicitly drawing comparisons between the "communism" of these countries and those that allow their citizens to freely obtain abortions. However, under *Roe* and *Casey*, the United States did not allow abortion under all circumstances; instead, the law limited state barriers to abortion in the first trimester and ensured any restrictions later in a pregnancy allowed reasonable exceptions for the mother's health and life. Only two dozen countries in the world entirely ban abortions, and most of those are authoritarian states.

Roberts also sought to position his *Dobbs* opinion as consistent with his nomination testimony, portraying his preference for not overtly overruling *Roe* as an expression of restraint: "The

Court's decision to overrule *Roe* and *Casey* is *a serious jolt to the legal system*—regardless of how you view those cases. A narrower decision rejecting the misguided viability line would be markedly less unsettling, and nothing more is needed to decide this case" (emphasis added). A serious jolt? That is a good description of the public's reaction to having their rights stripped away. Rather than demonstrating judicial "restraint," Roberts's *Dobbs* decision is indicative of his seemingly political calculation that erosion is the way to avoid a "serious jolt."[14]

The reality is that slowly dissolving a precedent is a strategy that provides fewer opportunities for jolting the public into action, for grassroots mobilization against the Court, like the metaphorical frog being slowly boiled in a pot. In reality, a frog will jump out when water gets uncomfortably warm, but unfortunately humans are apparently much more complacent in response to a rising threat than the typical amphibian.

Alito and Roberts seem to have the same destination on the horizon: a land where women's rights are subordinate to a government more concerned about their breeding than their lives, their health, their families, or their dreams. But Roberts is more attentive to not provoking a political backlash that could ultimately thwart his larger agenda. *Dobbs* produced a "serious jolt" precisely because it led almost immediately to a destination a majority of Americans never wanted to see. Indeed, most Americans never thought the elimination of the constitutional right to abortion was actually possible until they woke up in 2022 and learned they had been profoundly mistaken.

I am tempted to recount the myriad ways in which Alito's majority opinion was deeply flawed and exhibited an unconscionable level of cruelty and profound indifference to women and the people and communities who love them. Instead, I invite the reader to seek out the powerful dissenting opinion by Justices Breyer,

Sotomayor, and Kagan, which expertly does this work. A few lines from their dissent suffice:

> Now a new and bare majority of this Court—acting at practically the first moment possible—overrules *Roe* and *Casey*. It converts a series of dissenting opinions expressing antipathy toward *Roe* and *Casey* into a decision greenlighting even total abortion bans. . . . It eliminates a 50-year-old constitutional right that safeguards women's freedom and equal station. It breaches a core rule-of-law principle, designed to promote constancy in the law. In doing all of that, it places in jeopardy other rights, from contraception to same-sex intimacy and marriage. And finally, it undermines the Court's legitimacy. . . . With sorrow—for this Court, but more, for the many millions of American women who have today lost a fundamental constitutional protection—we dissent.

As legally comprehensive as their dissenting opinion is, Marge Piercy's words touch upon the inhumanity of banning abortion in a more visceral way, to me, in her poem "Right to life," which I have cherished since I first encountered it in law school in 1992:

> I will choose what enters me, what becomes
> of my flesh. Without choice, no politics,
> no ethics lives. I am not your cornfield,
> not your uranium mine, not your calf
> for fattening, not your cow for milking.
> You may not use me as your factory.
> Priests and legislators do not hold shares
> in my womb or my mind.
> This is my body. If I give it to you

I want it back. My life
is a non-negotiable demand.[15]

---

*Dobbs* jolted the public awake, into a nightmare, facilitated by the Roberts Court and supported by an intense network of antiabortion activists. Overturning *Roe v. Wade* was a personal goal of Leonard Leo, and it was in the Federalist Society's "DNA" from the very beginning. In 1982, the first Federalist Society event, held at Yale Law School, was about abortion. Since the Federalist Society's launch, its members have influenced government policy on abortion in every Republican administration. Its defenders have even bragged that "symbolic of their influence, members of the Federalist Society have presented oral arguments to the Supreme Court in every significant abortion case since 1992."[16]

Although the Federalist Society claims not to take a position on issues, its members' "ideas and tactics have shaped abortion law and jurisprudence since *Roe*, shining a light on the success that conservatives have had chipping away at the right to make abortion decisions." As noted by scholars who have studied the group, "Within the Federalist Society, the home of efforts to limit or overturn the constitutional rights related to personal sexual autonomy is the Religious Liberties Practice Group [which contends] that state or federal laws advancing gay rights, and access to contraception and abortion, offend the religious liberty of those who disagree. Such laws amount, some claim, to 'government-backed persecution.'"[17]

But how could a society of law students and lawyers accomplish such a dramatic rewrite of our laws? During the thirty-plus years that Leo has helped to guide the Federalist Society, it has focused on the courts and judicial appointments because personnel *is* policy. After all, all six of the Republican appointees to the US Supreme Court were confirmed with the help of Leo.

So perhaps it should come as no surprise that Leonard Leo had prescheduled an exclusive and very luxurious party at his mansion in Maine in conjunction with a conference hosted by George Mason's law school, just as the *Dobbs* ruling was about to be issued. As *ProPublica* described it,

> The party guests who arrived on the evening of June 23, 2022, at the Tudor-style mansion on the coast of Maine were a special group in a special place enjoying a special time. The attendees included some two-dozen federal and state judges—a gathering that required US marshals with earpieces to stand watch while a Coast Guard boat idled in a nearby cove. Caterers served guests . . . Winston Churchill's favorite Champagne. . . . The decadeslong campaign to overturn *Roe v. Wade*, which a leaked draft opinion had said was "egregiously wrong from the start," could come to fruition within days, if not hours. Over dinner courses paired with wines . . . attendees jockeyed for a word with the man who had done as much as anyone to make this moment possible: their host, Leonard Leo.[18]

The death blow that the Roberts Court dealt to *Roe* the next day unleashed chaos in the lives and destinies of women whose rights will be restricted for years to come—thanks to Leo and the backing of anti-choice billionaires.

What has happened since the Roberts Court overturned *Roe v. Wade*?

As Alito was doing his victory tour (including a speech in Rome underwritten by a clinic at Notre Dame Law School, which is one of a number of groups funded by Leo), Republican officials were using their new power to restrict abortion to impose an array of hardships, such as

- A $10,000 bounty for suing a mother who helped her daughter get an abortion just a few weeks after missing her period—an abortion made illegal when done more than six weeks after conception, which is when most people first learn they are pregnant;[19]
- Emergency room doctors, at the insistence of legal counsel, turning away terrified pregnant women in need of emergency medical care but apparently not close enough to death; and[20]
- An attempt to force a ten-year-old girl to carry a pregnancy, the result of rape, to term and to give birth against her will.[21]

Some states—like Georgia and Texas, captured by regressive political donors and with legislatures gerrymandered with the blessing of the Roberts Court—stood ready to exploit the Court's reversal of *Roe* by imposing six-week abortion bans that had recently been incorporated into so-called trigger laws. Other states, like Arizona and Wisconsin, had nineteenth-century restrictions that sprang into force. The Arizona Supreme Court, with all Republican appointees, issued a decree allowing its dormant 1864 abortion ban to go into effect, but the legislature passed a repeal, which Democratic Governor Katie Hobbs signed. The battle over Wisconsin's 175-year-old ban is ongoing. In 2023, a billionaire named Dick Uihlein spent millions through front groups, like Fair Courts America, to try to install Dan Kelly, an antiabortion evangelical, on the Wisconsin Supreme Court in order to secure an antiabortion majority. He failed. Two years later, in 2025, Uihlein was back trying to capture another seat on that state court, but this time his state-court-capture agenda was buttressed with more than $20 million spent by Donald Trump's biggest-known sponsor: billionaire Elon Musk. The judicial candidate favored by Musk and Uihlein lost. Notably, in both of those Wisconsin elections, an antiabortion group called Women Speak Out got most of its funding via one man: Uihlein.[22]

*Dobbs* was just the sort of lightning strike, startling the public awake from dreamy reverence for the US Supreme Court, that Roberts desperately wanted to avoid. It brought home what Planned Parenthood and other public interest groups and advocates had been saying in elections since before John Roberts was appointed: that women's reproductive rights were gravely at risk. Our rights could be rolled back by right-wing political operatives wearing judicial robes if we did not protect against the Right's efforts to capture the Court. During the summer immediately following *Dobbs*, in deep-red Kansas, voters rejected a proposal to amend the state constitution to say there was no right to abortion. In the 2022 midterm election that was forecasted to be a "red wave," Republicans did not capture the Senate. They barely won the House—and that was only because the Roberts Court had allowed election districts that favored Republicans to stand even though they violated the requirements of the Voting Rights Act.[23]

As Republican-dominated states began enforcing their bans and other restrictions on abortion, countless women—often with their partners—came forward to attest publicly to how they had been harmed by those limits. Some of them compellingly testified about how they had nearly died as hospitals refused to treat miscarriages with procedures associated with abortion services. A Georgia woman, Amber Nicole Thurman, died after a hospital refused to administer lifesaving health care to treat her miscarriage, paralyzed into inaction by a state law mandating that doctors withhold treatment until a woman was near death. Her preventable death left behind a six-year-old son to grow up without his mother. Tragically, Amber's family is not alone in losing a mother to the inhumane restrictions made possible by the Roberts Court.[24]

---

Less than two months after the *Dobbs* ruling, antiabortion extremists formed a new front group in Amarillo, Texas, to ensure that the case they filed would be assigned to the one federal judge assigned to that district: Judge Matthew Kacsmaryk. That front group, the Alliance for Hippocratic Medicine (AHM), was created in August 2022, just weeks after the *Dobbs* ruling. Even though it asserted that it had operations in Amarillo, its filing for tax-exempt status placed it in Bristol, Tennessee. In each of its first two years of operations, it had less than $50,000 in revenue and told the Internal Revenue Service it did not even have a website, but that did not stop it from bringing litigation to try to destroy the ability of American women to get medication abortions. AHM's president is listed as Donna Harrison, a Michigander whose day job is with the American Association of Pro-Life Obstetricians and Gynecologists (AAPLOG), which was also listed as a plaintiff in the case. AAPLOG seeks to impose its religious agenda on the practice of medicine, and it is notorious for promoting discredited claims about abortion and birth control, including the widely debunked assertion that abortion leads to breast cancer.[25]

Kacsmaryk is a go-to political operative installed in judicial chambers. Why? Before becoming a judge, he was the deputy general counsel at First Liberty, a nonprofit law firm launched in 1997 by antiabortion activist Kelly Shackelford, who is also a leader of Ziklag, a group trying to make US law conform to its view of the Bible. Kacsmaryk has claimed that LGBTQ rights and women's reproductive rights stem from the "radical" and "libertine" sexual revolution, and he has aggressively supported a religious-based right to discriminate against gays and lesbians. After Trump nominated him, Kacsmaryk even hid from the American people an antiabortion article he had written that had not yet been published. As a judge, he has sought to bar access to emergency contraception and even birth control at pharmacies.[26]

In response to AHM's challenge to the approval of mifepristone by the Food and Drug Administration, Kacsmaryk eagerly issued an injunction to rescind the FDA's approval of the abortion-inducing medication. Acting as if he were still a lawyer for the anti-abortion group that paid his salary for years, Kacsmaryk claimed that the FDA's approval process more than twenty years earlier had been flawed, basing his edict on biased, outlier studies asserting that mifepristone was dangerous. In reality, mifepristone has been proven safe by numerous studies in the United States and abroad; it is safer than many prescription and over-the-counter drugs. Since *Dobbs*, the most common form of abortion in the United States is through medicine and not surgery.

Kacsmaryk asserted that antiabortion doctors had standing to challenge the FDA's drug-approval process using absurd reasoning: because of the possibility that they might someday have to help save a woman's life by being forced to perform a surgical abortion, against their will, if mifepristone did not work. Republican appointees to the US Court of Appeals for the Fifth Circuit affirmed that ruling. One of the judges on that court, Trump-appointee James Ho, even asserted that a doctor has a legal interest in ensuring a fetus is born, even if the patient does not want to continue the pregnancy. As Orwellian as it sounds, Ho suggested a doctor's interest in seeing a pregnancy through to birth is stronger than a woman's right to terminate a pregnancy.

What did the Roberts Court do? True to Roberts's general approach of not wanting to spook people into action with a "serious jolt" in an election year, replicating the disastrous political consequences of *Dobbs* in 2022, the Court took the case but didn't issue a substantive ruling. Roberts received the headlines he surely preferred a few months before the 2024 presidential election: "Supreme Court Keeps Status Quo on Abortion Pill," "Supreme Court Rejects Challenge to Abortion Pill Mifepristone," and "Supreme Court Preserves Access to Abortion Pill." The headlines, for low-information voters, make John Roberts out to be the hero. He is not. The Roberts Court was just kicking the can down the road until *after* the 2024 election.

The Supreme Court sent that case back to the lower court on "standing" grounds, ruling on facts that were plain from the outset of the suit that the doctors' group did not sustain any legally cognizable injury from pregnant Americans having access to mifepristone—despite the outrageous machinations of Kacsmaryk and Ho to concoct such grounds. However, the Roberts Court did so with the knowledge that Kacsmaryk had already allowed Republican-led states to join the litigation. The Trump administration later moved to dismiss the case and began to consider revoking FDA approval.

---

The Roberts Court also took unusual actions in 2024 beyond how it handled the lawsuit seeking to deauthorize abortion medication. In *Moyle v. United States*, the Court took a case away from the US Court of Appeals for the Ninth Circuit, which was examining whether Idaho could block the enforcement of federal rules to protect the health of patients seeking emergency abortion care. Following *Dobbs*, the Joe Biden administration made clear that it interpreted a Reagan-era law, the Emergency Medical Treatment and Labor Act (EMTALA), as applying to abortion care. EMTALA requires hospitals that receive Medicaid reimbursement to protect the health of people seeking emergency treatment. Idaho objected to EMTALA's protections under its post-*Dobbs* law that makes it a state crime for a doctor to give abortion care to a woman who is not on the brink of death (or unless, for example, parents certify that their minor daughter became pregnant through rape). The Idaho attorney general hired the Alliance Defending Freedom's Erin Hawley, who clerked for John Roberts, to litigate the case.[27]

During the 2024 election year, after improvidently intervening in *Moyle v. United States* and hearing oral arguments, the Roberts

Court abruptly changed course, deciding to send the case back to the Ninth Circuit and await a decision on the merits, which is the normal sequence for appeals. Following Trump's inauguration, the federal government dropped its defense of EMTALA, making the case moot. That "places pregnant patients seeking emergency medical care in the state at risk of grave harms, including deaths" in states that ban abortion, as Physicians for Human Rights noted. In other words, more American women will perish.

---

Most Americans support access to abortion, which was protected by *Roe v. Wade*. Support for legal abortion access has only grown since the Roberts Court overturned that precedent and as reporters continue to document the deadly harms of restricting legal access to abortion care. Abortion is literally more popular than either the former or current president. It is more popular now than at any time since Dwight D. Eisenhower was president, decades ago. Even most Catholics in America support access to abortion. Many Jewish synagogues teach that women have a moral right to choose. Some Islamic schools instruct that abortion is permissible before "ensoulment," which is deemed to occur at 120 days (and also allow the procedure later to save a woman's life). American Buddhists generally support being able to make a choice whether to continue a pregnancy, as do many Christian denominations, such as the United Church of Christ, which views choice as a human right, and the Unitarian Universalists and other religious groups. Many secular groups devoted to ethics and freedom also support that choice.

But a vocal minority wants to block access to abortion for others, whose freedom in a secular democracy should not be bound by someone else's religious dictates. Recognizing the deep unpopularity of banning abortion, some of these very special interests—fueled mostly by rich men trying to make their personal agendas into binding law—have turned to the unelected, unaccountable Roberts Court to make their ambitions a reality.

Since John Roberts became the chief justice of the US Supreme Court, American women have been losing their liberty. Starting with the *Gonzales v. Carhart* decision through the *Dobbs* ruling and its aftermath, the Roberts Court has made it increasingly difficult for American women to get the medical care they need, to follow their doctor's advice to protect their health when they are pregnant and confronted with a heart-wrenching diagnosis like cancer that needs treatment or when a severe fetal abnormality is detected. Women are literally dying because John Roberts agreed that states can restrict access to abortion well before a fetus is viable. The result of Roberts's rule over our nation's highest court is that American women are less safe and less free. The dystopia that the narrow-minded Roberts has unleashed with the help of his fellow Republican justices is deeply destructive of our liberty and to women's power to choose their own destinies.

In the meantime, I will take some consolation from the fact that Roberts has lost his manufactured shield of faux neutrality, as more and more people understand that he and his Court cannot be trusted to do justice for all. That will have to suffice for now as we build a movement to reform the Court and repair the enormous damage his Court has caused to millions of people's rights.

CHAPTER 11

# GOD

MOST AMERICANS SAY religion is not the most important thing in their lives, but even as religious attendance is shrinking in the United States, inflating religious power has become a significant part of the political agenda of John Roberts and his fellow Republican appointees to the US Supreme Court. A recent Gallup poll found that 33 percent of Americans are Protestant, and another 13 percent describe themselves generally as "Christian." Another 7 percent are Jewish, Muslim, Buddhist, or Hindu. Another 22 percent are Catholics, a figure equal to those Americans who practice no religion at all, the 22 percent who are atheist or agnostic. However, fully 100 percent of the Republican appointees on the Roberts Court were raised Catholic (although one of them later became Episcopalian). What are the odds of that being random?[1]

If it seems as though this statistical anomaly could not happen unless they were handpicked, that would be correct. They were. Five of the six were chosen on the advice of Leonard Leo, and Leo helped the sixth, Clarence Thomas, win confirmation. Leo is a right-wing Catholic who has been determined to use the Court to impose his personal and political agenda—and the agenda of his superwealthy benefactors—to overturn the constitutional right to abortion, roll back gay marriage equality, tear down the wall between church and state, and more. "No one has been more dedicated to the enterprise of building a Supreme Court that will overturn *Roe v. Wade* than the Federalist Society's Leonard Leo," said his friend Ed Whelan, who led the Ethics and Public Policy Center, which Leo helps govern and C. Boyden Gray helped steer.

America is one of the most religiously diverse countries in the world. Religious worship has thrived here in part because there is no official religion. The wisdom of the Constitution expressly bans religious tests for public office, explicitly bars the establishment of a religion, and intentionally omits any use of the word "God." The way religion is treated in our Constitution reflects both the founding generation's commitment to the Enlightenment value of freedom of thought and a more practical interest in not being forced to subsidize someone else's church.[2]

These principles animate John F. Kennedy's response to opponents of his 1960 campaign for the presidency, who criticized him harshly for his Catholic faith:

> I believe in an America where the separation of church and state is absolute . . . where no church or church school is granted any public funds or political preference. . . . I believe in an America where . . . every man has the same right to attend or not attend the church of his choice; where there is no Catholic vote, no anti-Catholic vote, no bloc voting of any kind. . . . Whatever issue may come before me as president—on birth control, divorce, censorship, gambling or any other subject—I will make my decision in accordance . . . with what my conscience tells me to be the national interest. . . . But if the time should ever come when my office would require me to either violate my conscience or violate the national interest, then I would resign the

> office; and I hope any conscientious public servant would do the same.[3]

Although John Roberts and his Republican cohorts on the Court claim strict adherence to "text, history, and tradition," their rulings have sought to tear down that separation of church and state.

The Leo Five on the Supreme Court are John Roberts and Samuel Alito, plus all three appointees of Donald Trump: Neil Gorsuch, Brett Kavanaugh, and Amy Coney Barrett. The sixth Republican-appointed justice, Clarence Thomas, attended Catholic grade school and then enrolled in Conception Seminary College to become a Catholic priest before transferring to the College of the Holy Cross, the first Catholic college in New England. Shortly after attending Yale Law School instead of joining the priesthood, Thomas embarked on his political career, ultimately getting a seat on the Supreme Court in 1991, with the help of C. Boyden Gray. A few years later, Father Paul Scalia, one of Justice Antonin Scalia's sons and also an alumnus of Holy Cross, reportedly brought Thomas back to his Catholic faith.

By 2001, *Newsweek* was reporting that Justices Scalia and Thomas were reputed to be part of Opus Dei, a secretive, ultraconservative Catholic sect, although they could also have been unofficial collaborators. That article also reported that Scalia's wife, Maureen, had attended multiple Opus Dei "spiritual functions," according to a member of the sect who spoke with reporter Jack Evans. Opus Dei was created as a special prelature of the Catholic Church by Josemaría Escrivá, a priest with close ties to Spain's Fascist dictator, Francisco Franco. Journalist Gareth Gore recently noted that most Opus Dei members in the United States live in or near Washington, DC, and no government since Franco's has included as many Opus Dei members or collaborators as the first Trump administration. Two of Leo's closest allies in the dark-money financial engine that has captured the Court, Neil and Ann Corkery, have been part of Opus Dei. Leo also funds the Opus Dei headquarters in DC, the Catholic Information Center, and has received its highest award.[4]

Like Thomas, Neil Gorsuch was raised Catholic. He attended Christ the King Catholic School (a private Catholic academy in Denver) and then Georgetown Prep, an elite Catholic prep school in Washington, DC. Gorsuch, who joined the Episcopalian faith when he married, still "speaks frequently at conferences of Catholic legal scholars seeking to expand their influence on policy." Brett Kavanaugh also attended Georgetown Prep, a Jesuit school, as well as the Catholic private school Mater Dei. Kavanaugh grew up attending the Church of the Little Flower in Bethesda, Maryland, which reportedly has had some Opus Dei priests. Amy Coney Barrett was also raised in the Catholic Church and grew up as part of a controversial sect called the People of God. That group believes God talks directly to select believers who "speak in tongues," like her father. He is a former leader of the global oil and gas company Shell. When Samuel Alito, who attended public schools, was confirmed to the Court back in 2006, the Court had its first Catholic majority in US history: Alito plus Roberts, Thomas, Scalia, and Anthony Kennedy.[5]

John Roberts also attended Catholic grade school and prep school. When George W. Bush nominated him to the Supreme Court in 2005, Leonard Leo personally vouched for Roberts's devotion to his Catholic faith as making him suitable to be confirmed to the Court. As *The Washington Post* reported,

> Both he and his wife, Jane Sullivan Roberts, were observant Catholics, Mr. Leo told other allies. They had joined a church in Bethesda [Little Flower] to follow their priest, Msgr. Peter J. Vaghi, who was well known in the Washington area as an advocate of Catholic orthodoxy and opponent of abortion. "For people like me who are reading the

> tea leaves, it is another marker that we can breathe easy," said Austin Ruse, president of the Culture of Life Foundation, a conservative Catholic group.

Ruse is reportedly close with Monsignor Vaghi, a former lawyer who attended Holy Cross College, like Thomas and Paul Scalia. Vaghi helped baptize Robert Bork at the Catholic Information Center, when Bork converted later in his life. (Whether they were officially Opus Dei members or collaborators is unknown.)[6]

There is certainly nothing wrong with being an observant Catholic. I married into a big Catholic family. I spent some of my summers before then singing songs at Camp St. Malo and participating in the Catholic Youth Organization at the All Souls Parish in my hometown. Roman Catholics in America hold an array of political beliefs and views. Justice William Brennan, who was appointed by President Dwight Eisenhower, a Republican, voted with the majority in *Roe v. Wade.* President Barack Obama, a Democrat, appointed Sonia Sotomayor—a Catholic who attended Blessed Sacrament School and Cardinal Newman High School—and she voted against overturning *Roe.* Former president Joe Biden and Representative Nancy Pelosi are also both devout Catholics and Democrats, as are millions of other Americans.

Why does it matter that the current majority of the justices on the Roberts Court have roots in Catholicism, aside from the striking overrepresentation of one faith on the high court? It is not that the Supreme Court has more Catholic justices than at any point in history—though that is a remarkable historical anomaly—but that six of those justices were confirmed with the help of one man: Leo. (He opposed one Catholic nominated to the Court, Sotomayor.) No prior court majority in US history was constituted through the extraordinary insider influence of one man and the secretive money machine he has been tied to, which was first deployed to secure the confirmation of John Roberts.[7]

The underlying issue is not religious affiliation; it is that the Roberts Court rules on specific cases in ways that seem to advance a religious agenda. The centrality of conservative or orthodox Catholics to the right-wing legal movement allows Leo's PR network to claim that those who oppose the judges he handpicks are supposedly "anti-Catholic."[8]

Forty-five years after President Kennedy set down his marker for the qualities of public service, Leonard Leo began a project to put on the nation's highest court only people who would effectively impose their religious beliefs on America by destroying federal constitutional protection for abortion. When Donald Trump ran for the White House in 2016, he campaigned for the reversal of *Roe v. Wade*, and Leo played an essential role in providing Trump judicial candidates so that he could accomplish that reversal of women's reproductive rights. Leo advanced people *he* thought would get the job done, people who would *not* set aside their religious beliefs to protect the constitutional rights that a significant majority of other Americans believe people should be free to exercise in light of their own religious beliefs or values.

In 2019, after Kavanaugh's confirmation, Leo spoke at an event held by the Council for National Policy, a powerful right-wing Christian network created in 1981 to push Ronald Reagan further to the right. Leo was introduced as someone who "understands that elections may come and go, but judges with lifetime appointments . . . are going to be here for a long time. . . . And this is perhaps where Donald Trump is making his greatest, longest-lasting effort. But he's doing it based on a lot of the work by . . . Leo." In his speech in response, Leo announced that with Kavanaugh replacing Justice Kennedy, there were now five votes on the Court ready to accomplish their shared agenda of advancing "limited constitutional government." That is a euphemism for limiting *our* constitutional rights. Leo also confidently predicted that the Roberts Court was on the "precipice" of unfurling the agenda he and his funders sought, to restore what he called the "structural" Constitution. He said no one alive in that room had seen the kind of transformation in the law that was about to take place.[9]

In October 2022, a little more than three months after the Roberts Court reversed *Roe*, Leo gave a speech upon receiving the John Paul II New Evangelization Award from the Opus Dei–tied Catholic Information Center. He described how his mission of Catholic evangelization "extends to every facet of life, including law, public policy, and politics." He also claimed, "Catholicism faces vile and amoral current day barbarians, secularists, and bigots . . . [that] have been growing more numerous over the past few years. They control and use many levers of power, yet even so, we cannot lose hope in the ultimate success of the New Evangelization, with God all things are possible. . . . Our opponents are not just uninformed or unchurched, they are often deeply wounded people whom the devil can easily take advantage of. He has hardened their hearts and closed their minds which means reason alone will not win this struggle."[10]

Leo reprised these claims the following year in a graduation address at a Catholic college and even outlandishly suggested that secularists might try to stop people from going to church: "The barbarians are determined to threaten and delegitimize individuals and institutions who refuse to pledge fealty to the woke idols of our age. The secularists are fine with Catholics in the public square so long as we don't, you know, practice our faith. They want us to draw the curtains at home and keep it in the pews. And it remains to be seen how long they'll accept even that." Leo was articulating Opus Dei's core program of getting its adherents or allies into political power in order to use their posts to advance their beliefs. As the cult's founder, Josemaría Escrivá, wrote in his book *The Way*, "Have you ever bothered to think how absurd it is to leave one's catholicism aside on entering a university, or a professional association, or a scholarly meeting, or Congress, as if you were checking your hat at the door?" That passage is part of Escrivá's express attack on "nonsectarianism" and "neutrality."[11]

But neutrality and nonsectarianism are precisely what America's system demands of judges. The Supreme Court is not intended to be some kind of religious curia, imposing its pious hostility toward abortion through rulings like *Dobbs v. Jackson Women's Health Organization*. Under our system of "checks and balances," we entrust judges to make decisions *because* they are expected to apply the law with fairness and not favor the powerful, no matter how rich or powerful they may be, including religious groups. That means faithfully following the Constitution and legal precedents that protect our freedoms from politicians—and their billionaire backers—who may be inclined to transmute theocratic doctrines into law.[12]

Antiabortion / anti-LGBTQ rights zealots like Leonard Leo have failed to persuade majorities of their fellow citizens with their arguments. So, they are spending millions to circumvent the popular will and instead secure judicial decrees by like-minded right-wing activists installed as judges. In 2024, Leo made public a letter he had sent to numerous right-wing groups explaining that his focus is on "funding to operationalize or weaponize the conservative vision," to "crush liberal dominance at the choke points of influence and power in our society." Leo wasn't writing just as a person who controls a billion-dollar trust fund, which he has used to help orchestrate the reversal of *Roe* and more. *This* is the man who helped handpick the majority of justices on the US Supreme Court.[13]

---

Leo has sought to use the courts to impose his reactionary religious views on *all* Americans on issues beyond reproductive freedom. Leo and close allies like Robbie George, who operates the Witherspoon Institute, which has extensive ties to Opus Dei figures, have also sought to limit the definition of family in American law in order to block constitutional protections for gay and lesbian Americans to marry. Marriage is a religious sacrament in many faiths, but a secular society does not have to limit marriages to those only a church or a particular religious group would recognize. Over many decades, state laws have allowed judges or justices of the peace and other officiants to validate marriage contracts, while also recognizing marriage contracts officiated by clergy. But some religious groups have sought to block the ability of LGBTQ Americans to enter into such contracts. Civil marriage, outside of a church's blessing, has important and practical effects, like guaranteeing access to loved ones when in hospitals, providing a way to secure health insurance coverage through a spouse, easing the benefit of property transfers upon death, and protecting the ability to secure equitable property division if a marriage contract is dissolved, along with rights to raise children and make decisions about their health, education, and well-being.

Absurdly, some of the opponents of marriage equality have asserted that gay marriages threaten straight marriages, a false and completely illogical charge. Why, other than the desire to impose one's own religious beliefs on others, would anyone feel their marriage is threatened by two other people who love each other wanting to promise to spend the rest of their lives together, in sickness and in health? I can think of almost no greater expression of human freedom than to be able to marry the person you love. I can think of few things more painful or more invasive than for the government to say that an adult in America cannot marry another consenting adult in this land of freedom, just because some stranger does not like it based on their personal faith, which other Americans literally have zero legal obligation to follow.

During John Roberts's confirmation hearing, he affirmed that he did not believe that the Bible should be cited as a source of law or used for interpretation in judicial opinions. But when the question of marriage equality was taken up by his court, in *Obergefell v. Hodges*, Roberts cited as authority sources built on biblical claims. That was a neat trick, another sleight of hand.

For example, Roberts cites a book published by an Opus Dei–tied publisher and edited by Robbie George, which asserts that the movement for same-sex marriage has created a "crisis" for marriage. It also treats Christianity as authority on the relationship between "husbands and wives" and "man and woman" where "the family (headed by the husband) ruled itself." That essay, by law professor David Forte, which Roberts cites in his opinion, also asserts that the Founding Fathers relied on marriage as the foundation of a "free republic," "national morality," and "public virtue," based on one passage in one letter by John Adams asserting that marriage was necessary to rein in "private passions," whatever that means. This is one of the flimsiest readings to hang a ruling on that I have ever encountered in more than thirty-five years of reading Supreme Court opinions. By crediting Forte's essay, Roberts would have us accept that because almost 250 years ago only men and women could marry in America, therefore same-sex marriages cannot also be constituted of people contributing toward building an ethical culture of "public virtue." Whom you pledge your love to in marriage has nothing to do with whether you are virtuous in civil society or if your deeds contribute to the greater good of American society.[14]

The widely respected conservative Judge Richard Posner called John Roberts's objections in *Obergefell* "heartless" and utterly dismantled Roberts's dissent. Posner observed,

> Gratuitous interference in other people's lives is bigotry. The fact that it is often religiously motivated does not make it less so. The United States is not a theocracy, and religious disapproval of harmless practices is not a proper basis for prohibiting such practices, especially if the practices are highly valued by their practitioners. Gay couples

> and the children (mostly straight) that they adopt (or that one of them may have given birth to and the other adopts) derive substantial benefits, both economic and psychological, from marriage. Efforts to deny them those benefits by forbidding same-sex marriage confer no offsetting social benefits—in fact no offsetting benefits at all beyond gratifying feelings of hostility toward gays and lesbians, feelings that feed such assertions as that heterosexual marriage is "degraded" by allowing same-sex couples to "annex" the word marriage to their cohabitation.[15]

Posner also took aim at Roberts's posturing as a historian:

> The chief justice criticizes the majority for "order[ing] the transformation of a social institution that has formed the basis of human society for millennia, for the Kalahari Bushmen and the Han Chinese, the Carthaginians and the Aztecs. Just who do we think we are?" We're pretty sure we're not any of the above. And most of us are not convinced that what's good enough for the Bushmen, the Carthaginians, and the Aztecs should be good enough for us. Ah, the millennia! Ah, the wisdom of ages! How arrogant it would be to think we knew more than the Aztecs—we who don't even know how to cut a person's heart out of his chest while he's still alive, a maneuver they were experts at.

The Carthaginians, by the way, also ritually sacrificed their children to the gods. The San nomads have required that women be segregated when menstruating. And several Han Chinese emperors were bisexual or had male lovers. But, to Posner's point, why should any of those examples be persuasive or binding on civil society in America, on the nontheocratic rules for a modern democracy contending with the meaning of liberty for its diversity of people?[16]

The Roberts Court is enthralled with its power to impose the majority's religious views on all Americans, without regard to *our* legal precedents. As Judge Posner noted, Roberts's approach to the dissent puts other major precedents at risk, specifically *Loving v. Virginia*, which barred states from banning interracial marriage, although Roberts tries to manipulate his argument to avoid that obvious consequence. Justice Thomas, in his concurrence in the *Dobbs* case overruling *Roe*, expressly urges the Court to overrule *Obergefell*, which extended constitutional protections to same-sex marriage. Thomas also targeted *Griswold v. Connecticut*, which recognized Americans' liberty and privacy interests in obtaining birth control. As surprising as it may seem, that really is where these theocrats on the Roberts Court are headed.[17]

In Roberts's dissent on *Obergefell*, he asserts that the purpose of marriage is to procreate, even though many people get married who cannot conceive or do not wish to have children—something that Roberts knows firsthand, as his two children are adopted. The claim that having children is the purpose of marriage (and sex) sounds very similar to the 1968 encyclical of the Catholic Church, *Humanae vitae*, which decreed that marital procreation is the only "meaning and purpose" of sex. It also condemned abortion and decried medicine or devices that prevent pregnancy as immoral for "separating sex from reproduction." As one scholar emphasized, "That encyclical is not directed only at Catholics, but also makes a direct appeal to 'public authorities,' urging the 'rulers of nations' to adopt policies that aid families and facilitate population control without violating the 'moral law'" as defined by the church.[18]

Perhaps, then, it should come as no surprise that under John Roberts the Supreme Court has focused on transforming freedom of worship from a shield into a sword, a weapon for legalizing discrimination against gay Americans. In *Masterpiece Cakeshop v. Colorado Commission on Civil Rights*, a baker who was asked to make a wedding cake for a gay couple asserted that his cake decorations were a form of art to honor God, who would be displeased if he decorated a cake for a gay couple. The opinion in that case, written by Justice Kennedy, states, "Our society has come to the recognition that gay persons and gay couples cannot be treated as social outcasts or as inferior in dignity and worth. For that reason, the laws and the Constitution can, and in some instances must, protect them in the exercise of their civil rights. The exercise of their freedom on terms equal to others must be given great weight and respect by the courts." But, in ruling in favor of the baker, the Roberts Court found that the Colorado commission did not accord the baker's religious beliefs sufficient respect. The majority tried to distinguish its new interpretation from prior precedents that rejected a Bible-based assertion of a right to discriminate against Black customers, as with *Newman v. Piggie Park Enterprises, Inc.*

With Justice Kennedy onboard, the Court affirmed that its ruling in the baker's case still "recognized the 'general rule' that religious and philosophical objections to gay marriage 'do not allow business owners and other actors in the economy and in society to deny protected persons equal access to goods and services under a neutral and generally applicable public accommodations law.'" The American Civil Liberties Union praised the Court for preserving that rule. But five years later, with a change in personnel due to Kennedy's retirement and Ruth Bader Ginsburg's death, the Roberts Court took another bite of the apple. Justice Gorsuch wrote a new opinion on these matters and issued a sweeping ruling in *303 Creative LLC v. Elenis*, which was joined by only the Republican appointees. That edict sided with a website designer who claimed she had a "free speech" right to block the mere possibility she might be asked to create a website for a gay couple. As Justice Sotomayor noted in her dissent,

> Today, the Court, for the first time in its history, grants a business open to the public a constitutional right to refuse

> to serve members of a protected class. . . . "What a difference five years makes." [Citation omitted] And not just at the Court. . . . This is heartbreaking. Sadly, it is also familiar. When the civil rights and women's rights movements sought equality in public life, some public establishments refused. Some even claimed, based on sincere religious beliefs, constitutional rights to discriminate. The brave Justices who once sat on this Court decisively rejected those claims.

This case is also an example of the pattern of the Roberts Court taking up manufactured cases and ignoring the factual findings of the courts below.[19]

In this instance, the business owner, Lorie Smith, who was recruited by Alliance Defending Freedom (ADF), "does not offer wedding-related services to anyone, and thus she was never asked to offer, nor did she refuse to offer, marriage-related services to LGBTQ couples." This extraordinary approach is "part of a nationwide experimental legal strategy spearheaded by ADF to advance a broader anti-LGBTQ project. . . . ADF seeks to secure an advance judicial permission to engage in what is currently forbidden after the fact: refusals to transact with LGBTQ parties. . . . These businesses sue before they deny anyone service and thus, by definition, without being challenged by any legal authority." The Constitution does not provide for the Supreme Court to sit around issuing advisory opinions on hypothetical questions; it expressly requires a "case or controversy." But that requirement seems no longer to apply at the Roberts Court, bent on its agenda to legalize discrimination against gay Americans. The reversal of *Obergefell* is on the horizon.[20]

The Roberts Court has also allowed assertions of religious beliefs by a corporation to override the statutory rights of actual humans to get access to contraceptives, as it did in *Burwell v. Hobby Lobby Stores, Inc.* In that case, a huge craft supply retail chain company owned by the tremendously wealthy Green family asserted that it had a right to refuse to follow Affordable Care Act (ACA) protections for access to birth control. Justice Alito, with John Roberts and the other Republican appointees on board, carved out an exception for the corporation's "conscience" and allowed it to deny basic coverage under health insurance to help prevent pregnancy through use of IUDs, for example.

The Bible makes no mention of methods of birth control—or the sacred elements of cake decorating or website design, of course—although it does contain a specific prohibition on theft. After this ruling, in which a big box store's religious beliefs resulted in the loss of birth control coverage for thousands of its employees, the company purchased thousands of religious and historic artifacts it had been warned were likely looted from archeological sites and museums in the Middle East. The artifacts were acquired to stock the Green family's Bible Museum. Hobby Lobby later agreed to a fine of $3 million for bringing thousands of looted artifacts into the United States. So much for the asserted moral constraint of religious obedience to the Bible.[21]

Numerous Leo-tied groups also weighed in on this case as part of the amicus racket Leo and his billionaire funding allies have supported in order to undermine the Affordable Care Act. For example, the year after the Leo-tied Judicial Education Project (JEP) secretly funded Ginni Thomas's income through one of Leo's uberrich backers, that group began aiding attacks on the ACA in briefs to the Supreme Court. After JEP filed an amicus brief in the *Hobby Lobby* case, the Roberts Court adopted many of JEP's arguments that the ACA violated Hobby Lobby's "right" to freedom of religion by preventing it from barring access to birth control.

---

At the manufactured invitation of Leo-funded groups and his allies, the Roberts Court has also taken up a series of cases intended to destroy the wall of separation between church and state. Back in 2005, during Roberts's hearing for the Court, Senator Dianne Feinstein noted,

> Justice Sandra Day O'Connor said it so well in the recent Ten Commandments decision, and I quote: "At a time when we see around the world the violent consequences of the assumption of religious authority by government, Americans may count themselves fortunate: Our regard for constitutional boundaries has protected us from similar travails, while allowing private religious exercise to flourish. . . . Those who would renegotiate the boundaries between church and state must therefore answer a difficult question: Why would we trade a system that has served us so well for one that has served others so poorly?" . . . [Quoting from John F. Kennedy's speech:] "I believe in an America where the separation of church and state is absolute." My question is, do you?

Roberts dodged at first, and then when pressed, he responded, "I don't know what that means when you say absolute separation. I do know this, that my faith and my religious beliefs do not play a role in judging. When it comes to judging, I look to the law books and always have."

John Roberts subsequently used his position as chief justice to methodically undermine that separation. Just days before the *Dobbs* ruling, the Roberts Court issued a decree, in *Carson v. Makin*, overruling decades of precedent to assert that taxpayer money may actually be *required* to fund the tuition of private religious schools. That is a radical restructuring of the law and is contrary to one of the things that the generation who wrote the Constitution found most offensive in former colonies that had established an official religion: the requirement to subsidize other people's religious indoctrination. Although the Roberts Court has tried to frame this issue as private religious schools being unfairly denied money, the reasoning is distorted because it is a personal choice not to send your kids to public school, and the public should not have to subsidize your tuition any more than it should have to subsidize your country club fees if you prefer the private golf course to one at a public park, regardless of your religious beliefs.[22]

This is another instance of John Roberts lying in wait to accomplish his political agenda through his judicial office. While serving in the Ronald Reagan administration, Roberts "wrote a memo in which he referred approvingly to then-Justice Rehnquist's effort to 'revolutionize Establishment Clause jurisprudence' by overturning the Supreme Court's long-established criteria for determining when government laws and policies violate the Establishment Clause." In another Reagan administration memo, Roberts asserted that Supreme Court precedents against "voluntary" prayer, or so-called moments of silence, in schools seem "indefensible."[23]

Fast-forward to 2022: The Roberts Court issued a ruling that prayer sessions led by a public high school football coach did not violate the Establishment Clause. Roberts and Thomas joined Justice Gorsuch's opinion in that 6–3 decision decreeing that the supposedly "quiet and private" prayers led by the coach were not coercive or disruptive. Notably, when Roberts was the political deputy solicitor general in the Justice Department, he approved a brief urging the Supreme Court "to uphold school-sponsored prayer at graduation ceremonies, contending that the practice was not coercive," but the Rehnquist Court rejected his assertions in a case called *Lee v. Weissman*. Now, thirty years later, Roberts had a case he could use to win on an issue he lost back then, through remaking the law in *Kennedy v. Bremerton School District.*

Justice Sotomayor, joined by Justices Stephen Breyer and Elena Kagan, dissented. They noted that the majority had "misconstrued the facts" to such a degree that they felt compelled to include in their opinion a photo of the activities on the fifty-yard line, which showed this to be very public prayer that had the effect of appearing as though the school district endorsed it. They stressed that the ruling "elevates one individual's interest in personal religious exercise over society's interest in protecting the separation between church and state, eroding the protections for religious liberty for all," especially for impressionable high school athletes who might feel peer pressure (or coach pressure) to join such prayers.

That case, brought by Kelly Shackelford of First Liberty, was supported by numerous amicus briefs by groups in Leo's funding stream. To this day, First Liberty's misleading claims asserting that the case was about a coach's "silent fifteen-second prayer" and his right to "live out his faith" continue to be broadcast on Google ads. The public interest group Americans United for Separation of Church and State—and its leader, Rachel Laser, who represented the public schools—correctly characterized the Roberts Court's edict as "the greatest loss of religious freedom in our country in generations." Laser warned that First Liberty will "try to expand this dangerous precedent—further undermining everyone's right to . . . believe as we choose."[24]

John Roberts's antipathy toward the separation of church and state dates back more than four decades now, despite his evasion of Senator Feinstein's questions. For example, in his review of a speech by the Reagan administration's education secretary, William Bennett, Roberts approved remarks that asserted that the separation of church and state reflects "a hostility to religion not demanded by the Constitution." In that speech, Bennett singled out a 1980 ruling in *Stone v. Graham* that struck down a Kentucky law requiring every public school classroom to post a copy of the Ten Commandments. Justice Rehnquist issued a dissent in that case; Roberts was clerking for him at the time and in all likelihood played a role in drafting or editing it.[25]

Fast-forward to 2024: The Republican-controlled legislature in Louisiana adopted a law requiring every public school classroom to display the Ten Commandments (while rejecting federal aid for kids growing up in poverty to address their hunger in the summer when there are no school lunches). That case is now making its way to John Roberts and the Supreme Court.[26]

---

One of the most stunning things about John Roberts's tenure on the Supreme Court, once you examine it up close, is how rigid, extreme, and doctrinaire he has been. It seems that Roberts is still adhering to the biased opinions he formed in his twenties. Indeed, shortly after he was confirmed as chief justice, Roberts gave a speech at the Reagan Library, where he described his work in the Reagan administration as "making bricks." Those bricks, the legal work he was doing, had a purpose: "President Reagan never let us forget that what we were doing was building a cathedral," Roberts said. He has continued to build that "cathedral" brick by brick through his rulings from the bench of the US Supreme Court.[27]

The Reagan administration's attacks on the separation of church and state were both philosophical and political, something that Roberts seems to understand all too well. The Reagan administration helped orchestrate an effort to peel Catholics away from the Democratic Party. It also sought to peel them away from taking action for social justice and toward the issue of banning abortion, just as Pope John Paul II sought to redirect religious sympathies away from activism on behalf of poor people and toward protests for embryos and against abortion. The political component of this agenda lined up almost seamlessly with the creation of the Federalist Society, with the aid of right-wing activists who had become law professors and then federal judges, like Antonin Scalia and Robert Bork. That effort did not just materialize out of nowhere but was staked by superrich white men who saw the political advantages of taking on abortion.

To advance this ideological and political agenda, Leonard Leo and the Federalist Society have targeted the US Supreme Court, lower federal courts, and state supreme courts to install lawyers aligned with their legal policy agenda. I don't think they want them to be fair judges but to be *their* judges. Chief Justice John Roberts sits at the top of that program to rewrite the law through judicial power, and he has associates—literally associate justices on the Supreme Court—who are part of the scheme, even if they do not all agree all the time on all the details. The big picture is that—as Senator Sheldon Whitehouse has explained in his speeches, books, legal briefs, law review articles, and other work—the US Supreme Court has been captured. It has been captured by those who control billion-dollar fortunes—including, but not only, Leo—and who want a return on their investment in terms of policies that remake our world to suit their worldview, whether the public likes it or not.[28]

Tearing down the wall between church and state appears to be a price Charles Koch is willing to pay to grow ever richer and secure his ability to continue his fossil fuel exploitation with fewer regulations, which insiders say is job one for all core Koch operations in his nonprofit and for-profit empires. Some naive journalists actually credit Koch every two years when he claims he has changed his approach to politics or for supposedly being "pro-choice" as a "libertarian." If they bothered to examine his actual record, however, they would see that he has put his money on antiabortion politicians and political operations in thousands of elections by deploying his get-out-the-vote efforts to back Republicans 99 percent of the time, year after year, for decades.[29]

A newer player in these efforts is Kevin Roberts (no relation to John Roberts). Kevin Roberts, who also has ties to Opus Dei, helms the multi-million-dollar Heritage Foundation and its Project 2025 agenda, which the Trump administration is actively implementing, despite Donald Trump's efforts to distance himself from it in advance of the 2024 presidential election. That Heritage Foundation blueprint has been made possible in part due to Leo's funding of a significant number of the groups involved in Project 2025. As chief justice, John Roberts has also aligned the Court with the desires of far-right religious groups seeking to impose their beliefs as binding law on nonbelievers, one of the objectives of key portions of Project 2025.[30]

Rich and powerful people have always tried to rig the rules in their favor. Now they are trying to take America backward and control who we can be, who we can love, and how we can care for our bodies, our families, and our world. They are putting the weight of their wealth on the scales of justice to diminish other people's freedoms. The billionaires who helped capture the Supreme Court have a guaranteed freedom to exercise their religion in America, just as all Americans have the freedom to worship or not, as they choose. But the billionaire-backed effort to use the US Supreme Court to impose those views as law on abortion and other social issues is profoundly at odds with our nation's founding as a place of refuge *from* state-imposed religion.

On each of these issues—abortion, contraception, gay rights, and the wall of separation between church and state—John Roberts and the Roberts Court are out of step with the views of most Americans. Roberts seems untroubled that he is doing the bidding of billionaires and that he is politicizing and discrediting the Supreme Court in striking ways. Rather, he seems increasingly dedicated to arrogating more and more power over the American people to himself and the Court—and if the American people do not like it, as he told C-SPAN shortly after getting the best job and the most powerful role in the judiciary, "it's more or less just too bad."[31]

# PART V

# DOMINATION

CHAPTER 12

# VOTING

THE ACTIONS OF John Roberts and his right-wing majority on the Court have resulted in a spate of judicial edicts that undermine the Constitution's promises and damage our rights. This is especially true of the right to vote, a foundational freedom in our democracy because it is the primary means of securing other rights as well as policies that serve the public's interest.

In America, voting rights have always been deeply connected to race: Decades ago regressive white politicians pushed literally hundreds of measures to make it harder for Black Americans to vote until the landmark Voting Rights Act of 1965 put a stop to those manipulations. But then John Roberts undid some of those key protections and unleashed scores of efforts in the past decade to make it harder for Americans to vote and to have their votes count.

When Roberts was nominated to the Supreme Court, he was questioned intensely about his views on the Voting Rights Act. The questioning largely centered on his work in the Ronald Reagan administration, where he left a troubling paper trail assailing efforts to protect voting rights. In response, Roberts repeatedly claimed this work was in the distant past and he had been just a young "staff lawyer" supporting his boss. But the hundreds of hours he spent fighting a key component of enforcing the Voting Rights Act amounted to some of the most seminal work of his career. At various points in his confirmation hearings, Roberts told senators his view of the law "was not something [any]body was interested in," and he asserted he "was not shaping administration policy." Contrary to Roberts's characterization of himself as a deferential underling, however, in reality he held powerful posts in the top echelon of the Reagan administration—as special assistant to the attorney general and as associate White House counsel—where he wielded enormous influence over civil rights law. As David Daley extensively documents in his book *Antidemocratic*, Roberts was also part of a clique of young ideologues who were shaping the administration's position, pulling the older politicians above them further to the right on the law and public policy. In short, Roberts was a determined proponent of an extreme legal policy agenda; and, more than that, he was a driving force in trying to limit important gains in voting rights in America, in particular.[1]

During the hearings on his nomination to become the chief justice of the Supreme Court, Roberts dodged questions from Senator Ted Kennedy and others about his writings during that period. Those memos revealed his central role in the fight against restoring vital protections in Section 2 of the Voting Rights Act. They document Roberts's aggressive opposition to federal courts considering the racially discriminatory *effect* of a voting process. As Senator Kennedy noted at the hearing on Roberts's nomination,

> I am deeply troubled by the narrow and cramped, and perhaps even a mean-spirited view of the law that appears in some of your writings. In the only documents that have been made available to us, it appears that you did not fully appreciate the problem of discrimination in our society. It also seems that you were trying to undo the progress that so many people had fought for and died for in this country. . . .

> You wrote that violations of Section 2 of the Voting Rights Act, and I quote, "should not be made too easy to prove since they provide a basis for the most intrusive interference imaginable by Federal courts into State and local processes." I am deeply troubled by another statement that you made . . . and I quote, "there is no evidence of voting abuses nationwide supporting the need for such a change." No evidence? I was there, Judge Roberts, both the House and the Senate had extensive hearings. We considered detail-specific testimony from affected voters throughout the country.[2]

After Roberts was confirmed as chief justice, even more information about his work became available through the National Archives, the Reagan Library, and published books. Some of these resources further revealed that Roberts was a powerful player pushing narrow-minded views, as Senator Kennedy had warned, and not merely a follower in the Reagan administration. Roberts was a key opponent of considering racially disparate effects, and he routinely sought to limit protections against racial discrimination so that they could only apply if racially discriminatory intent were proven, a threshold that can be very difficult to meet.

During the hearings on his nomination, Roberts, the polite and charismatic ideologue, used his advocacy skills to create a misleading portrait of both his prior role (just following orders) and his future role (just an umpire), which facilitated his confirmation to the Supreme Court. Once on the Court, Roberts has acted in alignment with the political positions he took while playing a top policy-making role in Republican administrations. As chief justice, he has led the Court to eviscerate Section 4 of the Voting Rights Act, through which Congress required that certain states and cities get approval—called "preclearance"—from the Civil Rights Division of the Justice Department before making changes to voter registration and voting rules because those jurisdictions had a history of using changes to make it harder for Black Americans to vote.

Roberts has also used his judicial post to gut federal judicial review of "gerrymandered" voting maps, unfairly drawn maps that make it harder for voters to get fair representation in the legislature. Roberts has also made it easier for Republican-controlled legislatures to move Black voters out of their voting districts as long as they claim their target is Democrats, not Blacks. And, as of this writing, John Roberts is poised to constrict the ability of Section 2 of the Voting Rights Act to limit disparate racial impact, the very section Roberts spent hundreds of hours trying to block during the Reagan administration. That provision, which bars voting procedures and practices in any state or locality that have the effect of denying equal access to the political process based on race, is one of the last remaining enforcement tools left in the Voting Rights Act, after John Roberts's other rulings have decimated that landmark law.

---

Republicans know that, for every position of power, "personnel is policy." How did George W. Bush know Roberts was the right man for the job on the Supreme Court? Because in addition to his work in the Reagan and George H. W. Bush administrations, Roberts stood on the shoulders of right-wing "giants."[3]

John Roberts sought out and procured a clerkship with the then most right-wing member of the US Supreme Court: William H. Rehnquist. Rehnquist was a racist who had personally intimidated countless Black voters in the racially segregated neighborhood of Bethune on the west side of downtown Phoenix, Arizona, and he had trained other Republicans to do so too. Rehnquist denied this conduct, under oath, despite multiple witnesses who *saw* him do it, but he was never charged with perjury. Rehnquist claimed his actions, dubbed "Operation Eagle Eye" (which included using an empty camera to make a pretense of surveilling Black voters), did not target Black residents but were focused on challenging Democrats who just happened to be Black, and so he'd done nothing wrong. The Roberts Court would later loudly reprise this Rehnquist-esque defense and impose it as law in 2024 in *Alexander v. South Carolina State Conference of the NAACP*, letting Republicans get away with moving Black Democrats out of their long-standing congressional district to dilute the impact of their votes.[4]

Rehnquist's racism and authoritarian proclivities targeting Black voters in the 1960s were a prelude to his career in Washington, DC, where—surprise, surprise—he worked to undermine racial integration for the Richard Nixon administration. As the assistant attorney general in charge of the Justice Department's Office of Legal Counsel, Rehnquist wrote memoranda in support of Nixon opposing busing to racially integrate schools, for example. Although Nixon could not remember Rehnquist's name at times, he knew the man got things done. (Rehnquist even wrote a memo for Nixon to authorize the declaration of martial law in response to the May Day protest against the Vietnam War; Nixon did not do so and instead ordered a harsh crackdown resulting in more than 12,000 arrests, the largest mass arrest in US history to date.)

In 1971, Nixon rewarded the forty-seven-year-old Rehnquist's devotion to his right-wing legal program with a nomination to the US Supreme Court—the same day Nixon nominated Lewis F. Powell Jr. to the Court. Powell was a tobacco lawyer who had just penned a nonpublic memo to the US Chamber of Commerce urging rich corporate CEOs to get much more involved in politics and particularly in the courts. Powell had also been the chairman of the school board in Richmond, Virginia, the former capital of the Confederacy, where—as Representative John Conyers (D-MI) testified—Powell had used his power to maintain a "patently segregated school system, characterized by grossly overcrowded Black public schools [with] white schools not filled to normal capacity."

Conyers noted that Powell had also backed measures for state reimbursement of private school tuition to aid white flight in response to the Supreme Court's unanimous 1954 ruling in *Brown v. Board of Education of Topeka* that "separate is inherently unequal." Similarly, as a law clerk Rehnquist had written a memo titled "A Random Thought on the Segregation Cases," urging Justice Robert Jackson to dissent in *Brown* and arguing, "I think *Plessy v. Ferguson* was right and should be re-affirmed." The 1896 *Plessy* case legalized decades of racial apartheid in America—separate schools, entrances, drinking fountains, swimming pools, and bathrooms—and more that stigmatized Black Americans and systematically denied them the "equal protection of law" promised by the Fourteenth Amendment.[5]

The dissent of John Marshall Harlan (an appointee of Rutherford B. Hayes) in *Plessy* included the now-famous line "Our Constitution is colorblind," a declaration only very belatedly embraced by right-wing politicians. The embrace happened only after *overt* anti-Black racial discrimination was barred by the Civil Rights Act of 1964. Major right-wing politicians in America have deployed the concept of a "color-blind" Constitution not in order to protect racial minorities from discrimination and mistreatment but rather to protect the white majority from efforts to redress racial inequities. Notably, in 1964, as Senator Barry Goldwater (R-AZ) ran for the White House, he deployed that incantation during his campaign when he "masterfully co-opt[ed] the language of civil rights to oppose integration as a moral evil. 'It has been well-said that the Constitution is colorblind. . . . And so it is just as wrong to compel children to attend certain schools for the sake of so-called integration as for the sake of segregation,'" he said to the applause of his white audience. That speech was crafted by none other than Bill Rehnquist for one of the few senators who voted against the Civil Rights Act. Goldwater lost by a landslide.[6]

After the Civil Rights Act of 1964 and the Voting Rights Act of 1965 rebuked the rigged rules that had disenfranchised and discriminated against Black Americans, some "conservatives" became quick converts to the notion that being blind to color was the essence of equality. Denied their "right" to use color as a weapon, right-wing apparatchiks in the Reagan administration sought to use color blindness to block efforts to redress policies adversely affecting Blacks. The right-wing converts to the rhetoric of equality but not the reality of it—like Reagan—often invoke the Reverend Martin Luther King Jr. and his historic "I Have a Dream Speech," where he expressed hope that someday his children would "not be judged by the color of their skin but by the content of their character." That 1963 address at the Poor People's March, where a racially integrated crowd of tens of thousands filled the National Mall, was not an endorsement of *inaction* on civil rights through blindness to injustice; it was a call to *action* to redress anti-Black and antipoor policies that had thwarted access to the American dream and the levers of democracy for those whose ancestors were enslaved and others who were oppressed.[7]

Once equality was promised anew in the mid-1960s, "conservatives" of both major parties took refuge in a rationale that only intentional bias, or what I call "out-loud bigotry," was actionable. This was directly contradicted by the Supreme Court's finding that the Constitution, as amended after the Civil War, prohibits "sophisticated, as well as simple-minded, modes of discrimination," as Chief Justice Earl Warren emphasized in *Reynolds v. Sims* in 1964. That landmark decision is famous for protecting the principle of "one person, one vote." It cited a precedent from one of the early cracks in the wall of America's racial apartheid, when in 1939 Justice Felix Frankfurter (a Franklin D. Roosevelt appointee) used that phrase to strike down an Oklahoma voter-registration law that was neutral on its face but excluded Blacks from voting.[8]

Although the Right attempts to portray color blindness as high-minded idealism, in my view, it is really a kind of cynical political sophistry propounded by mostly privileged and "conservative" white men, like John Roberts. The phrase gives cover to acting blindly toward policies that demonstrably and disparately hurt Black Americans while claiming the moral high ground of supposedly seeing beyond race and ignoring the real-world effects of anti-Black racism.

---

The appointments of Rehnquist and Powell must be viewed as part of Nixon's racist "Southern Strategy." The chairman of the Senate Judiciary Committee at that time, James Eastland (D-MS), was himself a racial segregationist. He was notorious for spewing Hitlerian racist garbage that attacked Black soldiers as "inferior" in every way, even while they were still sacrificing life and limb for America in World War II. Eastland had also harshly criticized President Harry Truman's efforts to advance racial integration and equal rights for Blacks, calling such measures an attack on the Southern "way of life." So, of course, the senator known as "the voice of the White South" backed the appointments of Rehnquist and Powell to the US Supreme Court. Unfortunately, a bipartisan majority of senators also voted to confirm them. Initially Rehnquist's controversial nomination was met with a filibuster, but he was ultimately confirmed 68–26. Powell was confirmed 89–1, despite the valiant opposition of the National Association for the Advancement of Colored People (NAACP) and a single devoted advocate for racial equality, Senator Fred Harris (D-OK). (Two earlier Nixon nominees to the Supreme Court, Clement Haynesworth and G. Harrold Carswell, Southerners who used their offices and their social stature to aid racial segregation in various ways, were blocked by the Senate.)[9]

Even after Nixon was vanquished, the next Republican elected to the White House carried his Southern Strategy forward, with

Lee Atwater and Ed Rollins helping Ronald Reagan deploy dog whistles about busing and crime. To help cloak and even rationalize his extreme agenda, Reagan also invoked a nonexistent "color-blind" society as a tool to help turn back efforts to redress systemic anti-Black racism. On his way to the White House, Reagan bear-hugged the far right in the party. As journalist Sidney Blumenthal concisely recapped,

> [Reagan] opposed the Civil Rights Act of 1964, opposed the Voting Rights Act of 1965 (calling it "humiliating to the South"), and ran for governor of California in 1966 promising to wipe the Fair Housing Act off the books. "If an individual wants to discriminate against Negroes or others in selling or renting his house," he said, "he has a right to do so." After the Republican convention in 1980, Reagan traveled to the county fair in Neshoba, Mississippi, where, in 1964, three Freedom Riders had been slain by the Ku Klux Klan. Before an all-white crowd of tens of thousands, Reagan declared: "I believe in states' rights."[10]

Blumenthal, in summing up Reagan on civil rights, remarked, "The past is not dead. In fact, it's not even past," aptly quoting from the vaunted but controversial novelist William Faulkner.[11]

At the start of Roberts's career in Washington, DC, he chose to serve Justice Rehnquist and then President Reagan after getting his Harvard law degree. In 1980, just a few months before Roberts began his clerkship on the Supreme Court, Justice Rehnquist joined a ruling in *Mobile v. Bolden*, a lightning bolt of a decision that sought to turn back the progress made in the fifteen years since the Voting Rights Act was adopted in 1965. In that case, a plurality of Republican-appointed justices—Potter Stewart (an Eisenhower-Nixon administration appointee) and three Nixon appointees, namely Warren Burger, Rehnquist, and Powell—allowed at-large city elections that had the effect of electing only white politicians in Mobile, Alabama. In "at-large elections" representatives run citywide and do not represent specific neighborhoods or districts.

In that case, the Supreme Court ruled that such a procedure did not violate Section 2 of the Voting Rights Act. The relevant portion of the act reads, "No voting qualification or prerequisite to voting, or standard, practice, or procedure shall be imposed or applied by any State or political subdivision to deny or abridge the right of any citizen of the United States to vote on account of race or color." But in light of the ruling in *Bolden*, even if geographic districts would allow Black Americans to elect someone from their neighborhood to represent them in city management, at-large elections—where their votes would be diluted by the white majority in a racially segregated city—were deemed legal.

The language of Section 2 did not require discriminatory intent, but the plurality's ruling engrafted a requirement of invidious intent onto it, declaring that a facially neutral law does *not* violate the law unless it is proven to be motivated by discriminatory intent. That decree, a variant of color blindness, forced lower courts to disregard the effects of voting-related legislation as proof of a violation of the Voting Rights Act. Justice Thurgood Marshall dissented, observing that the consequence of *Bolden* was that "in the absence of proof of intentional discrimination by the State, the right to vote provides the politically powerless with nothing more than the right to cast meaningless ballots," because, in his view, at-large "districting schemes unconstitutionally diluted" the votes of Blacks. Justices William Brennan and Byron White agreed with Marshall and dissented too.[12]

That summer, as Roberts was moving to Washington, DC, to work for Rehnquist, members of Congress and the civil rights community were already making plans to correct the ruling that Rehnquist helped make possible. Key provisions of the Voting Rights Act were up for reauthorization in 1982. The new judicially imposed intent requirement had immediately made it harder for the Jimmy Carter administration to use Section 2 to challenge at-large election schemes. Plus, *Bolden*'s analysis put at risk the preclearance provisions in Sections 4 and 5 of the Voting Rights Act that limited voting changes in congressionally designated states and cities. Those potent provisions had successfully blocked numerous proposed voting changes *before* they caused a discriminatory effect.[13]

During John Roberts's year by Rehnquist's side, the Court did not hear arguments in any voting rights cases, but fellow clerks took notice that Roberts was fully aligned with his boss and mentor. As one fellow Supreme Court clerk told Ari Berman for his critically acclaimed book *Give Us the Ballot*, "Rehnquist reinforced John's pre-existing philosophies. . . . He was definitely in sync with Rehnquist. John was not a believer in the courts giving rights to minorities and the downtrodden. That was the basic Rehnquist philosophy."[14]

While Roberts was clerking for Rehnquist, the House Subcommittee on Civil and Constitutional Rights held dozens of hearings on a Voting Rights Act reauthorization bill introduced on April 4, 1981, which intended to overturn *Bolden* and make clear that discriminatory effects can be considered in voting rights cases. Key portions of those hearings critiqued how Rehnquist and his Nixon-appointed compatriots had willfully ignored the thorough documentation of the discriminatory effects of at-large/citywide elections on the inadequate city services provided to Black neighborhoods compared to the white enclaves in Mobile, another emblem of racial apartheid in America. Some of the witnesses supporting the reauthorization rebuked the Supreme Court for making it harder for the Justice Department to protect the ability of Black Americans to elect people to represent them and serve their communities—the essence of representative democracy. As President Lyndon B. Johnson had noted, "This right to vote is the basic right without which all others are meaningless. It gives people, people as individuals, control over their own destinies." When he signed the Voting Rights Act into law, he declared, "The vote is the most powerful instrument ever devised by man for breaking down injustice and destroying the terrible walls which imprison men because they are different from other men."

After choosing to be a kind of paid stagiaire to the most regressive justice on the Supreme Court, John Roberts got the nod for a job at the very top of the Department of Justice to work as a special assistant to Attorney General of the United States William French Smith. Justice Rehnquist had called Ken Starr, Smith's counsel, to recommend Roberts for a post in the leadership of the Justice Department. Smith and Starr hired Roberts and put him in charge of the Voting Rights Act reauthorization issues. Roberts had no actual experience working on voting rights, and his only seeming "qualification" for the job was clerking for Rehnquist, who was a prominent *opponent* of voting rights. From his new vantage point in the executive branch, Roberts seemed determined to do everything he could to preserve his judicial mentor's ruling in *Bolden* and block Congress from amending the Voting Rights Act to nullify the judicially concocted discriminatory intent requirement that ignored disparate impacts on Black Americans. According to his close colleague Michael Carvin, Roberts was working sixty-five-plus hours a week—writing arguments, developing talking points, and drafting op-eds on the Voting Rights Act. Such was his single-minded devotion to blocking Congress from restoring that law and his determination to exclude the effects on Black voters as proof of a violation.[15]

In his memos to the attorney general and Starr, Roberts crafted administration talking points with press-friendly, deceptive rhetoric. Roberts claimed, for example, that the Reagan administration *supported* reauthorizing the Voting Rights Act but that Congress wanted to "change" the law, eliding the fact that Congress was trying to restore the law it had passed and the Court tried to dismantle in *Bolden*. It was attempting to undo the damage Rehnquist and the other Republican appointees had done to the Voting Rights Act, necessitating those amendments.

During this period Roberts wrote to Judge Henry Friendly on the US Court of Appeals for the Second Circuit, rhapsodizing, "This is an exciting time to be at the Justice Department, when so much that has been taken for granted for so long is being seriously reconsidered." How exciting it was for Roberts to help take away people's hard-fought rights![16]

After President Reagan himself briefly wavered on blocking the restoration of the discriminatory-effects standard to the Voting Rights Act, the attorney general apparently raced to the White House to convince the president to stick with Roberts's strategy, which was to support reauthorization for ten years but oppose any changes to overturn *Bolden*. Reagan deferred, and Roberts won a temporary reprieve, but his attacks ultimately failed: The Voting Rights Act was eventually amended to make clear that Section 2 allowed proof of a discriminatory *effect* as well as a discriminatory *intent*. The Senate report noted that the amended "totality of the circumstances" test "included several factors . . . such as historical discrimination in a jurisdiction; the extent of racially polarized voting; use of at-large elections; whether political campaigns were characterized by racial appeals; and the extent to which discrimination affected education or employment." The vote to reauthorize the Voting Rights Act was overwhelming, 469–32, counting both the House and the Senate, despite all of the administration's efforts to block the amendment to restore that landmark law. On signing the reauthorization bill into law, Reagan, ever the actor, asserted, "The right to vote is the crown jewel of American liberties, and we will not see its luster diminished"—even though he had actively opposed the Voting Rights Act in 1965 and had resisted the reversal of *Bolden*, as Roberts had tirelessly urged.[17]

The 1982 bill extended the law's enforcement provisions not for the ten years targeted by Roberts but until 2007. Fortuitously for John Roberts, that deadline was slated for just after he was confirmed as chief justice of the Supreme Court. In that post, he would have much greater power than he had had as an influential palace whisperer to the attorney general and president of the United States. From his perch atop the Supreme Court, with other Republican appointees by his side, he could use the judicial power to dictate the fate of the Voting Rights Act, no matter what Congress overwhelmingly approved and a duly elected president signed into law. Meanwhile, in 1982, he was promoted to a job in the White House.

---

In Congress, the 1982 amendment and reauthorization of the Voting Rights Act represented a rare area of bipartisan agreement on policy in a sharply divided period. Republican legislators, like Representative Jim Sensenbrenner (R-WI), worked closely with Democrats to extend the preclearance provisions for another twenty-five years, based on a detailed factual record demonstrating the need for continued federal oversight of election processes in certain states, counties, and cities. The initial formula in Section 4 of the act required preclearance under Section 5 of the act of any proposed changes to voting procedures and voting locations in places where literacy tests had been used. In 1965, that list included all of Alabama, Georgia, Louisiana, Mississippi, South Carolina, and Virginia and parts of Arizona, Idaho, and North Carolina. When the Voting Rights Act had been reauthorized in 1970, the formula for coverage had been updated to cover certain counties in ten states, and the 1975 reauthorization expanded jurisdictions even further in order to secure bilingual access to the ballot. Despite John Roberts's efforts to limit reauthorization and uphold Rehnquist's attempt to bar the consideration of racially disparate effects, the 1982 reauthorization of the act did not change the formula under

Section 4 or the related preclearance procedure under Section 5. The reauthorization did, however, provide a "bailout" provision for jurisdictions that could prove nondiscrimination.

In 2005, Congress took up the Voting Rights Act again in advance of the potential expiration of Sections 4 and 5 in 2007. Civil rights and civil liberties groups worked to provide extensive documentation of the ongoing need for reauthorization of those preclearance provisions. For example, the American Civil Liberties Union (ACLU) issued a report detailing recent discrimination in voting procedures, including documenting the more than 300 cases it had brought since 1982 to help protect voting rights. It also issued a report showing how the Voting Rights Act had blocked some procedures with disparate impacts and had increased access to voting by Black Americans and other racial and ethnic minorities. The National Commission on the Voting Rights Act noted that more than 1,000 attempts to change voting rules had been denied under Sections 4 and 5 and that there had been more than 600 successful Section 2 cases. The commission also found, "The evidence demonstrates unfortunately that the persistence, degree, geographic breadth, and methods of voting discrimination are substantial and ongoing." The NAACP, the ACLU, and other public interest groups also urged Congress to redress judicial decisions of the Rehnquist Court—such as *Reno v. Bossier Parish School Board* (2000) and *Georgia v. Ashcroft* (2003)—that had weakened the preclearance provisions.[18]

The Republican-controlled Congress responded overwhelmingly to this detailed evidence and voted 98–0 in the Senate and 390–33 in the House to reauthorize the Voting Rights Act in 2006, ahead of schedule. Despite the nearly unanimous congressional support for the legislation, the leader of the tiny, all-white opposition to the legislation in the House, Lynn Westmoreland (R-GA), announced, "We needed 218 votes in the House but we'll only need five votes on the Supreme Court. Justice will prevail. The honor of

Georgia will be restored." It turns out that Representative Westmoreland wasn't merely a sore loser: He was right.[19]

The new chief justice, John Roberts, was lying in wait to strike down the law. A major challenge to the constitutionality of the newly reauthorized Voting Rights Act was accepted for oral argument for the first time right before Barack Obama was sworn in as the first Black president of the United States in January 2009. But in that case, *Northwest Austin Municipal Util. Dist. No. One v. Holder*, Roberts announced out loud that he was biding his time, stating that the constitutionality of preclearance under the Voting Rights Act "has attracted ardent briefs from dozens of interested parties, but the importance of the question does not justify our rushing to decide it. Quite the contrary: Our usual practice is to avoid the unnecessary resolution of constitutional questions. We agree that the district is eligible under the Act to seek a bailout"—that is, to invoke the clause allowing a jurisdiction to escape the application of preclearance in certain circumstances. Like his judicial role model, Rehnquist, Roberts planned his next chess move well in advance, using that majority opinion to tuck in language he would later use to accomplish his broader objectives, while claiming consensus. "Things have changed in the South," he wrote, planting language to use later when he chose to strike down those provisions.[20]

Roberts waited until three days after Obama was reelected in 2012 to accept another case on the constitutionality of the Voting Rights Act, a case out of the Deep South known as *Shelby County v. Holder*. It was brought by Shelby County in Alabama, a state with a legacy of racial terror lynchings and a history of vote dilution efforts. The respondent was Eric Holder, the first Black American appointed attorney general in US history. That was the vehicle Roberts handpicked to destroy the preclearance provisions of the Voting Rights Act.[21]

Invoking the words he wrote in *Austin*, Roberts reprised his theme that "things have changed in the South" in his judicial decree in *Shelby County*. Then he went about arrogantly disregarding congressional expertise and rejecting a mountain of factual findings in contradiction of his political agenda. This is exactly what Roberts did from within the Justice Department when he sought to dismiss the congressional findings on the Voting Rights Act in 1982. But by the time he was appointed to the Court, Roberts had a phalanx of secretly funded right-wing groups backing him up in asserting that the preclearance protections were no longer needed.

Carrie Severino filed one of the first amicus briefs in the case under the rubric of the Judicial Education Project, the shadowy group closely tied to Leonard Leo. The Severino / Judicial Education Project brief was submitted on behalf of some of the men Roberts had conferred with repeatedly in the Reagan administration on policies to weaken enforcement of the Voting Rights Act and other civil rights laws: Brad Reynolds and Roger Clegg.

A dense network of right-wing "legal interest groups" also filed briefs seeking to destroy the preclearance provisions of the Voting Rights Act. One was submitted by the Justice and Freedom Fund, a group created by James Hirsen, a founder (along with Leo insiders Neil Corkery and Gary Marx) of the Judicial Crisis Network (JCN), which ran ads to help get John Roberts and Sam Alito confirmed to the Supreme Court. By 2013, JCN was helmed by Severino. An amicus brief was also submitted by the Cato Institute, a group fueled by Charles Koch, who had actively promoted and funded the John Birch Society at the height of its opposition to the Reverend Martin Luther King Jr. and the civil rights movement. Some state attorneys general—part of the pay-to-play Republican Attorneys General Association, which would become a major beneficiary of donations from Leo-tied groups—also weighed in.[22]

Unlike the amicus briefs by right-wing operatives that assailed the Voting Rights Act, the amicus briefs that supported the legal validity of the preclearance provisions were submitted by organizations that collectively represent millions of Americans, including the NAACP Legal Defense Fund (LDF), the Leadership Conference on Civil and Human Rights, and Asian American and Latino public interest groups. The Voting Rights Act defenders were bipartisan—there were briefs from Representative Sensenbrenner and former Reagan and George H. W. Bush Attorney General Dick Thornburg, as well as from Senator Harry Reid. A particularly poignant brief was submitted by Representative John Lewis (D-GA), who detailed how the history of voting rights in America had been one of "recurring retrenchment" rather than uninterrupted progress. The nonpartisan American Bar Association, which serves the largest group of attorneys in the nation, also supported the Voting Rights Act, along with the National Bar Association, which is the largest network of Black American attorneys in America, and the National Lawyers Guild, the oldest group of progressive attorneys in the country. Other amicus briefs in support of preclearance came from the Congressional Black Caucus, the Navajo Nation, and numerous legal scholars.[23]

Supreme Court justices, like all appellate judges, are expected to follow precedent and defer to the factual findings of the courts below them and to Congress. But in *Shelby County* Chief Justice Roberts did not behave like an appellate judge. Instead, he gave scant consideration to the detailed findings of Congress and to the arguments of the groups submitting amicus briefs in defense of the Voting Rights Act, including those that provided detailed evidence to support the extension of the law. Following Georgia Representative Westmoreland's wish list, Roberts produced the antidemocratic outcome he desired but that the majority of the people's representatives overwhelmingly rejected. Roberts declared, despite congressional findings to the contrary, "The conditions that originally justified these measures . . . no longer characterize voting in the covered jurisdictions."

Justice Ruth Bader Ginsburg, joined by Justices Stephen Breyer, Sonia Sotomayor, and Elena Kagan, dissented. They noted,

"Throwing out preclearance when it has worked and is continuing to work to stop discriminatory changes is like throwing away your umbrella in a rainstorm because you are not getting wet."

What happened next was completely predictable.

Voting restrictions started going into effect immediately, within minutes of John Roberts announcing his decimation of the preclearance protections under the Voting Rights Act.

The GOP had already been waging a decade-long campaign asserting falsely that Democrats were engaged in widespread voting fraud. Karl Rove peddled those claims in the lead up to the 2004 election, and secret funders stood up an operation called the American Center for Voting Rights Legislative Fund, which pushed restrictive ID rules for voting that the Roberts Court approved in 2008. Then, after Obama was elected with enormous turnout in cities with large populations of Black Americans, a Koch-funded group called the American Legislative Exchange Council (ALEC) gave top priority to adopting voter ID restrictions that make it harder for Americans to vote. In 2009, ALEC's model bill on voter ID restrictions was secretly voted on at a task force meeting cochaired by the National Rifle Association, but the newly reauthorized Voting Rights Act's preclearance provisions were standing in the way in several states.

Now, in June 2013, as John Roberts announced the *Shelby County* ruling, Republican politicians rejoiced. The decision unleashed a massive wave of changes to voting procedures, many of which have made it harder for Black Americans to vote—which was, as some proponents let slip, precisely their objective, though others cloaked their intent. States "previously covered by preclearance rushed to enact new voter laws that would restrict access to the ballot, especially for Black voters, because they were now unobstructed by the preclearance requirement." For example, Greg Abbott, then the attorney general of Texas, announced that the state's voter ID restrictions would go into effect immediately. As the NAACP Legal

Defense Fund noted, the Texas law "imposes significant burdens on young African-American student voters in Texas, many of whom have previously relied on student IDs to vote in past elections. Texas's restrictive voter ID law would have a disproportionate effect on voters of color throughout the state. Nationally, only 8% of white voting age citizens, while 25% of African-American voting age citizens, lack a government-issued photo ID. Under the proposed law, concealed handgun licenses would be acceptable forms of photo ID, but student IDs would not."[24]

Without the Voting Rights Act's preclearance provisions blocking it, Alabama enacted voter ID restrictions that targeted IDs often used by urban Black voters who relied on public transportation and did not have a driver's license to register to vote. It did so by "eliminating options that were previously accepted such as Social Security cards, birth certificates, Medicaid or Medicare cards, and Electronic Benefits Transfer (EBT) cards." Meanwhile, the US Court of Appeals for the Fourth Circuit struck down voter ID restrictions in North Carolina after finding the state's GOP legislature had enacted "one of the largest restrictions of the franchise in modern North Carolina history" and "target[ed] African-Americans with almost surgical precision."[25]

That wave of voter restrictions was extended in the years that followed and accelerated after President Donald Trump made claims of "voter fraud" a centerpiece of his attacks on the 2020 presidential election. His false claims fueled "Stop the Steal" groups to organize the January 6 rally on the National Mall, where he incited the deadly insurrection at the US Capitol. The lesser-known part of his speech that day focused on numerous changes to state voting laws he wanted Republican-controlled legislatures to enact going forward. Since 2021, many of those restrictions were adopted at the urging of right-wing groups such as the Honest Elections Project, an alias of the Leo-tied Judicial Education Project.[26]

The onslaught of voting restrictions was not the only devastating effect of Roberts's *Shelby County* decision. Access to polling places has also been constricted dramatically. As the NAACP Legal Defense Fund noted, "Research from the Leadership Conference Education Fund demonstrates [that between] 2012 and 2018, counties with past histories of racial discrimination in voting closed at least 1,688 polling places." That trend has continued in more recent years, too, in aid of the extraordinary efforts pursued by the Trump campaign during the 2020 election to block legislative and judicial actions that protected alternative ways for Americans to vote during the deadly COVID-19 pandemic. Trump lost the litigation he pursued against voter access in 2020, but in 2024 he continued to spread debunked claims about voter fraud and immigrant voting—until he narrowly won. Then, suddenly, his hype around voter fraud stopped cold, until he reprised it in March 2025 by issuing an executive order attempting to dictate state voter qualification rules in advance of the 2026 midterm election.[27]

Roberts's *Shelby County* edict also unleashed more voter purges. As LDF noted, "Voter purges are often-inaccurate processes of deleting names of registered voters, which can prevent eligible voters from casting a ballot when done incorrectly. While voter purge practices may appear neutral, they often have discriminatory impacts, such as disproportionate purges in neighborhoods with more voters of color or disproportionate purges of voters with 'non-citizen' names, leading to more voters of color showing up at the polls and being unable to cast a ballot," or being allowed to cast only a provisional ballot.[28]

LDF also flagged scientific analysis finding that "the *Shelby County* decision led to a significant increase in voter purge rates in counties previously covered by preclearance," which "could be indicative of racially motivated voter suppression." This is John Roberts's legacy.[29]

These voter suppression techniques work hand in glove with unapologetically partisan redistricting efforts. The structural changes to American democracy made by the Roberts Court "obviously confer electoral and financial benefit on the GOP and its corporate benefactors, and so often violate judicial norms to deliver the goods," as Senator Sheldon Whitehouse has detailed. The Leo- and Koch-fueled ALEC has also aided extreme partisan gerrymandering at the urging of Trump advisor Cleta Mitchell, who guided state legislators on how to draw superpartisan voting maps and urged them to delete their notes on her presentations to hide these orchestrations from the public and the press. Drawing distorted maps is another means of giving Republicans an unfair electoral advantage by ensuring that the proportion of GOP legislators far exceeds the proportion of their actual electoral support in a state.[30]

Roberts's major assault on fair electoral maps occurred in a ruling called *Rucho v. Common Cause*. That decision was issued in 2018, two years before the mandatory 2020 census that triggered another round of map drawing for legislative districts. In *Rucho*, John Roberts declared that federal courts had no jurisdiction to address hyperpartisan redistricting in North Carolina or any place else, even though a three-judge panel had struck down North Carolina's congressional map from 2016 under long-standing judicial precedents recognizing that the map was an illegal partisan gerrymander that diluted votes. Roberts joined the North Carolina case with one brought against a Democratic-drawn map in Maryland to try to make his ruling appear nonpartisan, yet another sly move more befitting a politician than a judge. But his decree that federal courts cannot intervene primarily aids Republicans. For example, in North Carolina and Wisconsin, Democrats can win statewide offices where the map is the whole state, but the Republican-drawn maps allowed Republicans to dominate the state and federal legislature. As Justice Kagan, joined by Justices Ginsburg, Sotomayor, and Breyer, wrote in dissent in *Rucho*,

> For the first time ever, this Court refuses to remedy a constitutional violation because it thinks the task is beyond judicial capabilities. And not just any constitutional violation. The partisan gerrymanders in these cases deprived citizens of the most fundamental of their constitutional rights: the rights to participate equally in the political process, to join with others to advance political beliefs, and to choose their political representatives. In so doing, the partisan gerrymanders here debased and dishonored our democracy . . . enabl[ing] politicians to entrench themselves in office as against voters' preferences. . . . They encouraged a politics of polarization and dysfunction. If left unchecked, gerrymanders like the ones here may irreparably damage our system of government.[31]

As with the *Shelby County* case, in *Rucho* an array of right-wing groups that mostly do not represent any significant number of actual voters submitted amicus briefs. Numerous public interest groups that cumulatively represent millions of Americans opposed the hyperpartisan gerrymandering. All of these arguments and substantial documented evidence of damage to fair representation had no impact on John Roberts's decree in *Rucho*.

Although his ruling in *Rucho* severely harmed representative democracy, he dangled the promise that the federal courts could still strike down *racial* gerrymandering. The opportunity to make good on that promise arrived when *Alexander v. South Carolina State Conference of the NAACP* made its way to the Supreme Court. After the 2020 census, the South Carolina legislature drew new lines for the state's 1st Congressional District to "bleach" more than

30,000 Black residents out of that district, which has long included the Gullah Geechee community, part of the distinctive culture of the descendants of people who had been enslaved. That amounted to moving 62 percent of the Charleston area's Black voters out of the district that narrowly elected Representative Nancy Mace and into the district of Representative Jim Clyburn, a Black Democrat. That maneuver changed a swing district previously represented by a Democrat, Representative Joe Cunningham, into a statistically safe seat for Mace and the Republican Party. A panel of three federal judges evaluated the facts and found that the legislature's new map for the 1st District was a "stark racial gerrymander" designed to suppress the power of Black voters. The ruling found that map illegal and ordered new maps drawn.[32]

After the Roberts Court agreed to hear the case, the parties agreed to expedited briefing and oral arguments so the case could be decided before the spring 2024 primary, in time for the printing of ballots and voting district maps. By October 2023, all of the materials had been submitted to the Court. The Roberts Court slow-walked the case, letting the printing deadline pass, ensuring that no matter how the Court ruled, the map the lower court declared to be an illegal racial gerrymander would be in effect in the 2024 election. In the summer, though, the Roberts Court reversed the lower court and let the old map stand even though lower court judges determined that it deliberately bleached out thousands of Black voters.

As Justice Kagan noted in her dissent, joined by Justices Sotomayor and Ketanji Brown Jackson, the lower court had conducted extensive fact-finding, holding "a 9-day trial, featuring some two dozen witnesses and hundreds of exhibits. It evaluated evidence about South Carolina geography and politics. It heard first-hand testimony about the redistricting process. And it considered the views of statistical experts on how the State's new district lines could—and could not—have come about." The lower court did not give credence to the assertions of state officials that they had not considered race. It made factual findings that the evidence proved that the state "mapmakers were experienced and skilled in the use of racial data to draw electoral maps; that they configured their mapmaking software to show how any change made to the district would affect its racial composition; that the racial makeup they landed on was precisely what they needed, to the decimal point, to achieve their partisan goals; and that their politics-only story could not account, as a statistical matter, for their large-scale exclusion of African-American citizens."

In an opinion that John Roberts assigned to Sam Alito, the Court overturned the lower court, 6–3, and declared that the map had been drawn for partisan purposes and so did not constitute *racial* gerrymandering. Alito disregarded the factual findings of the lower court, which under long-standing judicial precedents can be set aside "only for clear error." There was none. The partisan Republican majority on the Roberts Court simply imposed a declaration that the state legislature supposedly acted in "good faith," despite the evidence to the contrary. In light of the *Alexander* decision, it is now open season for Republican legislatures to consider race in drawing legislative districts as long as they assert their maps are drawn for partisan purposes.

John Roberts is not done playing games with our elections. Two days before the 2024 election, the Roberts Court chose to accept a case where right-wing politicians in Louisiana and other Southern states were seeking to overturn Section 2 of the Voting Rights Act and block the 1982 amendments that allow courts to consider the disparate racial impact of a voting procedure or practice. That is the very section that Roberts spent hundreds of hours trying to stop from passing during the Reagan administration.[33]

Back in 2022, however, the Roberts Court allowed the use of Alabama's maps for US House races even though they violated Section 2, and the Court ordered the maps redrawn only *after* the midterm elections. In 2023, when the State of Alabama openly ignored the Court's order to redraw the maps to ensure there were two Black voting districts, key state legislators orchestrating this defiance boasted they had "intel" that Justice Brett Kavanaugh had the votes to overturn Section 2, and so they did not really need to redraw the maps. The word "intel" suggests more than the legislators' inference of Kavanaugh's position based on his concurrence in the Alabama ruling, as key Leo-tied operatives were aiding the state in its highly unusual noncompliance with a Supreme Court order. Alex Aronson, my partner at Court Accountability, helped bring this information to light, which seemed to stop that scheming in its tracks.

But the damage was already done. Because John Roberts had let Alabama and a few other states proceed with legally faulty maps in the 2022 midterm elections, control of the US House of Representatives flipped from Democratic to Republican, ending the January 6 Committee's investigation into Trump and putting up a two-year barrier to the Joe Biden–Kamala Harris legislative agenda. In 2025, with Trump back in the White House thanks in part to John Roberts's unprecedented intervention in the 2024 presidential election, Roberts could do even greater damage to Americans' voting rights, which a Republican-controlled Congress would be highly unlikely to undo before the 2026 midterms, no matter how egregious.

---

What kind of person—a white man in his twenties, no less—makes it a priority to block the restoration of a key provision of the Voting Rights Act, which was built on the backs of millions of Black Americans striving to exercise the most fundamental right in our democratic republic? I confess I find it really odd that Roberts, a privileged young man who had just left the stately halls of the ivory tower, would have developed such hostility toward the then-just-fifteen-year-old Voting Rights Act. It is both disturbing and deeply sad that time and experience did not diminish his destructive impulses toward a statute that was won after decades of enormous sacrifice—lives lost, people battered, and dreams shattered—to help make the promises of the Civil War amendments to our Constitution real, to help our multiracial democracy thrive.

Is this the result of personal racial animus? Bruce Fein, who worked with John Roberts at the Justice Department, does not think so, claiming Roberts doesn't have "a racist bone" in his body. Similarly, there is no indication Roberts is ill-mannered toward colleagues or friends, like Clarence Thomas, because of their race. But John Roberts's actions in some ways comport with Lee Atwater's description of the Southern Strategy and its euphemisms. Until the unexpected rise of Donald Trump, the racism of the establishment in the modern Republican Party was not "out loud," although its effect was to serve and preserve white domination without admitting it. Elites were usually not racist in an overt way, such as using the N-word or speaking in the doltish and unfounded Trumpian way, such as calling Black-majority cities and countries "shitholes." That is far too lowbrow. (As noted film director Paris Barclay, one of the first Black students to attend the La Lumiere School and a classmate of Roberts, told the *Los Angeles Times*, "No one ever called me the N-word. . . . They were too sophisticated for that." Barclay was speaking to the culture he and his brother, Neil, experienced at La Lumiere in the early 1970s.)[34]

That said, Roberts's personal beliefs regarding race are largely beside the point; indeed, speculating about them can serve as yet another distraction. Whether or not Roberts is racist in the rank of his mentor Rehnquist, his actions as a jurist are racist in effect. His rulings have had massive adverse consequences for Black Americans' rights, and he literally fought battles to prevent the law from considering such effects. More to the point, the effect of Roberts's work has been to uphold laws that make it harder for many Black Americans to vote and have their vote meaningfully count in securing representation as America's largest minority group. Whether intended or not it serves John Roberts's political agenda too, since Black Americans consistently have voted overwhelmingly for Democrats, who have fought to protect the Voting Rights Act.[35]

The result is that Roberts has given constitutional cover to racist policies and practices. Over and over, Roberts's rulings have undermined Americans' voting rights under a mirage of supposedly neutral principles, all the while advancing a reactionary agenda shared by a billionaire elite to which he seems deeply beholden. Roberts attacked the Voting Rights Act not as a subordinate following distasteful orders or like a fair-minded umpire, but like a man on a mission. His tenacity could harken back to the lessons he learned as a member of his high school wrestling team. Wrestling is a sport of strength, endurance, and leverage where you resist and contort your opponent until he or she submits to your will. Although he failed in his grand ambitions during the Reagan administration, as the chief justice of the US Supreme Court John Roberts has succeeded in bending the Voting Rights Act to his will—to the detriment of millions of Americans and the health of our democracy.[36]

## CHAPTER 13

# CLASS

JOHN ROBERTS IS by far the richest member of the Supreme Court, with a net worth of more than $25 million. That high net worth makes him wealthier than 99.9 percent of the US population. Back in 2003, when he was appointed to the DC Circuit court, his net worth was about $3.5 million, based in part on over $1 million in annual income as a partner at a law firm. His salary as chief justice, at $280,500 a year, is more than what members of Congress make.

Roberts was born on third base, the son of a Bethlehem Steel executive, with access to the best private schools money could buy. But his wealth has surged since he was appointed to the Supreme Court because his wife, Jane, has made a fortune as a headhunter. She has been paid large commissions for placing elite lawyers at elite law firms that litigate before the Supreme Court and other courts. As you might imagine, some law firms appear very eager to hire the spouse of the chief justice to help them recruit lawyers. At least one of her associates has suggested that law firms might feel pressure to accept her solicitations or recommendations. In response to reporting about this potential conflict and the appearance it raises, one of her employers crowed that she was the highest-paid legal-placement recruiter they had, which in this context raises more questions than it answers. John Roberts does not disclose to the public which prominent lawyers his wife has placed at big corporate law firms, and so there is no way to know how much of their lifestyle is effectively being underwritten by lawyers who appear before the Supreme Court or sign on to briefs to the Court.

Jane Roberts was an accomplished lawyer who became a legal recruiter *after* her husband became chief justice. Has the prestige of his office aided her recruitment? Do they never discuss the lawyers she has placed or the law firms that have paid her commissions? Shouldn't there be new rules to better address potential conflicts of interest that could arise from the employment or contracts or other activities of the spouses of justices on the Supreme Court?

Although John Roberts has the most wealth of all of the justices, every justice on the nine-member Supreme Court is a millionaire on paper. Most of the other justices' net worths are in the seven figures due in part to the valuation of their homes in the expensive Washington, DC, real estate market. It is Clarence Thomas, however—not John Roberts—who is living the life of a billionaire, due to the luxury trips, private jet travel, and fabulous vacations showered on him by billionaire benefactors, while he remains perhaps the most reliable vote to advance the Republican political agenda. Samuel Alito has also shown a penchant for rubbing elbows with right-wing billionaires, including uber-rich, right-wing foreign royalty.

The ranks of US Supreme Court justices have often included the sons of wealthy or powerful families, and many have attended elite colleges and law schools. It is certainly not a moral fault to be born rich or to become rich; it is a common aspiration of many. But the federal judicial oath includes a solemn promise where judges—including Supreme Court justices—swear they will "do equal right to the poor and to the rich." The germane question is whether the Roberts Court's right-wing majority is using judicial power in ways that favor the rich over the poor. The answer, unfortunately, is a resounding yes, in almost every case where it could matter.[1]

---

In 2020, as the death toll from the COVID-19 pandemic was hitting thousands per week, Joe Biden ran for office on a platform that included forgiving some of the student loan debts of American workers. After he was elected, Biden invoked a provision of the 2003 Higher Education Relief Opportunities for Students (HEROES) Act, signed into law by President George W. Bush, in order to accomplish this goal. That law expressly allows the secretary of education to forgive student debt in times of national emergency. The Biden program was designed to allow people with less than $125,000 in income to cancel $10,000 in student loan debt. This was a targeted effort to provide modest relief to millions of Americans.

In a case known as *Biden v. Nebraska*, John Roberts took it upon himself to write the majority opinion striking down President Biden's student loan debt relief program. That case should not even have been before the Court, because the parties attacking the program—six Republican-controlled states—did not have "standing" to sue to block their residents from getting their student debt forgiven. Long-established rules regarding standing require that a party to a case actually be injured, and because there was literally no injury to those states, their claims should have been dismissed with prejudice. Instead of following uncontroversial legal precedent, Roberts justified his arrogant intervention by connecting the lawsuit to the work of the Missouri Higher Education Loan Authority, which helps administer student loans, while ignoring the fact that this "legally and financially independent public corporation" was not a party to the lawsuit.[2]

Roberts's miserly interpretation of the statute also blots out the law's plain language allowing such debt forgiveness in emergencies, which are not by statute confined to wartime. Roberts asserted that even if the statute allowed such forgiveness, which it does, Congress should have passed new, more specific legislation to allow this kind of forgiveness. That is because the policy offends a new (fake) doctrine manufactured by the Roberts Court that Congress, not administrative agencies applying existing law, must first address so-called major questions, like student loan forgiveness during a deadly pandemic. The failure of the student loan forgiveness plan occurred in a period when people saw massive debt forgiveness for corporations that collectively received billions of dollars in COVID-19 relief.[3]

That is, John Roberts accepted a "case" that was really just a political argument brought by Republican states with no legal standing under existing precedents, and then he and his Republican cohorts on the Court ignored the plain language of the law in order to block a signature policy of the Democratic administration. In doing so, Roberts handed President Biden a political loss that could serve to alienate potential voters—many of whom were counting on that student loan debt relief—in the 2024 presidential race. Put simply, Roberts countenanced the manufacture of a political "case" to reach a political result for his political party. There was nothing modest or neutral about it. He was not acting as a fair umpire, merely calling balls and strikes. The dissenting justices, led by Justice Elena Kagan, with Sonia Sotomayor and Ketanji Brown Jackson joining, pointed out these deep flaws in his approach, concluding, "In a case not a case, the majority overrides the combined judgment of the Legislative and Executive Branches, with the consequence of eliminating loan forgiveness for 43 million Americans."[4]

The articles about the student loan debt relief litigation almost always failed to tell the story of the special interest campaign behind it. In this instance, the suit was brought by the Republican attorneys general of several states who owed their offices in part to

Leonard Leo, whose groups have been the biggest funders of the Republican Attorneys General Association (RAGA) over the past decade. The state attorneys general who complained about the student loan debt relief program hailed from Nebraska, Missouri, South Carolina, Iowa, Arkansas, and Kansas. The residents of those states were not clamoring for them to block student loan relief, but the partisan political actors who opposed Biden were. Other RAGA attorneys general weighed in, part of a "flotilla" of amicus briefs, as Senator Whitehouse has called them, giving Roberts a bounty of biased material favoring Republicans from which to craft his opinion.[5]

The authors of these amicus briefs—which support what would have been deemed, in a prior era, dubious cases brought for purely political reasons—enrich their organizations by getting money to weigh in on what are now quite predictable partisan victories. Many of these nonprofit groups pass through big sums of their revenue to for-profit law firms to actually write the briefs, effectively allowing their benefactors to get a tax write-off for ultimately funding a law firm's six-figure fees, a neat little loophole for those who can afford to play the game. This racket helps sustain the right-wing echo chamber under the guise of participating in the marketplace of ideas, when in fact the die is cast, and the fix is in almost every time.

---

Another recent example of the Roberts Court predictably ruling against the poor is the 6–3 decision in *City of Grants Pass v. Johnson* allowing cities to make it a crime for Americans to sleep outside. That ruling transforms a fictional phrasing into a miserable reality for unhoused Americans. As Anatole France wrote in *The Red Lily*, "The law, in its majestic equality, forbids the rich as well as the poor to sleep under bridges, to beg in the streets, and to steal bread." John Roberts assigned the opinion to Neil Gorsuch, whose $2 million house and millions in investments make him the third-richest person on the Supreme Court.[6]

The case arose out of a city code against sleeping outside, which provided fines and exclusion orders that could be turned into criminal violations. It was adopted by the City of Grants Pass in Oregon. Lower federal courts found the code unconstitutional. As the US Court of Appeals for the Ninth Circuit ruled in a similar case called *Martin v. Boise*, "The Eighth Amendment prohibits the imposition of criminal penalties for sitting, sleeping, or lying outside on public property for homeless individuals who cannot obtain shelter." Gorsuch, along with all the other Republican appointees to the Court, rejected the *Martin* injunctions against penalizing people for sleeping in public. One of the plaintiffs, an elderly, disabled, unemployed woman named Debra Blake, testified, "I am afraid at all times. . . . I could be arrested, ticketed, and prosecuted for sleeping outside or for covering myself with a blanket to stay warm." She died while the case was pending, with $5,000 in past-due fines for sleeping outside while homeless.[7]

Justice Sotomayor, joined by Justices Kagan and Jackson, wrote a stinging dissent, noting, "Sleep is a biological necessity, not a crime." She continued, "For some people, sleeping outside is their only option. The City of Grants Pass jails and fines those people for sleeping anywhere in public at any time, including in their cars, if they use as little as a blanket to keep warm or a rolled-up shirt as a pillow. For people with no access to shelter, that punishes them for being homeless. That is unconscionable and unconstitutional."

Both the majority opinion and the dissent used words acknowledging the challenges facing both people who are unhoused and cities contending with the rise in homelessness. But where the dissenters relied on these facts in finding that it was unconstitutional to punish unhoused people for their profoundly unfortunate conditions, the Republican majority merely feigned compassion and understanding. Instead, the majority chose to set aside long-standing legal precedents in order to side against Americans with nothing besides the Constitution to protect them from punishment for being in dire straits. As the dissent noted, this "leaves the most vulnerable in our society with an impossible choice: Either stay awake or be arrested. The Constitution provides a baseline of rights for all Americans rich and poor, housed and unhoused. This Court must safeguard those rights even when, and perhaps especially when, doing so is uncomfortable or unpopular."[8]

---

John Roberts's ruling on the Affordable Care Act (ACA) is often cited as an example of him putting principle above politics, precedent, or expedience. It is certainly the case that when Roberts voted to protect the ACA, many Republicans in Congress and their donor class were dismayed, as though they were entitled to win 100 percent of the time. In fact, despite the hyperventilating protests of Republicans, this appears to be another example of Roberts acting as a consummate politician, intervening to protect the GOP from its own worst instincts. To any astute observer it was clear that striking down the Affordable Care Act in its entirety—with its protections for people with preexisting conditions and more—during the 2012 presidential election would cause a "jolt" to the system that could damage the GOP's electoral prospects.

Back in 2009, the Barack Obama administration began efforts to provide more affordable access to health insurance for the millions of Americans who needed it. Obama advisor Rahm Emanuel apparently thought that by adopting the plan that Mitt Romney had embraced as the Republican governor of Massachusetts—a plan built on creating health insurance exchanges that had initially been proposed by the right-wing Heritage Foundation—he would secure strong bipartisan support and a bipartisan victory for expanded access to health insurance. Progressives had been promoting a much more ambitious plan, dubbed "Medicare for All," that would have expanded that popular program to reach people beyond senior citizens. Emanuel sought to crush that effort—and progressives, politically—and insisted on a market-based plan rather than purely government-funded insurance. He grossly miscalculated. Even though Democrats held fifty-eight seats in the Senate and had a 257–178 margin in the House, Emanuel squandered Barack Obama's supermajority mandate by spending months seeking Republican support in vain, wasting time and valuable political capital. Meanwhile Republicans maneuvered to run out the clock and used their expanding propaganda machinery at FOX and other right-wing outlets to lie to their followers by painting Obama's modest proposal, inspired by a Republican plan, as "socialism," a smear amplified by big GOP funders like Charles Koch. Republicans also planted the pernicious but false notion that it was a plan for government "death panels," even though the real death panels rejecting coverage sought by doctors and their patients are actually run every single day by huge health insurance corporations, with denials now aided by their AI programs.[9]

Prior to the ACA becoming the law, Republican operatives were already lining up litigants to file suit against the measure, arguing that it was unconstitutional. Major GOP funders—specifically Charles Koch and Republican strategist Karl Rove—contrived to use the National Federation of Independent Businesses (NFIB) as a front group to take up the political fight against the ACA. The NFIB is a trade organization whose stickers are on the doors of thousands of small businesses, which get AAA-like discounts for paying dues of $195 per year. In 2010, the year it filed suit against the ACA, the NFIB received more than $3.7 million from Republican strategist Karl Rove's political machine, called Crossroads GPS. That was an unusual gift for a group that labels itself "the voice of small business" to accept. NFIB and its affiliated nonprofits also accepted $2.5 million from Koch's Freedom Partners Chamber of

Commerce, whose minimum annual membership fee of $100,000 is so steep that few small businesses could ever afford it. That is, the trade group that says it represents small businesses accepted millions of dollars from the nonprofit tied to Koch Industries, one of the biggest corporations in the world and the second-largest privately held company in America. NFIB also accepted more than $1 million from DonorsTrust, a right-wing donor-advised fund with ties to the Koch network of billionaires and other wealthy right-wing funders.[10]

The Republican Party expected that the Supreme Court would strike down the ACA when it agreed to hear *National Federation of Independent Businesses v. Sebelius* in 2012. Michael Carvin, John Roberts's old friend, represented NFIB in claiming the ACA was unconstitutional under the Commerce Clause. The Obama administration defended the ACA as legislation consistent with the very deferential legal precedents under the Commerce Clause. It also argued that the part of the law called the individual "mandate," which required people to obtain insurance or face a tax penalty, was within congressional power to make policy through tax law.

According to Jan Crawford's reporting for CBS after the Supreme Court announced its decision, John Roberts initially voted to overturn the individual mandate as unconstitutional under the Commerce Clause because that provision had never been used to require a person to buy a product, as opposed to allowing government to regulate a product. Roberts assigned the writing of the opinion to himself, but he apparently sought to separate the Commerce Clause claims from a ruling that would declare the entire act unconstitutional, even the very popular requirement that health insurance provide affordable coverage for preexisting conditions, which affect tens of millions of Americans. The other Republican appointees to the Court refused to budge on that point. Meanwhile, the Democratic appointees to the Court were trying to keep the ACA's expansion of Medicaid intact, under long-standing precedents upholding that federal program, even though the ACA's provision played real hardball with the states by requiring them to accept either a federally subsidized expansion of Medicaid for poor people living just above the poverty line or the total loss of funding.[11]

When Roberts switched gears to uphold the ACA under the power to tax, the initial dissenters, the Democratic appointees, agreed to join him in his opinion upholding the ACA but striking down the Medicaid expansion. As Joan Biskupic wrote, "Perhaps Roberts' move was born of a concern for the business of health care. Perhaps he had worries about his own legitimacy and legacy, intertwined with concerns about the legitimacy and legacy of the court. Perhaps his change of heart really arose from a sudden new understanding of congressional taxing power." Jan Crawford's investigative reporting added additional observations that shed light on how Roberts approached the highly watched ACA ruling: "Roberts pays attention to media coverage. As chief justice, he is keenly aware of his leadership role on the court, and he also is sensitive to how the court is perceived by the public. There were countless news articles in May warning of damage to the court—and to Roberts' reputation—if the court were to strike down the mandate. Leading politicians, including the president himself, had expressed confidence the mandate would be upheld."[12]

Republican politicians were furious, as was one of their main organs, *The Wall Street Journal*'s editorial board. So was Carvin, who apparently thought he had the win in the bag. Besides the political implications of overturning the law, supporters of a complete repeal of the ACA had overlooked the role that the "mandate" to purchase insurance played in the legislation. The power to make policy choices through the tax code—through incentives and penalties—is a long-standing tool of Congress, and it unquestionably aids big business and the wealthy more than anyone else in America. Striking that down would throw open an array of challenges to wealth-benefiting tax provisions that provide numerous loopholes that favor the rich.

When the case was heard I was convinced John Roberts would not undercut the policy-making power of Congress under its tax authority. I also believed that Roberts was calculating the effect of tearing down the ACA just four months before the presidential election and how invalidating the widely popular preexisting condition coverage would play with the electorate. I also thought it would be bad optics to cancel health insurance coverage for more than 20 million Americans on election eve. Roberts's opinion was clearly a carefully crafted political decision, though it appears that he underestimated how intensely some Republicans would claim he had betrayed their cause, despite upholding what had been the health insurance plan pioneered by Romney and the Heritage Foundation. After all, as the US Chamber of Commerce's own polling would show, most business leaders subsequently said that the most important health care–related issue for them was "keeping health care costs low for American families," not eliminating the ACA. Roberts's ruling was consistent with the view of most business elites.[13]

While protecting some of the core provisions of the ACA, Roberts also provided a roadmap for ways to undermine it, and he later took up cases that made carve-outs to the ACA's coverage. For example, two years later in 2014, Roberts joined Sam Alito's opinion blocking the ACA from requiring for-profit corporate employers to provide access to contraceptives if they assert a religious objection, in *Burwell v. Hobby Lobby Stores Inc.* In 2020, Roberts also joined an opinion written by Clarence Thomas exempting the nonprofit Little Sisters of the Poor from the ACA's provisions on access to contraception, even though it did not qualify as a church.[14]

---

John Roberts and the Republican appointees on the Supreme Court routinely side with the US Chamber of Commerce in the vast majority of cases in which it files a brief. In a recent five-year period, the Court "decided more than 90 cases in which the Chamber filed a brief. In just two of those cases did the Court reverse a lower-court victory for corporate interests. But during the same period, the Court reversed nearly 50 lower-court victories for plaintiffs or the government." The Chamber promotes itself as the voice of American business writ large, but, as the public interest group Public Citizen has detailed, the vast majority of its funding comes from a few dozen major donors, which include some of the biggest corporations in America and the world. And those mega-corporations' profit motives put them at odds with the interests of ordinary people when it comes to issues like access to health care, labor rights, consumer protections, progressive taxation, and more.[15]

At one point, polling conducted by Chamber pollster Frank Luntz showed that the position of the national and state chambers was at odds with more than 1,000 business leaders he surveyed who supported paid sick leave, raising the minimum wage, and other progressive policies. Rather than alter its position, though, the Chamber provided talking points on how to overcome that "empathy." That is, the Chamber was not really representing the positions of most businesses leaders but was actively advancing the agenda of the most powerful few.[16]

The Chamber's more recent successes before the US Supreme Court have their roots in the Powell Memo, the now-famous and then-secret memorandum distributed by tobacco lawyer and racial segregation abettor Lewis Powell on August 23, 1971. The thirty-four-page memo was filled with breathless rhetoric claiming that America had fallen prey to socialism. It included ridiculous claims for the world of 1971, such as "As every business executive knows, few elements in American society today have as little influence in government as the American businessman, the corporation, or even the millions of corporate shareholders. . . . [I]n terms of political influence . . . the American businessman is truly the 'forgotten man.'"[17]

A month after Powell penned that memo, Supreme Court Justice Hugo Black, a former US senator from Alabama and former member of the Ku Klux Klan, died. A month after that, Powell was nominated to replace him. The public did not learn about Powell's memo until almost a year after he was confirmed, when investigative reporter Jack Anderson published excerpts. That explosive piece from 1972 questioned whether Powell could be considered fair in ruling on any business case that came to the Supreme Court. Powell's memo assailed consumer advocate Ralph Nader, who had fought to keep dangerous cars, like General Motors' "unsafe-at-any-speed" Corvair, off the highways. At the time of Lewis Powell's memo, Republican Richard Nixon was president and headed toward reelection—it was nearly a year before Nixon's henchmen broke into the Watergate Hotel to try to steal strategy documents from Democratic headquarters. Nixon was battling what was dubbed "stagflation," a slow economy with inflationary pressures. In response, Nixon announced tax cuts along with wage and price controls. A few years earlier, with a Democratic Congress, Nixon had provoked the Chamber of Commerce's ire by signing bills that protected workers from being killed or maimed on the job through the new Occupational Safety and Health Administration (OSHA). Growing numbers of Americans had also expressed concerns about pollution in the years after Rachel Carson published her influential book *Silent Spring* about the toxic chemicals used in agriculture. After a blowout on an off-shore oil rig in the Santa Barbara Channel flooded the ocean and shore with nearly 100,000 gallons of oil in 1969, Americans organized the first Earth Day on April 22, 1970. Weeks later, Nixon created the Environmental Protection Agency (EPA).[18]

It was in this context that Powell penned his secret memo. Superwealthy heirs to family fortunes, like oil man Charles Koch and Joseph Coors of the Coors beer dynasty, stepped up to fund new nonprofit groups to respond to Powell's metaphorical call to arms. In 1973, for example, Coors worked with Paul Weyrich and Ed Feulner to launch the Heritage Foundation. The following year, in 1974, a contingent of pro–Ronald Reagan Republicans launched the American Legislative Exchange Council to promote a Heritage Foundation–aligned business agenda with state legislators. That year, Charles Koch gave a speech to the Institute for Humane Studies arguing that Powell did not go far enough: "We have accepted the concept that the corporation has a broad social responsibility beyond its duty to its shareholders. When the businessman does this, he is in fact preaching pure and unadulterated socialism. . . . The development of a well-financed cadre of sound proponents of the free enterprise philosophy is the most critical need facing us at the moment. . . . The system can be restored if business will re-examine itself and undertake radical new efforts to overcome the prevalent anti-capitalist mentality." There is no evidence that John Roberts read Koch's speech as an undergraduate student at Harvard, but within a few years he would be embracing that agenda from within the Reagan administration.[19]

To win the presidency, Reagan bested both Jimmy Carter and Walter Mondale on the Democratic Party ticket and Ed Clark and David Koch on the Libertarian Party ticket (a third-party run that received a paltry 1.1 percent of the popular vote). The Libertarian Party's platform, underwritten by the Koch family fortune, called for abolishing OSHA, the EPA, the Securities and Exchange Commission, the Department of Education, and more. It was decades ahead of Donald Trump and Project 2025 on those matters, seeding the field or salting the earth, as it were. The Koch-funded Libertarian platform also asserted that corporations had a right not to recognize unions and also called for the repeal of the National

Labor Relations Act. Having lost that third-party bid, Charles Koch turned his focus toward getting the Reagan administration and Republicans to embrace his extreme political and judicial agenda, a long-term project that proved highly successful over the following four decades.

---

In early 1981, the newly elected Reagan administration charted its own course, including a particularly surprising one for a president who had once led one of the most influential unions in the nation: the Screen Actors Guild.

In August 1981, after John Roberts finished his Supreme Court clerkship with Bill Rehnquist and walked into the attorney general's suite of offices on the fifth floor of the Justice Department, the nation's air traffic controllers had just gone on strike. By the afternoon of Monday, August 3, the majority of flights had stopped. The Professional Air Traffic Controllers Organization (PATCO) had called the strike of more than 11,000 union members after negotiations with the Federal Aviation Administration broke down. The air traffic controllers had been negotiating for better wages and working hours that addressed the intense stress of managing flights in and out of busy airports. Robert Poli, PATCO's leader, attested that many air traffic controllers never received their pensions because they died too young from on-the-job stress. Many of PATCOs members were military veterans, and the union had affirmatively endorsed Reagan, who had promised better working conditions. So PATCO's leaders and members believed they would prevail in their strike and negotiations. However, at midweek, President Reagan ordered the controllers back to work. Less than 10 percent of the strikers returned to the control towers to work alongside active military and retirees who had crossed the picket lines, working as scabs.[20]

At the end of that first full week of August, Reagan fired every single traffic controller who had not returned to work. He also issued an order barring them from federal employment, a bar finally rescinded by President Bill Clinton more than a decade later. The PATCO strike was the first time the federal government had actively shut down a strike since the Pullman railway strike of 1894. The Reagan administration's decision to act as a strike breaker sent a powerful signal to the private sector, undermining a potent union tactic and emboldening employers for years to come. Thirty years later, in 2011, then-Governor Scott Walker stripped public employees in Wisconsin of their collective bargaining rights, invoking "Reagan's handling of PATCO as he prepared to 'change history' by stripping public employees of collective bargaining rights in a party-line vote. 'I'm not negotiating,' Mr. Walker said." In *The New York Times*, historian Joseph A. McCartin wrote, "With Mr. Walker's militant anti-union views now ascendant [and] workers less able to defend their interests in the workplace than at any time since the Depression, the long-term consequences continue to unfold in ways Reagan himself could not have predicted."[21]

In the two decades before Reagan crushed PATCO, federal workers had engaged in thirty-nine work stoppages in the course of negotiating new contracts. But since that week in August 1981, there have been none. The Reagan administration's blitz against PATCO augured a weakening of the power to strike as a potent collective bargaining tool.

During the televised hearings on John Roberts's nomination to the Supreme Court in 2005, he was not asked about labor unions. Andrew Stern did, however, submit a letter raising serious concerns on behalf of the Service Employees International Union (SEIU). Stern noted that Roberts had, in his brief time as a judge on the DC Circuit, voted against unions in several cases. He also noted that, as a lawyer in private practice, Roberts had taken positions against workers' rights. For example, Roberts represented a poultry industry trade group arguing that "low-wage primarily African American workers"—in Stern's words—who caught and brought chickens for processing were not entitled to unionize under the National Labor Relations Act. The Rehnquist Court rejected Roberts's claims.[22]

As Stern pointed out, Roberts also represented coal mining corporations numerous times in ways that hurt workers' rights. In one particularly noteworthy case, Roberts argued to the Supreme Court that the United Mine Workers of America were not entitled to a trial by jury before being fined a staggering $74 million for a strike over pensions and health benefits for retired or disabled coal miners at the Pittston Coal mines. The Rehnquist Court rejected John Roberts's position in a 9–0 decision. Roberts's father—his namesake—had worked as an executive for Bethlehem Steel, which divested from its coal mining business and stopped most of its operations just as Roberts was starting his career with the Reagan administration. In its heyday, the company produced steel for many of the cannons the United States fired in World War I, many of the warships deployed in World War II, and the infrastructure of public and private works like the Golden Gate Bridge, the Hoover Dam, the George Washington Bridge, and the Empire State Building. The company also had racially segregated bathrooms and imposed employment tests that had a racially disparate impact, which took years to redress through federal civil rights enforcement. Ultimately, with changes in technology, Bethlehem Steel could not compete with more modern Japanese steel mills. It had also padded its profits by lowballing the cost of pensions and health benefits fought for by unions, making promises it failed to keep, which the federal pension board was forced to redress.[23]

As Roberts was ascending to the bench during the George W. Bush administration, right-wing funders were gathering to expand their assault on unions. Documents from the Bradley Foundation reveal how, in 2003, it launched a Working Group on Employee Rights that was really about *undermining* workers' rights. Grover Norquist, the right-wing operative who infamously said he wanted to shrink government down to the size that it could be drowned in a bathtub, joined the effort, as did the National Right to Work Committee, the Mackinac Center, and the Illinois Policy Center, among others. This union-busting coalition soon broadened to include the American Legislative Exchange Council, a front group called the Center for Union Facts, the State Policy Network, and the Randolph Foundation, led by Heather Higgins, an heir to the Vicks VapoRub fortune. After Roberts and Alito were confirmed to the Court, numerous cases assailing unions would be teed up for the Court. The litigation targeted public employee unions, just as Governor Walker had done in Wisconsin, because "if unions are dealt a blow in the public sector, private sector businesses might see decreased pressure from pro-labor forces on issues ranging from the minimum wage to paid sick leave and other employee benefits."[24]

The Bradley Foundation's files make quite clear that it was targeting unions because their support has long been a "pillar" of the Democratic Party's strength, even though union members are not required to fund political activities. In 2015, the Roberts Court took up a case called *Friedrichs v. California Teachers Association.* The lower courts had rejected Rebecca Friedrichs's challenge to allowing teachers' unions to collect "fair-share fees" from nonunion members to support collective bargaining activities that secure pay and benefits for all employees, based on the long-standing Supreme Court precedent in *Abood v. Detroit Board of Education.* When the Roberts Court agreed to hear that case, the Republican-appointed majority clearly intended to affirm Friedrichs's claim that mandatory payment of the fees violated the First Amendment. Then Justice Antonin Scalia died unexpectedly in February 2016, and the Roberts Court deadlocked 4–4 over the claims. The lower court's ruling rejecting Friedrichs's argument would stand, at least for the time being. (Friedrichs herself become a kind of celebrity speaker in the Right's efforts to assail public schools.)[25]

But the Bradley-fueled groups had another case in the wings: *Janus v. American Federation of State, County, and Municipal Employees, Council 31.* In that case, a social welfare worker named Mark Janus also claimed that being required to pay fair-share fees violated his First Amendment rights. This time Neil Gorsuch was there to break the tie, reversing nearly forty years of legal precedent. Numerous groups funded by the Bradley Foundation and DonorsTrust submitted amicus briefs, and the Trump administration's solicitor general sided with Mark Janus too. John Roberts assigned the opinion in the case to Sam Alito, who asserted that the fair-share rule created a "windfall" for unions. Alito's opinion, which Roberts joined, allows workers like Janus to be free riders who get benefits and wages negotiated by unions without paying any fees—that's the real windfall. As the dissenting justices noted, the Roberts Court's majority was weaponizing the First Amendment to undo precedents that the new majority disliked; they were reversing the law in *Abood* based not on any material change in the law or circumstances but just because John Roberts had the numbers to do it.[26]

The decision also gave Charles Koch and his family a major victory in their multigenerational attack on unions. By a single vote, the Roberts Court's 5–4 decision reversed decades of legal precedent that had obstructed part of the Koch family's pro-corporate agenda. That vote was secured with Charles Koch using his fortune to bankroll efforts that included helping to maintain a GOP Senate majority; helping the Senate block President Obama from filling the February 2016 Supreme Court vacancy, which could very well have denied Roberts a majority to accomplish this reversal and other parts of the Right's agenda; and helping to win the confirmation of right-wing corporatist Neil Gorsuch. After that ruling, Bradley-funded groups formed brigades to urge public-sector workers to stop paying dues, through door-to-door campaigns and apps, using public records laws to identify people to target. Those groups bragged about potentially taking away hundreds of millions of dollars from unions, weakening them and, along with them, a key part of the get-out-the-vote efforts for Democrats.

That is, the Roberts Court's decision helped pave the way for a core objective of Bradley and Koch funding when it comes to labor: to "defang and defund" unions as a way to weaken the chances for progressives to win in politics and policy. This harkens back to a memo that Roberts wrote in 1983 for the Reagan administration. That memo discussed a potential rule to prohibit federal grantees from using money for lobbying, which progressive groups said would harm their advocacy. Roberts snidely wrote, "It is possible to 'defund the left' without alienating [defense contractors] TRW and Boeing, but the proposals, if enacted, would do both"—that is, they would harm not just the Left but corporations too.[27]

The effort to roll back federally protected union rights began nearly a century ago, as wealthy industrialists objected to the National Labor Relations Act of 1935, known as the Wagner Act, which secured the right to collective bargaining in the United States. Many tycoons of the time, like Alfred Sloan, the head of General Motors, opposed those rights, as well as other business reforms of Franklin Delano Roosevelt's New Deal. Fred Koch, cofounder of the corporation that later became Koch Industries, harshly criticized American workers under New Deal policies in 1938, extolling the economic policies of Emperor Hirohito, Adolf Hitler, and Benito Mussolini and claiming American workers were lazily "feeding at the public trough."[28]

Only recently, through the investigative work of Jane Mayer, has the public learned that the Koch fortune was built on contracts that aided not just the tyrant Joseph Stalin but also Adolf Hitler. Fred Koch helped create a factory to refine high-octane fuel needed for Hitler's air force, the Luftwaffe, which became "a key component in the Nazi war machine." Koch's praise of Germany came after Hitler's air bombers murdered 136 men, women, and children in

Guernica in the Basque region of Spain in aid of the far-right military coup led by Francisco Franco. That tragedy was made famous by the enormous, evocative mural painted by Pablo Picasso.[29]

After World War II, industrialists like Sloan and Koch pursued efforts to undo New Deal reforms. In 1947, Congress amended the Wagner Act with the Taft-Hartley Act, which gave states the power to pass "right-to-work" laws that undermined collective bargaining. A decade later, Fred Koch helped win the so-called right to work in Kansas, where, *The New York Times* reported, antiunion views had taken hold due to relatively massive last-minute spending: "More campaign efforts and more money were expended on the emotion-provoking issue than on the campaigns of all Republican and Democratic state and Congressional candidates combined. . . . For the last 10 days or so before Election Day an organization called Kansans-for-the-Right-to-Work flooded newspapers, television channels and other advertising media with appeals to 'vote yes.' These by far outnumbered the 'vote no' advertisements of unions opposing the amending." A month later, Fred Koch joined Robert Welch and ten other men in Indianapolis to found the extreme right-wing John Birch Society. In 1960, Koch published his polemic "A Business Man Looks at Communism," which makes a variety of hysterical claims, such as that labor unions were dominated by communists, Earl Warren's Supreme Court issued pro-communist decisions, and that even President Dwight Eisenhower was soft on communism.[30]

Following his father's efforts to launch the Birchers, Charles Koch embraced strident antiunion sentiments. For example, he repeatedly touted F. A. Harper's 1957 book *Why Wages Rise*, which absurdly argues, "Wages rise not because of unions or government action, but because of marginal productivity gains—people get more money when they produce more value for other people." Koch called reading this a "revelation," a "peak experience" in his life, though it has been disproven, repeatedly, over the past four decades as CEOs and shareholders have hoarded productivity gains while workers' wages have stagnated. Charles Koch personally fund-raised for the Birchers before parting ways over the Vietnam War, and he later supported the National Right to Work Committee, which ultimately helped bring the *Janus* case to fruition, in order to fuel supposedly "respectable" arguments like "Compulsory unionism itself violates the dignity of the individual worker, regardless of how the forced union tribute is spent." That argument is embodied in the Roberts Court decision in *Janus*, though it is framed not as a supposedly moral claim but as a First Amendment right.

Through Roberts's rule on the Supreme Court, what's old is new again. *Janus* dealt a devastating blow to union organizing, but the Roberts Court was not done undermining union rights.

---

In *Cedar Point Nursery v. Hassid*, John Roberts delivered another blow to union organizing with his own words. Writing for the 6–3 Republican majority in that case, Roberts struck down a forty-six-year-old law that allowed union organizers a "right of access" to an agricultural employer's property to protect agricultural employees' right to freedom of association in order to organize. Roberts asserted that the right to organize in the farm fields constituted a "taking" under the Fifth Amendment.

As Justice Stephen Breyer, joined by Justices Sotomayor and Kagan, noted in dissent, the law provided that "union representatives can enter the property only 'for the purpose of meeting and talking with employees and soliciting their support'; they have access only to 'areas in which employees congregate before and after working or 'at such location or locations as the employees eat their lunch.'" The rule was designed to allow union organizing in an agrarian working environment, where organizing is more challenging due to the itinerant nature of the work and workers. As the SEIU stated in its brief:

> California's farmworkers, nearly all of whom are seasonal workers who move from employer to employer as different crops become ready to harvest—and many of whom do not speak English and are illiterate even in their native tongues—were, as a practical matter, inaccessible to union organizers interested in communicating with them about the advantages of self-organization. Even among those farmworkers who did not live on the land of their employers, many lived in transient dwellings such as motels. (Internal citations omitted).[31]

But John Roberts disregarded those factual findings in his effort to protect corporations from union organizers that they want to exclude. While he dressed up the case as grounded on the Takings Clause of the Constitution, his decision harkened back to the *Lochner* era from 1897 to 1937, when the Supreme Court routinely struck down efforts to organize unions and to protect worker's rights under the invented notion that the "freedom of contract" overrode such rights.

Time and again, the Supreme Court's decrees show that Roberts is committed to rolling the law back to before the New Deal, to the robber baron era when corporations reigned supreme and when the Supreme Court helped protect the rich from the demands of the poor, putting the interests of corporations above those of workers. Although supporters of the Roberts Court often claim that its decisions are not "politically motivated" and are just a matter of "judicial philosophy," the math tells a different story. As Professor Scott Budow concluded after analyzing the justices' votes in fifteen major rulings in labor and employment law,

> Supreme Court justices collectively cast 134 votes in the 15 cases [that] spanned civil procedure, constitutional law, and statutory interpretation. There is no unifying judicial

> philosophy—such as originalism or textualism—that neatly explains why conservative justices would reliably vote in one manner and liberal justices in the opposite manner for these cases. Yet, if all one knew was that conservative justices favor employers and liberal justices favor workers, that person would have correctly predicted 132 of the 134 votes cast (98.5%). If judicial philosophy rather than political motivation explained the underlying dynamics, and we assume that judicial philosophy in the abstract is no more likely to favor employers than workers, then the Court's collective votes are the equivalent of flipping a coin 134 times and getting heads 132 times. Statistically, this is virtually impossible (internal citations omitted).[32]

---

One of the more curious things about John Roberts's history is that, according to the Reagan Library, the file folder from the Reagan White House labeled "Affirmative Action" is entirely empty. Nobody knows what content was in it, why that content was removed, or what became of it. Fortunately, the bulk of Roberts's memos and notes from that period remain. Those files include numerous instances of his objections to so-called racial quotas and his embrace of the myth of color blindness. It is clear from a review of the Reagan archives that Roberts was the go-to guy in the White House Counsel's Office on every major case involving affirmative action, minority set-asides, employment tests, or racial discrimination either brought by the Civil Rights Division or considered by the Solicitor General's Office between 1982 and 1986. That includes supporting the Reagan administration's efforts to use equal employment law to advance the concept of "reverse discrimination," the claim that policies to redress racial discrimination against Blacks supposedly discriminated against whites.

During John Roberts's twenty years on the Supreme Court, he has helped make it almost impossible to mitigate America's established history of structural racism through affirmative action or diversity, equity, and inclusion (DEI) initiatives. In 2023, for example, Roberts took it upon himself to write the majority opinion in *Students for Fair Admissions v. President and Fellows of Harvard College*. His ruling struck down the affirmative action policies of Harvard University and the University of North Carolina, claiming that they violated the Fourteenth Amendment's equal protection clause. This ruling upended decades of efforts through admissions policies to increase the racial diversity of universities and, with those policies, to increase the chances for *all* Americans to share in the opportunities that those educational institutions provide for class mobility.[33]

Roberts's edict, joined by all the other Republican-appointed justices, sided with an array of Leo-tied groups that secretive billionaires have given millions of dollars to in order to attack affirmative action and DEI policies in the public and private sectors. In this area, as with voting rights, Roberts has embraced a blinding kind of color blindness that views America not as it is but as the color-blind society it has never been, consistent with the approach of the regressive mentor Roberts apprenticed with: Justice Rehnquist. Notably, when previous affirmative action cases were argued before the Supreme Court, such as *Fisher v. Texas* in 2015, Roberts expressed disdain, such as asking with a straight face, "What unique perspective does a minority student bring to a physics class?" This so-called color blindness consistently favors whites, and particularly white Republicans or "conservatives" seeking to preserve or remake America in their image. It is a willful blindness that has served to enable the history-denying rise of Donald Trump and his mostly white base of people who call themselves Christian nationalists.

Roberts's ruling is now being used by Trump to bully public universities and private companies to stop their efforts to create more inclusive spaces where people of all races, ethnicities, and circumstances can thrive. The man who was the public face of the anti–affirmative action litigation, Edward Blum, has also parlayed that ruling into something of a full-employment gig for lawyers at Consovoy McCarthy, a right-wing law firm. One of the firm's partners is one of only three trustees of Leonard Leo's billion-dollar trust fund, Marble Freedom Trust, and several of its partners are former clerks for Leo's friend Clarence Thomas. Since the affirmative action ruling, a new nonprofit Blum established has attacked law firms, aerospace companies, and venture capital firms for programs they instituted to diversify their workplaces. With the help of John Roberts's rulings in this area and others, Leo has helped generate potentially endless business opportunities for bullying litigation by the professional right-wing operative clique. Roberts's decree is already having an adverse impact on admission rates for Black students at universities and Trump's threats to universities will only do more damage.

Roberts's ruling has paved the way for an emboldened second Trump administration to assail affirmative action and DEI measures across the federal government, too. This hysteria briefly led to the erasure of important markers in American history at the Department of Defense, such as recognition that one of the men who raised America's flag after the brutal battle on Iwo Jima was a Native American and the acknowledgment of the vital role Navajo code talkers played in America's victory in World War II. The Trump administration has also taken what should be viewed as insurgent and coercive authoritarian actions to try to bully the private sector, public universities, and the states over their use of DEI. There is no doubt that John Roberts's use of the judicial power to destroy affirmative action has led to a cascade of destructive edicts damaging to the pillars of civil society.

---

During his work in the Reagan administration, John Roberts also routinely used his powerful perch to assail women's equality rights, including the proposed Equal Rights Amendment, which provides simply that "equality of rights under the law shall not be denied or abridged by the United States or by any state on account of sex." His writings show him to be arrogant and sarcastic on the subject. *The Washington Post* first reported in 2005, for example,

> His remark on whether homemakers should become lawyers came in 1985 in reply to a suggestion from Linda Chavez, then the White House's director of public liaison. Chavez had proposed entering her deputy, Linda Arey, in a contest sponsored by the Clairol shampoo company to honor women who had changed their lives after age 30. Arey had been a schoolteacher who decided to change careers and went to law school. In a July 31, 1985 memo, Roberts noted that . . . Arey had "encouraged many former homemakers to enter law school and become lawyers." Roberts said in his memo that he saw no legal objection to her taking part in the Clairol contest. Then he added a personal aside: "Some might question whether encouraging homemakers to become lawyers contributes to the common good, but I suppose that is for the judges to decide."[34]

In another memo, Roberts "criticized a report that lauded strides by states to combat sex discrimination in the workplace [asserting that] 'many of the reported proposals and efforts are themselves highly objectionable.'" That included a "proposal to require women to be paid the same as men for state jobs considered of comparable worth." He repeatedly attacked "comparable worth" measures to ensure that women were paid a comparable amount for similar work, calling such workplace measures "anticapitalist" and "staggeringly pernicious."[35]

Even though Roberts subsequently married a woman who practiced law and has hired numerous women—such as Erin Hawley—to be his law clerks, many of his rulings from the bench have continued to deal blows to women's economic rights, in addition to hampering their ability to access contraception or abortion care. For example, John Roberts joined a ruling against Lilly Ledbetter, who had sued the Goodyear Tire and Rubber Company for discriminating against her because of her gender. A jury found that the company had discriminated against her in pay and promotions and awarded her $3.5 million in damages, although the trial judge unilaterally reduced that award to $350,000. On appeal, the Roberts Court issued a 5–4 ruling in 2007 that ordered the dismissal of her complaint. The Court also declared that the courts could consider only the most recent 180-day period as actionable and no prior pay disparities could be added in as damages. This reading of the statute had to be reversed by an act of Congress, which adopted the Lilly Ledbetter Fair Pay Act of 2009.[36]

Notably, however, the Roberts Court took a strikingly different approach to statutes of limitations when it came to claims by corporations, in a case called *Corner Post, Inc. v. Board of Governors of the Federal Reserve System*, where John Roberts joined an opinion written by Amy Coney Barrett. As Justice Jackson noted in her dissent, with Justices Sotomayor and Kagan joining her, "The Court's baseless conclusion means that there is effectively no longer any limitations period for lawsuits that challenge agency regulations on their face. Allowing every new commercial entity to bring fresh facial challenges to long-existing regulations is profoundly destabilizing for both Government and businesses. It also allows well-heeled litigants to game the system by creating new entities or finding new plaintiffs whenever they blow past the statutory deadline."[37]

---

The bottom line is that John Roberts has presided over a Supreme Court that routinely limits the rights of ordinary people while elevating the rights of corporations and the powerful. The dramatic changes to the scope of legislative, executive, and judicial power that Roberts has orchestrated have strengthened both presidential power and corporate power in ways that make us less free and less safe and that even put the future habitability of our planet at greater risk.

## CHAPTER 14

# POWER

John Roberts helped pave the way for Donald Trump to become the forty-seventh president of the United States.

If the Justice Department's case against Trump for alleged crimes relating to the insurrection on January 6, 2021, had proceeded, then the months leading up to the 2024 election would have included news coverage of the testimony in that trial, detailing Trump's attempted coup and the deaths and destruction he unleashed in an attempt to stay in power. A federal jury may have found Trump guilty of committing serious crimes. But Roberts used the nation's highest court to effectively pardon Trump, a power that the Supreme Court does not have under our Constitution. Roberts and his fellow Republican appointees on the Supreme Court also sent a message to the American voter in the summer of 2024: Trump did no wrong in the actions for which he was criminally indicted by a grand jury in Washington, DC, and the Justice Department's actions to prosecute him were illegitimate. There would be no trial.

In 2023, the Roberts Court had been asked to expedite the resolution of Trump's assertion of presidential immunity in *Trump v. United States* but declined to do so. Then, after the three-judge panel of the US Court of Appeals for the DC Circuit issued a detailed opinion that compellingly and unanimously rejected Trump's claim of immunity from criminal prosecution, the Roberts Court took up the case. The Court pushed the oral argument in the case as far into its term as possible, running out the clock and all but ensuring that no criminal trial could take place before the election, no matter the outcome of the appeal.

Then, in its ruling, the Roberts Court eliminated key portions of the indictment by asserting—out of thin air—that Trump should be given broad presidential immunity. Roberts orchestrated this astonishing and reckless result despite the lack of precedent for such immunity. The Constitution's text provides no such immunity for a president, no such escape hatch.

John Roberts's unprecedented decree was that Trump had committed no crimes, and could have committed no crimes, as long as he was acting in his official capacity as president. The chief justice's declaration that Trump's speech and actions in connection to his so-called official acts could not be used as evidence also interfered with other indictments and even potentially his conviction in one of the other cases. No court in American history had ever made such a ruling—the effect of which was to give Donald Trump a supreme exclusionary rule, in that almost nothing he said or did as president could ever be used against him in a criminal proceeding. What Roberts did was choreograph a shocking and atrocious political intervention by political judges to protect a political candidate from their political party from facing the consequences for major crimes that substantial evidence indicated Trump had committed.

This was, essentially, a judicial coup.

The majority ruling in *Trump v. United States* is the most nakedly partisan political act the US Supreme Court has ever engaged in, surpassing even the Rehnquist Court's disgraceful intervention to stop the counting of ballots in *Bush v. Gore*, a 5–4 ruling that Justice Sandra Day O'Connor years later said she regretted joining. Roberts's *Trump v. United States* is singular, though, in its retrospective and prospective harm to the proper functioning of our system of government. As Michael Podhorzer has noted, if we saw a high court in another country with a majority of judges appointed by that country's leader—half of whom were appointed by him—decree that their party's leader was immune from criminal prosecution, we would consider that to be a deeply illegitimate act. We would see it as a coup d'état—or, at the very least, as coup d'état adjacent, since it set the stage for Trump's tiny margin of victory in 2024.

John Roberts and the Republicans on the Court did not act alone: A slender majority of American voters selected Trump over Kamala Harris—although, when all the votes for all political parties are counted, a majority of American voters chose candidates other than Trump. We will never know how many voters Roberts's ruling helped persuade to back Trump, but there is no doubt that John Roberts's extraordinary intervention helped buoy Trump. He helped validate Trump's absurd claims that he had done nothing wrong and that the Joe Biden administration had weaponized the Justice Department against him, although nothing could be further from the truth.

Before John Roberts interceded in the 2024 presidential election by granting Trump wide-ranging criminal immunity, Roberts intervened in *Trump v. Anderson*, a case contesting a decision by the Colorado Supreme Court that Trump was ineligible for federal office and should not be on the ballot in that state, because he had engaged in an insurrection against the United States. In that case, Roberts helped invent a requirement for Congress to pass legislation to implement the Fourteenth Amendment's bar on insurrectionists holding office, even though that amendment says the opposite: that only a supermajority vote in Congress can *remove* that bar. But Roberts helped strike down the effect of the

Constitution's language and interposed a completely invented hurdle to that provision in a cowardly anonymous majority opinion by five of the Republican justices. (Four other justices concurred only in the result of not having one state alone keep Trump off the ballot, not in the requirement that Congress must pass implementing legislation to effectuate the bar despite text and historical practice to the contrary; notably, those concurrences were initially listed as dissents in the Court's online filing system.)

Had the Roberts Court not blocked Colorado from keeping Donald Trump off the ballot, perhaps other states would have had the courage to do so too. Trump lost Colorado anyway, by more than 350,000 votes, but again the Roberts Court's ruling had the effect of signaling to some portion of the electorate that Trump did not engage in office-barring insurrection, despite the detailed factual findings and compelling legal analysis of the Colorado Supreme Court.

Plus, Roberts never should have had the votes for that anonymous (per curiam) opinion in the first place because, if Justices Clarence Thomas and Samuel Alito had any professional integrity, they would have recused themselves. There is no way that Roberts did not know about Ginni Thomas's deeply reported role in goading the effort to subvert the votes of the American people in the 2020 election—she even asked state legislators to appoint alternative (fake) electors for at least two states' Electoral College votes—and yet John Roberts made no public objection to Clarence Thomas participating in the case to help steer it in the direction Roberts wanted. Thomas should have recused himself under the federal statute requiring justices to do so to avoid the appearance of bias, as well as actual bias. Alito also should have recused himself, knowing that a symbol of the insurrection—an upside-down flag—had flown over his home for weeks in 2021. Another flag tied to the January 6 insurrection—the Appeal to Heaven flag—had also flown over his summer home for weeks in 2023. Had Thomas and Alito properly recused themselves, John Roberts would have been in the minority in that ruling, not in the five-justice majority.[1]

Then there is the case of *Fischer v. United States*, which involved a claim by an aggressor in the January 6 insurrection that his actions did not fit the definition of the crime with which he was charged: obstructing an official proceeding. John Roberts reassigned the majority opinion in that case to himself after *The New York Times* reported the Alito flag controversy, but he still let Alito participate in the ruling alongside Thomas, both of whom again should have recused themselves. Instead, John Roberts wrote an opinion they joined, in which suddenly he was interested in the "intent" of the statute used to charge some of the Trump followers who had committed acts of violence on January 6. Again, ignoring the plain language of the law that made it a crime to obstruct an official proceeding, Roberts wrote that the provision was originally intended to apply only to interfering in investigations, even though the plain language of that criminal statute specifies that it applies to "official proceedings," which can reasonably be construed to include congressional proceedings to count the Electoral College vote. Unfortunately, Justice Ketanji Brown Jackson—a former criminal defense attorney—was persuaded to join Roberts in his ruling, which gave him cover. That left Amy Coney Barrett to author a powerful dissent, joined by Justices Sonia Sotomayor and Elena Kagan. She noted,

> Joseph Fischer allegedly joined a mob of rioters that breached the Capitol on January 6, 2021. At the time, Congress was meeting in a joint session to certify the Electoral College results. The riot forced Congress to suspend the proceeding, delaying it for several hours. The Court does not dispute that Congress's joint session qualifies as an "official proceeding"; that rioters delayed the proceeding; or even that Fischer's alleged conduct (which includes

> trespassing and a physical confrontation with law enforcement) was part of a successful effort to forcibly halt the certification of the election results. Given these premises, the case that Fischer can be tried for "obstructing, influencing, or impeding an official proceeding" seems open and shut. So why does the Court hold otherwise? Because it simply cannot believe that Congress meant what it said.[2]

Whenever it suits Roberts's political agenda, he ignores the literal language of the law. This trio of rulings about January 6 shows that for John Roberts it is politics first and principles second, with "judicial modesty" or judicial restraint cast aside when expedient for the ends he seeks.

John Roberts chose to protect some of Trump's most determined followers on January 6 by removing one of the legal bases for their convictions. Meanwhile, Trump promised to actually pardon all of them of all charges if he was reelected—appallingly calling them the "January 6 hostages"—and he did. After he became president, Trump released numerous January 6 violent offenders from prison.

Over two decades of Roberts's rulings in criminal cases, never—with the notable exception of *Snyder v. United States*, dealing with Mayor John Snyder's shakedown of constituents for cash after steering a big contract to them—has Roberts acted with such seeming concern for the rights of those accused or convicted. For example, the same year that Roberts partially exonerated at least fifty of the (almost all white) Trump rioters who stormed the Capitol, the Roberts Court refused to stay the imposition of the death penalty for Marcellus Williams, who had been wrongfully convicted of murder after a botched trial. The attorney who prosecuted him admitted there were serious errors at trial, said Williams was innocent, and asked the courts "to correct this manifest injustice." The Roberts Court let Williams be executed anyway.[3]

Under Roberts, the Court remained seemingly untroubled by miscarriages of justice involving the execution of potentially innocent people or disparate racial impacts in general. During the last year of Donald Trump's first term, at the urging of his administration, the Roberts Court allowed federal executions to resume after a twenty-year moratorium. The four then-serving justices who had been appointed to the Court by Democratic presidents dissented. They noted that significant evidence showed that "the death penalty is often imposed arbitrarily," with people who commit the same crime getting different sentences in racially disparate ways. The Roberts Court has also been generally disinterested in protecting the wrongly accused, the illegally arrested, and those brutalized or killed by police violence, at least based on its rulings.[4]

Along these lines, Roberts has written or joined numerous opinions in cases involving the notion of "qualified immunity," a judicially concocted doctrine that protects government officials, including law enforcement officers, from liability for violating the law "while acting in their official capacity." The effect of the Roberts Court's devotion to that "doctrine" has made excessive-force "claims against a police officer . . . difficult, although not impossible, to sustain." Some cities or counties do settle excessive-force claims under public pressure in response to undeniable misconduct or brutality caught on video. One example of the rare circumstance where a state actually prosecuted law enforcement officers for murder, for killing a person in their custody, happened in Minnesota after four Minneapolis officers suffocated George Floyd to death and were caught on camera ignoring his pleas that he could not breathe and his cries for his mother. Four states (Colorado, Montana, Nevada, and New Mexico) have now banned police officers from using qualified immunity as a defense at all. But, overall, the Roberts Court has made it more difficult to prevent police brutality, which is demonstrably more likely to occur when it is Black Americans who are seized or pursued by law enforcement.[5]

In Trump's first administration, the Roberts Court also granted Trump "broad discretion" to issue a "proclamation" banning Muslims from designated countries from traveling to the United States. This is significant because immediately after being elected in 2024 Trump announced that—just as the Heritage Foundation's Kevin Roberts had promised—he would invoke "emergency powers" to seize immigrants. Trump called them invaders to try to justify the use of the US military to help carry out these policies. He has also cited statutes that can only be invoked in response to invasion.

Significantly, in the first Trump administration, John Roberts chose to write the opinion in the "Muslim ban" case, *Trump v. Hawai'i*, overturning the lower court's injunction against Trump's travel ban. It was a 5–4 decision, with all the Republicans joining together to let Trump's ban proceed. Long-standing law under the Immigration and Nationality Act had barred discrimination on the basis of nationality in the granting of visas. However, because Trump had not banned *all* Muslims from *all* of the majority-Muslim countries, just all those from the Muslim countries he singled out as national security risks, Roberts and his fellow Republicans ruled that the policy had "sufficient national security justification."

Justices Stephen Breyer and Elena Kagan dissented on the grounds that the factual record was insufficient to assess how Trump's proclamation and the potential waivers it included were really being applied. Justice Sonia Sotomayor, with Justice Ruth Ginsburg, dissented on the merits, noting that Roberts was "ignoring the facts, misconstruing our legal precedent, and turning a blind eye to the pain and suffering the Proclamation inflicts upon countless families and individuals, many of whom are United States citizens." They also noted that Trump's order could not withstand even the lowest level of constitutional scrutiny because it constituted a "total and complete shutdown of Muslims entering the United States" from several countries. The country-specific exclusions were similar to the Japanese exclusion orders issued during World War II in the sense that Trump's order applied to people without any individualized assessment of wrongdoing or risk. President Trump's 2017–2018 orders were not predicated on an act of war, however, and fortunately did not result in mass internment. How the Roberts Court will rule on the second Trump administration's extreme removal orders is uncertain, as of early 2025.

---

Chief Justice John Roberts is obviously not directly engaged in organizing the second Trump administration, but he has been working for years to ensure that a president's power is as unchecked as possible. In addition to the immunity ruling, Roberts has advanced the "unitary executive theory," which basically envisions a president who can fire anyone in the executive branch at any time at will. Project 2025 asserts that a president has absolute authority over the executive branch and all of its employees, and it calls on Trump to demand that the Roberts Court formally overrule a case called *Humphrey's Executor v. United States*, which approved certain kinds of independent agencies whose directors could not be removed without cause.

Five years ago, in *Seila Law v. Consumer Financial Protection Bureau*, John Roberts authored the Court's declaration that Congress did not have the authority to protect the director of the Consumer Financial Protection Bureau (CFPB) from removal even though Congress specified that CFPB's director could only be removed on the grounds of inefficiency, neglect, or malfeasance. (The CFPB was created by the Dodd-Frank reforms after the subprime mortgage crisis and Wall Street crash during the George W. Bush administration.) John Roberts asserted that those conditions for termination violated the "separation of powers," although he did not expressly overrule *Humphrey's Executor*, a unanimous 1935 Supreme Court decision holding that President Franklin Delano

Roosevelt could not fire or force the resignation of the head of the Federal Trade Commission, who had been appointed by his predecessor, President Herbert Hoover. Roberts left the door open for a more propitious time to continue his quest to advance the right-wing program to overturn legal precedents targeted by Leonard Leo and his cadre.

Similarly, the Roberts Court has already been taking up part of the Project 2025 agenda to strip administrative agencies of their powers to adjudicate violations through administrative law judges, asserting that the "separation of powers" prevents executive branch agencies from engaging in judicial-type functions. Such procedures have long helped America contend with the complexity of our economy and the growth of our nation, providing vital tools for enforcing our laws without making every matter into a federal court case. A recent example of the massive disruption orchestrated by John Roberts is his ruling in *Securities and Exchange Commission v. Jarkesy.* Again, Roberts chose to pen that decision, striking down decades of administrative law practice to declare suddenly that Congress cannot assign the administration of civil penalties for securities fraud to the Securities and Exchange Commission (SEC) and that instead such cases must be tried in federal court. This dramatic change in the law will make it far more difficult and expensive for the SEC to enforce the rules on trading securities, rules that protect American investors.

As Justice Sotomayor wrote in dissent, with Justices Kagan and Jackson concurring,

> Throughout our Nation's history, Congress has authorized agency adjudicators to find violations of statutory obligations and award civil penalties to the Government as an injured sovereign. The Constitution, this Court has said, does not require these civil-penalty claims belonging to the Government to be tried before a jury in federal district

> court. Congress can instead assign them to an agency for initial adjudication, subject to judicial review. . . . The majority today upends longstanding precedent and the established practice of its coequal partners in our tripartite system of Government. . . . Because the Court fails to act as a neutral umpire when it rewrites established rules in the manner it does today, I respectfully dissent.[6]

The delegation of such enforcement to administrative agencies was long-settled law, repeatedly reaffirmed by decades of Supreme Court decisions. Roberts's edict did not just affect the SEC. As the dissenters stated, it has unleashed chaos in the enforcement of "more than 200 statutes authorizing dozens of agencies to impose civil penalties for violations of statutory obligations."

This is the kind of wreckage that Federalist Society Executive Vice President Leonard Leo was conjuring when he boasted about the coming successes to the dark-money funders and operatives at the Council for National Policy in early 2019, after his friend Brett Kavanaugh was confirmed to the Supreme Court. Swapping in Kavanaugh for Justice Anthony Kennedy gave John Roberts the votes on the Court that he needed to accelerate the imposition of the Right's legal agenda that Leo has been advancing. Kennedy was a problem for them not just due to his defense of gay marriage but because he had affirmed administrative law precedents that Leo and his confederates opposed for supposedly violating the so-called structural constitution.

---

How can one make sense of the seemingly contradictory demands of the "unitary executive theory," which concentrates immense powers in the presidency, and the new judicial limitations on executive branch regulatory power that the Roberts Court is also imposing? The most straightforward way to understand this seeming contradiction is to realize that both "principles" support the same underlying political priority of protecting corporate power and prerogative. The Roberts Court is advancing a superficially more sophisticated version of the ridiculous claims ham-handedly advanced by Trump and his militants about needing to "drain the swamp" and smash a supposedly out-of-control federal government that they malign as the deep state.

Apparently, Trump was offended in his first term that federal agencies continued to do the business of the American people—endeavoring to protect the rights of workers, guard against discrimination, administer rules fairly, and develop policies based on provable facts and not capricious whims—instead of just becoming blunt instruments of the personality occupying the Oval Office and his loyalists. Trump also seems to have a visceral hatred of the "administrative state" precisely because rule following is not something he actually values, despite using rhetoric around "rule of law." The objective is to do away with the rules and regulations that protect ordinary people from corporate exploitation and that protect a democracy against autocracy.

The systematic destruction of properly functioning administrative agencies is a goal that the Republican majority on the Supreme Court has repeatedly embraced in recent years. That this embrace gives Trump more unchecked power is a short-term effect. The Roberts Court's thrust toward this goal would proceed even if Trump were not president because it is baked into the composition of the Court. It is key to the long-term objectives supported by and benefiting the billionaires who funded the court-capture machine. There is perhaps no better example of this interaction than the multidecade efforts of billionaire Charles Koch to block government rules that impinge on his quest to make as much profit as possible no matter the effects on others.

For example, Koch provided resources for assailing the Barack Obama administration's Clean Power Plan (CPP), which was proposed in 2014 as an initiative to reduce carbon emissions in the United States. Koch was not alone: The oil majors and the methane gas frackers, the gas compression companies, and other significant parts of the fossil fuel industry all sought to thwart the CPP and related regulations, despite the modest and indeed inadequate measures the CPP conceived to mitigate the destructive climate changes that are underway.

Leonard Leo played a role here, too. For example, early on, in 2010, one of his core allied groups, the Judicial Education Project (JEP), had designs on making the attorney general of West Virginia the public face of the litigation against Democratic efforts to mitigate climate change. The state was contending with a declining coal industry losing ground to cleaner energy sources. The purported sin of the Environmental Protection Agency (EPA) was that it was daring to set goals for utility companies to increase the percentage of renewable energy, such as from solar and wind, providing power to the grid. It took ten years for coal-producing West Virginia, through its new attorney general, Patrick Morrisey, to get the right case to the US Supreme Court, but when they got up to the plate, John Roberts helped make sure they hit a home run.

Koch also threw his voice through numerous amicus briefs, bellowing a chorus of attacks against the CPP. Of course, Morrisey's cause was joined by other members of the Republican Attorneys General Association, whose biggest funders over the past decade have been groups tied to Leo, another ventriloquist throwing his voice through the power of money.

Again, John Roberts took the pen. In *West Virginia v. EPA*, Roberts dealt a devastating blow to the power of the EPA. Roberts articulated the totally invented so-called major questions doctrine, which appears nowhere in the Constitution and had never appeared in any prior cases. This judicial invention asserts that federal agencies cannot use existing statutes to regulate on an issue that the Court deems to be a "major question" that Congress should first pass specific legislation to address. Under that "doctrine," Roberts and his fellow Republican appointees declared that the EPA did not have the authority to regulate carbon by setting targets for utility companies to expand reliance on renewables, even though the EPA has authority under the statute to regulate carbon and other pollutants. Roberts deployed the fabricated major question doctrine in order to require that Congress pass legislation authorizing the agency to address policies the Court disfavors, which all but assured that the vital issue would go unaddressed due to the fossil fuel industry's capture of the Republican Party in the US Senate.

Roberts also trotted out his favorite rationale for striking down federal laws, the bludgeon of separation of powers, to impose the "major questions" gambit. In reality, if Congress had objected to the CPP, it didn't need the Court; it could have withheld funding. As a politician who wears judicial robes, Roberts knows full well that Republicans have repeatedly used their powers—whether in the majority or minority—to block any really assertive climate-mitigation legislation, with the exception of the green energy investments the Biden administration folded into the Inflation Reduction Act to address the inflationary effects of the first wave of the COVID-19 pandemic. That is, Roberts knows the GOP is deeply dependent on Koch money for its electoral campaigns and for the dark-money spending unleashed in *Citizens United v. FEC*, which fund attacks ads and get-out-the-vote efforts through Koch's Americans for Prosperity, Concerned Veterans of America, and the Libre Initiative. Consequently, although the velocity of global warming is increasing, administrative regulations are the only way the federal government can effectively try to forestall a growing planetary crisis. Now, however, thanks to Chief Justice John Roberts, the power of any future Democratic administration to use existing statutes to issue regulations to reduce our dependence on fossil fuel has been greatly weakened.

Immediately before the Supreme Court reversed *Roe v. Wade* in 2022, John Roberts announced the Court's ruling against the CPP. Koch's team and the fossil fuel industry more broadly were ecstatic. The newsletter of Koch Industries' law firm, Quinn Emanuel Urquhart & Sullivan, LLP, extolled what the Roberts Court had accomplished for them:

> The decision was less important for what it did—the Clean Power Plan had never taken effect, the Trump Administration had repealed it . . . —than for what it portends for future regulatory efforts to solve major national problems. . . . We are entering a new phase of American law where traditional deference to regulators gives way to scrutiny and skepticism. Federal agencies should expect legal headwinds when they claim the power to enact fundamental changes. . . . For businesses, the "major questions doctrine" will be a powerful new tool to challenge undesirable regulations.[7]

With the Roberts Court's "major questions" stratagem, Koch had acquired a powerful weapon to assail major changes in environmental regulations he and his private conglomerate oppose, but that was not enough. As *The Guardian* reported in October 2023, "An economic policy strategist at the Koch network's central coordinating group, Stand Together, said that the new composition of the court amounted to a huge 'landscape opportunity, particularly on the administrative state. We're doubling down on this strategy.'" Another staffer with Koch's Americans for Prosperity group extolled their ability to "get the right cases to the supreme court" to rule in their favor.

That is just what Koch did.

His nonprofit empire spent millions of dollars funding two groups—the New Civil Liberties Alliance and Cause of Action—to get a case to the Roberts Court that would go beyond allowing corporations to challenge administrative rules on "major questions" and make it easier to challenge almost any rule they dislike unless Congress has been very specific in its authorizations. The vehicle that Koch and his allies supported, funded, and structured to accomplish their goals is a case called *Loper Bright Enterprises v. Raimondo.* On its face, *Loper Bright* is about sea captains opposing a regulation designed to protect wild fish in marine habitats from overfishing, but the case was about much more than marine life. It was about advancing the destructive legal agenda of one of the richest men in the world, whose enormous wealth comes from extractive industries. The case transcended Koch's individual pecuniary interests, however, and was designed to make it easier for other billionaires and corporations to assail an array of federal regulations across countless industries.

A close examination of the *Loper Bright* litigation reveals how it was orchestrated to secure a pro-Koch ruling by a Supreme Court with a newly constituted majority packed with judges Koch helped get confirmed. Ultimately, Koch's investment in Leo's operations to influence the Supreme Court nomination and confirmation process paid off by getting him a judicial ruling he long desired: the reversal of the legal precedent set in *Chevron v. NRDC. Chevron* was a unanimous 1984 Supreme Court ruling that required federal courts to defer to interpretations by federal agencies of statutory language when Congress did not specify the meaning of a particular word or term and the agency's interpretation was a reasonable policy choice. That ruling, in favor of the Ronald Reagan administration's interpretation of certain kinds of pollution sources under the Clean Air Act (interpretations that a pro-environment group opposed), came to be known as "*Chevron* deference." The effect of the ruling was that federal courts were not allowed to substitute their own preferences—or the desires of an opponent of a federal regulation—in place of reasonable policies adopted by a federal agency in response to broad or ambiguous statutory language. Over the course of forty years the *Chevron* case was cited more than 15,000 times by the courts and provided some stability to the setting of federal rules. It mandated judicial restraint by requiring federal courts to act with deference to the expertise of federal agencies, which use a notice and public comment process to get public, democratic input on complex issues.

*Chevron* was well-settled law until Charles Koch seized an opening to overturn that legal precedent. The plaintiffs in *Loper Bright* are described as four fishing companies with no parent corporations, and that is accurate, but the weak disclosure procedures for briefs submitted to the Supreme Court allowed this case to be almost entirely subsidized by secret sources—in this instance the Koch fortune. In 2022, the *Loper Bright* litigation was initiated by a group called Cause of Action (COA). COA is governed by the very top lieutenants of Koch's nonprofit empire—including Americans for Prosperity and Stand Together—along with the managing partner of the law firm defending Koch Industries from climate change litigation and other regulations, Quinn Emanuel. Some think the real underwriting of the *Loper Bright* litigation came through time donated by COA's attorneys, who work for Koch organizations. Who holds COA's financial books, it turns out? Koch's Stand Together arm.

Those ties were not readily visible on the surface of COA's website or the website created to promote the *Loper Bright* case and its photogenic plaintiffs. That lack of transparency makes it harder for the public to understand what was going on. COA is a vehicle for Koch to use the courts to rewrite our laws to suit his will, to constrain the public's ability to regulate corporations and limit their immense profits, or adopt regulations like those to protect thriving ecosystems, and more. But sometimes people inadvertently reveal the game being played, as when the vice president of legal and judicial strategy for Koch's Americans for Prosperity gleefully told followers, "By now you may know that the Supreme Court will hear *our* Cause of Action team's case asking the Court to overturn the 'Chevron doctrine'" (emphasis added).

Koch doubled his odds by also underwriting the litigation in a case called *Relentless, Inc. v. Department of Commerce*. Like Loper Bright, Relentless is a company that owns fishing vessels that catch and freeze fish at sea. Ostensibly, both cases were about who pays for federally mandated inspectors tasked with protecting against overfishing and limiting "bycatch" of other species that may be at risk of depletion or extinction. Koch's interest in the case had little to do with fishing and everything to do with capturing the government's ability to regulate activities affecting our planet's health.

As with *Loper Bright* and COA, the *Relentless* case was superficially propelled by another group. That group calls itself the New Civil Liberties Alliance (NCLA), and its objective has been to attack federal laws, including long-settled administrative law like the *Chevron* precedent. In 2017, the Charles Koch Foundation staked NCLA with $1 million, and millions more followed. The group was launched by Professor Philip Hamburger, who has made strident claims, like saying that the "administrative state" is the biggest threat to civil liberties in history.

NCLA's advent in 2017 coincided with Trump's appointment of Neil Gorsuch to replace Justice Antonin Scalia, who had died the year before—leading Koch, Leo, Senator McConnell, and other Republicans to help block President Obama from filling that vacancy on the Supreme Court. Having a Leo-approved, Trump-appointed judge on the Supreme Court in place of Scalia changed the equation for Koch's prospects for overturning the *Chevron* precedent, because Scalia had repeatedly affirmed *Chevron* since the 1980s. Gorsuch was part of the new breed of activists in Leo's pipeline to power who seemed eager to overturn long settled administrative law. By 2021, NCLA's annual spending had expanded to nearly $5 million.

Until the three Leo-Trump appointees were installed on the Supreme Court, John Roberts did not appear to have the votes to overturn the *Chevron* deference precedent. In 2014, before these right-wing additions to the Roberts Court, Professor Hamburger himself noted—in his book attacking regulations, *Is Administrative Law Unlawful?*—that no one thought it was possible that the US Supreme Court would consider reversing the *Chevron* precedent. Even Clarence Thomas, for example, had written an opinion in 2005, in a case called *National Cable & Telecommunications Association v. Brand X Internet Services*, that upheld and reaffirmed *Chevron* deference.

However, as *ProPublica* reported in 2023, billionaires rubbing elbows with Thomas at exclusive venues, including Charles Koch, were keen on getting *Chevron* reversed. In subsequent years, as Thomas accepted millions of dollars' worth of secret gifts and luxury travel from billionaires like Harlan Crow, his views "evolved." *ProPublica*'s Pulitzer Prize–winning 2023 investigation revealed for the first time that, in 2016, at the exclusive all-men's Bohemian Grove club, where Crow has a posh camp, Thomas told the assembled movers and shakers that he thought he had finally shifted Scalia's views on *Chevron*, meaning to support overturning that precedent—but then Scalia died. The Leo-Trump appointments, however, provided Thomas and Roberts with the 6–3 majority they needed to overturn *Chevron* and dramatically weaken the regulatory powers of federal agencies.

After the Roberts Court chose the *Loper Bright* and *Relentless* cases for argument, groups funded by Koch and Leo submitted an avalanche of amicus briefs to signal and bolster their desired outcome. Roberts again decided he would be the author, writing the decision in those joined cases. He apparently wanted to deal the death blow to *Chevron* deference himself. In so doing, Roberts did Koch's bidding by overturning forty years of legal precedents that help America tame the powerful private sector. As of the summer of 2024, federal judges no longer needed to defer to reasonable policy choices by experts at federal agencies in cases of broad statutory authorization. Now federal judges—which include more than 200 Trump appointees—can substitute their beliefs or slants for those of government scientists and other substantive experts employed by the public. The Roberts Court has opened up a free-for-all for hostile federal judges to assert that they know more about air pollution than the experts at the EPA—or, as is evident in the anti-abortion rulings of Trump-appointee Matthew Kaczmarek, that they know better than the Food and Drug Administration about approving drugs like abortion medicine. Roberts has thus introduced massive instability into the rubric of rules affecting our well-being.

In essence, John Roberts has declared countless federal regulations fair game for big-money-backed attacks. He has opened up new opportunities for corporate lawyers, like he once was—until such rulings can be reversed by a future Supreme Court or Congress. He has unleashed a torrent of future attacks on regulations on climate, clean air, clean water, and more, unsettling the law in ways that strengthen the influence of deep-pocketed polluters and others whose policies or practices harm the public and whose actions could have been constrained by regulators. This is a signature outcome long sought by Koch, Leo, and their comrades.

Recalling Roberts's earnest pronouncements about the importance of judicial restraint when he was vying for confirmation, an observer might have expected that he would have led the Court to act modestly in resolving who pays for fishing inspectors without sweeping away decades of settled law. The Roberts Court could have deferred to the agency if that regulation was deemed reasonable or struck it if it was not. But the case was never really about the fish.

It was about power.

---

Almost all of the Koch-funded groups use the catchphrase "limited government," but coming from the mouth(pieces) of a billionaire, that really means "limited democracy," as in limiting the ability of our government to regulate billionaires and their corporations. The illuminating American historian Nancy MacLean uncovered another Koch-tied operative describing Koch and his billionaire coteries' agenda as putting "democracy in chains." That sums it up quite accurately. They seek to limit the ability of federal agencies to protect the public's interest by regulating corporations, by using the power of the law to constrain behemoth companies and their owners. When the federal government is constrained from regulating carbon or making strides to reduce harmful pollution or limiting dangers in food processing, the safety and well-being of ordinary Americans is diminished, and the power and profits of corporations grow. Even before these rulings by the Roberts Court, corporations were already too powerful. Many of them, like Koch Industries, have greater wealth than whole countries across the globe.

Under Chief Justice John Roberts, the power of corporations has grown substantially and the power of the president has increased exponentially with the kinglike attributes Roberts has designed for Trump. But the power of Congress—the very institution the Framers imagined to be the heart of our democratic system—has been greatly diminished. For example, Roberts blocked Congress from extending the Voting Rights Act's key enforcement provisions. In *Citizens United v. FEC*, Roberts tackled Congress by limiting its power to regulate dark money in our elections. Then, in *Americans for Prosperity v. Bonta*, the Roberts Court handed another victory to Koch and his legal team by sacking rules that required nonprofits to disclose their biggest donors to state regulators as part of the privilege of not paying taxes on those revenues. That case extended the notion that money is speech, itself a result of litigation Charles Koch subsidized in *Buckley v. Valeo* (1976). In the *Americans for Prosperity* case, the Roberts Court ratified the Koch group's assertion that an agency's inadvertent disclosure of major donors could "chill" their speech—that is, inhibit their giving of secret gifts of big money to advance their agendas.

As chief justice, John Roberts has also sought to weaken Congress as a representative body by inviting primarily Republican legislatures to lock in extreme partisan gerrymandering that causes Republicans to be overrepresented in state legislatures and in the US House of Representatives. In states like Kentucky, that means that Republicans can manufacture supermajority rule in their legislature even if a Democrat can win the governorship in a statewide race. For Congress, it means that states like South Carolina can now bleach Black voters out of districts as long as the legislature claims that this racially disparate impact is just a side effect of a partisan objective to minimize Democrats' opportunities for fair representation. Under the Constitution, the US Senate was always going to be an institution prone to minority rule because of the Framers' compromise to give every state an equal number of votes no matter how small their population. The US House was designed to be the body expressive of the popular will, to represent the majority of Americans, but the gerrymandering Roberts has given constitutional protection to has undercut majority rule. It is also a major driver of divisiveness and extremism, because with gerrymandering the only real competition Republicans face is through primaries that pull to the right. It was also John Roberts who unleashed a historic wave of restrictions on voting after he usurped Congress's rightful role under the Constitution's express grant of authority to the legislative branch to implement the civil rights guaranteed by the trio of Civil War amendments, which include voting rights.

As for the power of the states, the Roberts Court both giveth and taketh away, depending on the result that the Republicans on the Supreme Court seek to achieve. The Roberts Court kicked the question of abortion access to the states but, in contrast, showed no deference to the State of Colorado in determining whose names get printed on its ballots, even though presidential ballots in states are always different depending on who qualifies to run. Most people living in the United States consider themselves Americans first and state residents second, living in states based on where their family is or where their jobs take them. But, with John Roberts steering the Court, Americans will have to think harder about which states will protect their rights and freedoms: where the air and water will be cleaner, where women and girls can access reproductive health care, and where families can raise LGBTQ children without fear that essential health care will be criminalized or that bullying will be tolerated or even exalted.

The overall trend is that the Supreme Court led by John Roberts is the first in US history to backslide on Americans' freedoms in most areas except for the two that are aligned with the Republican Party: guns and God. Will marriage equality survive the theocratic Roberts Court and Leonard Leo's desire to impose his personal opposition to gay marriage through the law by getting key legal precedents repealed? We shall soon see whether the right to marry the person you love gets stripped away and if Americans need to relocate to particular states to protect those rights. The same goes for religious indoctrination in public schools and so many other issues. Core rights and freedoms may soon depend not on whether you are living in America but on the state where you were born, go to school, or work. Year by year, John Roberts is working to roll back the clock to times when our freedoms were more limited and more precarious and when robber barons and their corporations ruled supreme.

---

Under Chief Justice John Roberts, the Supreme Court's power is perhaps not yet at its zenith. There are more cases to come that Roberts could use to overturn legal precedents he dislikes and further privilege presidential power and corporate prerogative over individual freedoms. Meanwhile—as the cloud of corruption surrounding his Court continues unabated and the majority of Republican appointees continue to align their rulings with their political party—the American people will continue to lose confidence in the Roberts Court, as they should. America deserves a high court worthy of public confidence, with genuinely fair judges held to the highest ethical standards. We do not have these nice things because right-wing funders and operatives captured the Court, and Roberts has delivered on their agenda. He is a player, a quarterback on the field, not the fair umpire he projected at the hearing on his nomination.

In the long run, if our democratic republic survives this period, the current crises that John Roberts has unleashed on America, including Trump's emboldened destructiveness, could ignite a powerful movement to restore and expand our freedoms—and reform the Court, too. America is facing enormous challenges from a trifecta of wealth, power, and repression, but America has faced and overcome similar challenges in earlier eras. As another chief justice said, more than 150 years ago, in remarks that seem even more on point today,

> There is a looming and new dark power. . . . The accumulation of individual wealth seems to be greater than it ever has been since the downfall of the Roman Empire. The enterprises of the country are aggregating vast corporate combinations of unexampled capital, boldly marching, not for economic conquests only, but for political power. For the first time really in our politics money is taking the field

> as an organized power. . . . The question will arise, and arise in your day, though perhaps not fully in mine. Which shall rule—wealth or man; which shall lead—money or intellect; who shall fill public stations—educated and patriotic free men, or the feudal serfs of corporate capital?[8]

That is indeed the question we are now facing, in the eloquent oratory of Chief Justice Edward Ryan of the Wisconsin Supreme Court circa 1875. In the decades that followed his remarks, reformers successfully organized for their freedoms and for our future.

Organizing takes energy, creativity, and courage, but together—if we do not lose hope—we can restore and expand our freedoms. We can consign John Roberts to history, to a brief period when America lost its way before we revived the values that made our country the land of the free, where together we renew our pledge to establish liberty and justice for all.

# EPILOGUE

BY THE TIME this book is published, John Roberts will have served as chief justice of the US Supreme Court for twenty years. During his tenure, he has presided over five inaugurations, where he has sworn in three men as president of the United States: Barack Obama, Donald Trump, and Joe Biden. Each time except the last one, he wore his signature red tie. On January 20, 2025, however, Roberts did not have to wear team colors. It was his decision in *Trump v. United States* that helped sweep Trump back into office and enthrone him with unprecedented immunity. Weeks later, at the State of the Union address, Trump made a point of patting Roberts on the shoulder and telling him, "I won't forget." Trump later claimed, implausibly, that he was just referring to the official act of administering the oath of office rather than what Roberts had done for him.

Roberts wore a red tie when he gaveled in the first impeachment trial against Trump in early 2020, when Trump was charged with soliciting foreign interference in the presidential election that year, abusing his power by conditioning US aid to Ukraine on getting a public announcement by Ukrainian President Volodymyr Zelenskyy that he would investigate Trump's political rival in the upcoming 2020 presidential election, Joe Biden. The Constitution requires that "when the President of the United States is tried, the Chief Justice shall preside." Roberts seemed to treat this as a largely ceremonial role, not a truly judicial one; for example, he gave no admonitions about fairness when Republicans blocked subpoenas and witnesses for that proceeding, making it a deeply flawed "trial." After several days of arguments about the law and facts, almost all of the Republican senators voted in lockstep to block Trump's conviction and removal, despite the compelling evidence he had abused his power and also obstructed Congress.

Trump was impeached again by the US House of Representatives on January 13, 2021, a week after the violent and deadly insurrection at the US Capitol on January 6, after he incited his followers to stop Congress from counting the Electoral College votes. But this time, John Roberts chose *not* to preside over the trial. Senator Patrick Leahy presided instead, as the Senate's most senior member. Why did Roberts avoid presiding over the second trial for Trump? Why did he duck out based on a technicality that Trump would no longer be president when the trial took place, even though Trump was being impeached for his actions while he was president? Perhaps Roberts's dodge should be seen as an omen of his role to come in 2024, in the ways his actions helped pave the way for Trump's return to power in spite of the January 6 insurrection.

At the conclusion of the second impeachment trial, a majority of US senators voted to convict Trump on the charge that his words on January 6 "encouraged—and foreseeably resulted in—lawless action" that "threatened the integrity of the democratic system, interfered with the peaceful transition of power, and imperiled a coequal branch of Government," constituting "a threat to national security, democracy, and the Constitution." This time the vote was 57–43, with all the Democratic and Independent senators voting to convict along with Senator Mitt Romney and six other Republicans; most of the Republicans voted to acquit. The verdict fell short of the two-thirds needed to bar Trump from office under the Impeachment Clause. Senator Mitch McConnell, who had condemned Trump's actions on the evening of January 6, voted against convicting him, although he stated, "There's no question that President

Trump is practically and morally responsible for provoking the events of the day." McConnell noted that, instead, Trump could be held responsible in criminal court for his actions, which reflected a widespread view of the law, until Chief Justice John Roberts would later make sure that was, in practice, impossible.[1]

The select committee that the Democratic-led Congress established to investigate January 6 held penetrating public hearings and issued a devastating report about Trump's actions and culpability in December 2022. That bipartisan investigation recommended criminal charges against Trump and others. A month before that congressional report was finalized, Attorney General Merrick Garland finally appointed a special counsel to investigate Trump, after what I consider to be unforgivable delay. Garland named a highly respected prosecutor, Jack Smith, to lead that independent review of the facts and law. That investigation led to a grand jury indicting Donald Trump on felonies for his actions, and Smith began proceedings to initiate a criminal trial for Trump in 2023.

John Roberts ultimately put a stop to these criminal proceedings in 2024, with his truly dangerous ruling creating presidential immunity from criminal prosecution for Trump. Roberts put Trump above the law.

How could Trump have won the election in 2024? The answer is simple: It is because Trump was not disqualified and jailed for crimes there was ample evidence he committed. That is directly due to John Roberts and his fellow Republican appointees on the Court. They may not donate to the Republican Party anymore, but they gave the party its biggest gift of all time: the illegitimate exoneration of the party's leader.

---

Roberts may have mortally damaged our democracy. Since January 20, 2025, Trump has been wreaking destruction and acting as though he is above the law. At inauguration, Roberts administered a presidential oath that he had rendered almost meaningless. Promising to "faithfully execute" the laws is the opposite of breaking them, which is what Roberts allowed Trump to do—so much for Roberts being an institutionalist. The Roberts Court even dismissed the hypothetical that Trump's own lawyer acceded to: that Trump could order the assassination of a political rival and be immune from prosecution under such a broad grant of immunity. In giving Trump kinglike powers, Roberts jeopardized the freedom of everyone living in this country—especially immigrants but citizens too. Trump even suggested that people who criticize "his" Supreme Court should be arrested, a reprehensible threat from someone who swore an oath on a Bible that he would "preserve, protect, and defend the Constitution of the United States," which expressly guarantees First Amendment protection for the freedom of speech and the freedom of the press in America.

Whatever extremes Trump pursues in 2025 and beyond, these sins must fall at Roberts's feet too. Roberts broke the central pillar upon which our Constitution is built: The American president is not a king. Neither is Elon Musk, the billionaire who has acted like Trump's unelected copresident. Together, they have slashed and trashed federal agencies and fired tens of thousands of federal workers in violation of rules and contracts—capriciously shuttering USAID and locking out our civil servants, closing national park ranger stations, and even trying to silence the Voice of America, something Russia sought to do for years. Trump and Musk have taken a chainsaw to government programs millions of Americans need. They even let Musk's minions get the keys to the kingdom, to the data of some our most important systems like Social Security and the Internal Revenue Service. Then there is the kleptocracy, like Musk trying to get the Federal Aviation Administration to hire his for-profit business to handle air traffic control. Meanwhile, Republicans in Congress let Trump get away with appointing the most unqualified, reckless, and dangerous cabinet in all of US history.

It has felt as though America has become a plane that has been hijacked by a brigade of ignorant and destructive pirates.

But all is not lost. The movement to restore American freedom and build a healthier economy, where the billionaires pay their fair share of taxes and where we can all thrive, is taking root. It started with simmering sparks of outrage at town halls and expanded with the fearless leadership of Americans from all walks of life who care deeply about our country and our Constitution. This movement will grow wider as Trump's erratic domestic and foreign policies damage our economy and our nation. Trump will almost certainly try to repress the movement to make America sane again, but I have faith that the American people will not give up.

---

We are going to have a lot of work to do in the coming years to clean up and rebuild, work that is beyond the scope of this book but within the purview of us all. Focusing in on the Court, however, what *can* be done to repair the substantive damage John Roberts has caused to the law and to address the culture of corruption he allowed to engulf the Supreme Court? A lot.

Members of Congress and public interest groups have proposed an array of reforms that could be adopted as soon as there is a willing Congress and president. Clearly it will not be possible to secure the needed reforms under the Trump administration and a Republican-controlled Congress, but it is vital to build on the existing base of support for reform. Success may seem a long way off, but there are also tipping points that open up real possibilities.

In our democratic system, change requires a committed group of people who will work for reform, an increase in the number of legislators who will fight for reform, and the election of a president who will sign such advances into law. We must adopt strategic patience to win moral battles like this, which are about matters of principles like the vital necessity of having fair courts and fair laws that reflect the will of the people and respect people's rights. We simply must not allow John Roberts's usurpation of the power of lawmaking to stand unchallenged.

Numerous reforms are needed to correct the decisions of the Roberts Court that have eviscerated constitutional provisions, limited our freedoms, or displaced commonsense policies. These include the following:

- Senator Chuck Schumer's No Kings Act would make clear that presidents are not immune from criminal prosecution. This legislation represents an important breakthrough in support for limiting the jurisdiction of the Supreme Court, which the Constitution permits.
- The John Lewis Voting Rights Restoration Act would restore key enforcement provisions—the preclearance rules—that Congress adopted in 2006 and that John Roberts dismantled.
- The Freedom to Vote Act, previously called S. 1, would bar extreme partisan gerrymandering and reverse the rulings in *Rucho v. Common Cause* and its progeny.
- The *Citizens United v. FEC* ruling must be overturned, and the Bipartisan Campaign Reform Act's rules on ads near Election Day should be restored; there are a number of proposals to accomplish this. The Disclose Act should also be adopted to require the disclosure of big donors to nonprofits spending significant funds trying to influence elections. Publicly traded companies that spend money in elections and on lobbying should also have to disclose that spending, and shareholders should be allowed to vote on political expenditures.
- The tax code obviously needs to be reformed to make sure billionaires pay their fair share, which should be at least 35 percent of revenue or more, with a limit on loopholes;

billion-dollar corporations should also be required to pay their fair share and post how much they actually pay in taxes to support our nation.

- A federal right to access abortion and contraception should be adopted. The Comstock Act, which Project 2025 suggested using to block the mailing of Mifepristone, should be repealed.
- We also need measures to underscore that the Environmental Protection Agency can regulate carbon, along with bills to restore *Chevron* deference by judges in reviewing regulations.
- Many other Roberts Court rulings need to be overturned or mitigated, including the decision where John Roberts hubristically blocked student debt forgiveness, the devastating *Janus* ruling that undermines labor unions, and the ridiculous decision that recast bribery as a form of acceptable "gratuity." Congress also needs to overcome the *Heller* and *Bruen* rulings and adopt commonsense gun regulations that protect public safety, including restoring the Assault Weapons Ban, barring bump stocks, and adopting other rules. These are just a few of the substantive reforms needed to restore the law to where it was before the Roberts Court began deconstructing it. Other bold measures can and should go beyond just restoring the law. I am excited for real progress on policies that can help our families, our schools, our communities, and our country thrive.

There are also many court reforms to build support around in the years ahead, including:

- Term limits: This would help address the aberrant way the Roberts Court was constructed and set reasonable limits on how long any justice could serve no matter who appointed them and no matter how old they are when appointed. A twenty-year term limit for all justices would be more than reasonable.

- Court expansion: Advocates have outlined a number of options to increase the size of the Court, including ensuring that each presidential term has at least one Supreme Court seat to fill (there were no vacancies during Jimmy Carter's term, but there were four in Ronald Reagan's two terms, for example).
- Ethics enforcement: The Supreme Court Ethics, Recusal, and Transparency Act that Senator Whitehouse and his colleagues proposed would strengthen transparency of justices' income and trips and improve the financial disclosure process. It would also make it easier to file motions asking justices to recuse and have those motions heard by a panel of judges who can enforce ethics rules.
- Limiting gifts: The High Court Gift Ban Act, which Representatives Jamie Raskin and Alexandria Ocasio-Cortez introduced, would bar the receipt of any single gift worth more than $50 or more than $100 in aggregate in a year; plus it would cap gifts of so-called personal hospitality, like stays at the palatial homes of people who have befriended a Supreme Court justice.
- Addressing the amicus racket: Senator Whitehouse's Assessing Monetary Influence in the Courts of the United States (AMICUS) Act would require disclosures about who is really paying for amicus briefs.

I would also bar public and private universities and other nonprofits from arranging special trips for Supreme Court justices to teach abroad, as George Mason's law school has done repeatedly. I would also require full disclosure of major sources of income of a justice's spouse, along with dollar amounts and, if I were writing the rules, I would require additional details to ensure that corporations or consulting firms could not be deployed to obscure the true funders or clients. To those who would object on the basis that a lawyer's clients are allowed to be secret, I would say that there should be an exception if your spouse is on the Supreme Court. That is a small price to pay to help ensure that our public servants in the judiciary do not have their nests secretly feathered by secret pay, like Leonard Leo arranged for Ginni Thomas.

More details about these and other reforms we can build support for in the coming years can be found on this book's website, WithoutPrecedent.info. It includes a comprehensive set of potential reforms and the rationales for them, along with links to actions people can take. It also includes helpful resources for learning more about the policies discussed in this book, as well as additional citations, reporters to read, and stories to share to illuminate these important issues.

---

How much John Roberts and the Roberts Court will further enable Trump's authoritarian tendencies is not yet known. Even if they were to block some of Trump's major transgressions of the law—and the Trump administration obeyed such court orders—that would not undo the vast amount of damage to the rule of law and to justice that John Roberts unloosed by keeping Trump out of jail. Even if Roberts repeatedly rebukes Trump for his crude efforts to intimidate brave federal judges who dare to protect what the law commands, that would do nothing to undo the damage that Roberts has caused to America's election process and the Voting Rights Act in particular, in addition to other wreckage.

I think John Roberts will go down as the worst chief justice in American history. The path of deep destruction he has carved through our laws and our democracy all but ensures it. He has sown the seeds for his fall from grace by opening the door to authoritarianism in America.

The Roberts Court will not last forever. The future of the Supreme Court is ultimately in the hands of the American people, and we do not have to accept the status quo. We, who care about liberty and justice, have a moral obligation to ourselves, to those who came before us, and to the future to help ensure that America's highest court is genuinely a fair one.

We must remember day by day that progress is possible. The future is still unwritten, and it is ours to make, if we combine hope with wise action. As the historian Howard Zinn observed, "Hope is the energy for change." Choosing hope is essential, even when the odds seem stacked against us. Indeed, that is when we need to employ hope, grit, and creativity most of all.

# ACKNOWLEDGMENTS

This book would not have been possible without the initiative of my very talented editor, Jeffrey Kusama-Hinte, who sought me out and asked me to share my analysis and observations. He, on behalf of Bold Type Books, has been a real partner in this endeavor to illuminate the truth about John Roberts. Our many conversations about this subject and public policy greatly helped inform the stories I tell here. I have such appreciation for Lisa Kaufman, whose edits patiently sought to make the best possible use of my propensity for digression. I am also grateful for the support of the Type Media Center, which Jeff chairs, and Type's executive director, Taya McCormack-Grobow, for their deep devotion to bold, accurate reporting and truth-telling books. I am also grateful to the Hachette Book Group publisher Lara Heimert, and its excellent editing team, Shena Redmond and Jennifer Kelland. Thank you also to Angie Messina at Basic Books and her publicity team, including Brooke Parsons.

I could not have written this book without the enormous support of my beloved husband and mother, who were my first readers and editors of every chapter. Their love, patience, kindness, and encouragement buoyed me throughout this process. Their belief in me and in this labor of love—along with their tender and strong support for endeavors to help make our nation and our world a better place—have really sustained me. My treasured brother-in-law Joseph Zweber, his wife Jane Zweber, her sister Lori, and her husband Tom have also cheered me on, and their views have also helped shape my approach to this work in positive ways. My sweet brother Alan and his wife, Mikayla, have also encouraged me with their kindness and patience. My godparents, Bev and Bill Frank, and their niece DeAnna Marler have also been lovingly supportive of my writing. I am blessed with an amazing pack of sisters-in-law and brothers-in-law—plus twenty-nine nieces and nephews and their children—who have gracefully tolerated many visits that also involved my working. Meanwhile, my rescue doggos have not so patiently put up with my distracted presence, but they seem to adore me anyway, as good dogs do.

My great-hearted adopted tribe on the East Coast—Adelaide Gomer, Benno Friedman, Kenny Bruno, Karen Kimball, Wrexie Bardaglio, Carolyn Fine, Sarah Stranahan, Donna Edwards, Ray Paultre, Jay Halfon, Alicia Wittink, Rachel Leon, and Michael Connor—also spurred me on. My best friend, the amazing Jeani Murray, and many other wonderfully talented friends encouraged me along the way to writing this book, including Yolanda, Nick and Julie, Victoria Smith, Paul Morris, Rebecca and Eric, Kathy Bonnifield, Kert Davies, Arn Pearson, Kris and Howard Matlack, Dezy and Claire Walls, Noam Chomsky, Kathy Togni, Marvin Waterstone, Kim Haddow, Clarince Thomas, Patty First, Christine Bremer Muggli, Ann Jacobs, Teresa Vilmain, Jamie Corey, Connor Gibson, Charlie Cray, Robin Powers, Jenny Branks, Tai and Chelsea, Molly, Sahana, Eric and Sue Sie, Carol Weiss and Joseph Ranney, Avner and Julie, Susana and Claudio, Chris, Brian, Clarisa, Edna Brillon, Trevor, Dave Merritt, Ellen Braune, Jan Miyasaki, Talia, Carlos, Cindy, Jack, Carter, Loesch, James Adams, Paige, Carol Didget Pomfret, Dalynda Morgan, Calvin Sloan, Fred Smith, Annabelle Anders, Sarah Gossage Kennedy, Michele McNulty, Judy Bode, John T., Katie, Roger Danis, Jim Coomber, LeAnn, Nancy and Howard, Cindy Baxter, Michael Fischer, Inger Stole, Dave Johnson, Alexis Marx, Kristin Cabral, Karen Hunold, Tyler Engel, Shanita Starks, Savita Gilbert, Karen Palmer, Sandra Nakasone,

Tami Frazier, Elanor, Danielle Fagan, Carlos Duque, Nate Timm, John Jack, Michal Spocko, Sari Williams, Phyllis Lawrence, Paige Asawa, Mattie Stevens, Ringuette, Rebecca Buckwalter-Poza, Tsoghig Hekimian, Kyoko and Larry, Lauren Windsor, Mary Bottari, Kate Martin, and the late Jerry Libin, Mark Glaze, Bob Sloan, Doug Kendall, Charles Cassell, Ken Katsuma, Gloria Starks, and Ed Werneke.

The superb investigative journalist Bob O'Harrow became a dear friend of mine after he left *The Washington Post*. He provided lovely encouragement to me in writing this book before he passed away, far too soon, while working on a magnum opus for Patagonia Books about the cataclysmic losses of the mayfly. Duncan Campbell has been an essential conversation partner with me about the Supreme Court, both on the air, on KGNU and his Living Dialogues program, and off. I have been inspired by on-air dialogues with Ian Masters, Amy Goodman, Nicole Sandler, Rose Aguilar, Laura Flanders, Edwin Eisendrath, Rick Smith, Brad Friedman, Joan Esposito, RJ Eskow, and Aly Muldrow. I also want to thank Tom Carter, who has tirelessly sought to raise the alarm about Leonard Leo's agenda. Ben Strader and the Blue Mountain Center crew also provided early support for writing this book.

I want to thank my wonderful team at True North and in particular Alyssa Bowen and Evan Vorpahl, along with our below-the-radar researchers, for being so devoted to the ideals in this book. I am also so grateful for my partners at True Compass, the visionary Alex Aronson, Naomi Aberly, Darcy McConnell, Jess Brady Reader, Laurie Rubiner, and our whole fantastic crew. Thank you also to my creative partners at the MeidasTouch Network, especially Michael Popok and the team at Legal AF on YouTube. I am grateful to my fabulous partners at The Five 8 and The Five 8 1/2: Greg Olear, LB Koff, and Nadine Smith. Many thanks also to the talented crew at Courier: Tara McGowan, Devin Moroney, RC Di Mezzo, and Lucy Ritzmann. I also so appreciate the Research Collaborative: Mike

Podhorzer, Anat Shenker Osario, and Tara Buss. It is also a joy to work from time to time with Hamilton Fish at *The Washington Spectator*, Jon Queally at Common Dreams, David Armiak at the Center for Media and Democracy, TruthOut, the Nation, Joel Bleifuss at the Barn Raiser, and *The Progressive* magazine.

I also want to express my deep gratitude to Senator Sheldon Whitehouse for being such a shining star in making the case for the protection of fair courts and the defense of our planet, along with his excellent communications and legal teams, as well as his colleagues like Senator Richard Blumenthal and Representatives Jamie Raskin, Alexandria Ocasio-Cortez, and Hank Johnson, among others. I am also so appreciative of the always insightful MSNBC host Lawrence O'Donnell for shining a bright light on these issues, along with MSNBC's other top-notch hosts and producers. I also want to express my deep gratitude to the writers of dazzling books like Jane Mayer, Nancy MacLean, Bill Moyers, Dahlia Lithwick, David Daley, Gareth Gore, Sidney Blumenthal, Sean Wilentz, Ari Berman, Anne Nelson, Kyle Spencer, Heather Cox Richardson, Jim Hightower, Elie Mystal, Maurice Cunningham, Thom Hartmann, Herman Schwartz, Nina Burleigh, Chris Leonard, Laurence Tribe, Ilyse Hogue, Elle Langford, Donald Cohen, David Brock, Randall Ballmer, Amanda Hollis-Brusky, Dominic Erdozain, Jackie Calmes, Jeff Nesbit, Jane McAlevey, Robert Reich, Dan Kaufman, Donald Cohen, Tom Sullivan, Ciara Torres, Lee Cokorinos, John Nichols, Isaac Kramnick, R. Lawrence Moore, Gordon Lafer, Ian Milhiser, Ralph Wilson, Isaac Kamola, Ruth Marcus, Steve Vladeck, Chris Geidner, Leah Litman, and the late Bob McChesney. I am also so grateful, of course, for the work of the eminent Supreme Court reporter Joan Biskupic, whose thoughtful books and ongoing reporting on Roberts inform this work. On the website that complements this book, I will also link to the excellent work of superb reporters—like Heidi Przybyla, Shawn Boberg, Josh Kaplan, Justin Elliot, Stephanie Kirchgaessner, Elie Mystal, Andy Kroll, Lauren

Windsor, Andrew Perez, Joe Patrice, Abbie VanSickle, and others—and amazing advocates, whose devotion to truth inspires me daily.

I am also deeply grateful to Senator Patrick Leahy for bringing me onto the Judiciary Committee staff and for being such a wonderful and inspiring boss. His staff—the Leahy family—overwhelmingly reflected his best traits too, including David Carle, Kevin McDonald, Susan Davies, Tara Magner, Bruce Cohen, Ed Pagano, Clara Kirchner, Phil Toomajian, JP Dowd, and Tracy Schmaler, along with the members of the Nominations Unit Response Team I adored: Kristine Lucius, Leesa Klepper, Andra Roy Chernack, Rachel Arfa, Shanna Hughey Singh, David Mickenberg, Chip Vance, Julia Franklin, Mona Lewandoski, and Marit DeLozier. I was so fortunate to work with other amazing Senate staffers, including Stephanie Jones, Bob Schiff, Jennifer Duck, Jonathan Meyer, Chris Rhee, Jeff Berman, Melody Barnes, Olati Johnson, Jim Flug, David Hantman, Beth Stein, Eric Columbus, Joe Zogby, Seth Bloom, Lisa Moore, Neil Kornze, Mark Keam, Joe Bryan, Mike Zubrensky, Jimmy Ryan, Jane Butterfield, and Roslyne Turner. I also appreciated the views of indefatigable advocates like Wade Henderson, Nan Aron, Nancy Zirkin, Marge Baker, Leslie Proll, Doug Kendall, Jason Rylander, Marsha Kuntz, Simon Lazarus, Kendra Sue Derby, Adam Shah, Glenn Sugamelli, Carlos Ortiz, Ralph Neas, and Elliot Mincberg, among others.

To this day, I remain deeply appreciative of having had the privilege of working with my first great mentor in the legal profession, Eldie Acheson, who is a real-life hero to me, along with Janet Reno. I am so thankful for the brilliant people on Eldie's team on judicial issues and legal policy, including Paul Morris, Harry Litman, Lisalyn Jacobs, Mark Greenberg, Brian Hoffstadt, Katrina Weinig, Robyn Thiemann, Kristine Lucius, Geoff Bestor, Peter Owen, Jeani Rhee, Wendy Patten, Jessica Rosenbaum, Sheila Joy, Matt Nosanchuck, Scot Bales, and others. I also loved working with Eric Angel and Sarah Wilson in the White House Counsel's Office and being Mike Dolan's deputy in the Article III Judges Division of the Administrative Office of the US Courts. I often recount the insightful advice Eldie and Mike gave me. What great good luck to have had the chance to work for them!

I also want to express my eternal gratitude to the devoted teachers and coaches who have inspired me over the years, including Christine McCann, Rita Homrich, Steve Shiffrin, JoAnne Miner, Cynthia Farina, Faust Rossi, Alan Freeman, Alan Bigel, Dave Beale, Bill Bielke, Kit Gibson, Ed Collins, Bev Bradshaw, Elizabeth Schramm, Karen McCubbin, and Virginia Hungerford. Their lessons illuminated my world. Meanwhile, I feel so fortunate to have basked in the love of my grandmothers, Eileen and Paula, who taught me the importance of honesty, kindness, determination, curiosity, and cultivating a really good sense of humor.

Finally, thank you, dear reader, for taking the time to dive into the ideas in my first book.

# NOTES

## INTRODUCTION

1. *Mitchell v. W. T. Grant*, 416 U.S. 600, 636 (1974) (Stewart, J., dissenting), cited in *Planned Parenthood v. Casey*, 505 U.S. 833 (1992).

## CHAPTER 1. CONFIRMATION

1. "Excerpts from Interview with Nixon About Domestic Effects of Indochina War [Frost-Nixon Interviews]," *New York Times*, May 20, 1977, A16.

2. David E. Rosenbaum, "Files from 80's Lay Out Stances of Bush Nominee," *New York Times*, July 27, 2005; Joan Biskupic, *The Chief: The Life and Turbulent Times of Chief Justice John Roberts* (Basic Books, 2019), 66 (Kindle).

3. "Roberts Confirmation Hearing [Before the Senate Judiciary Committee], Day 1," C-SPAN, September 12, 2005, 3:39:18.

4. George W. Bush, *Decision Points* (Crown, 2010), 98.

5. David Kirkby, "What Roberts' Friends Are Saying . . . David Kirkby, Former High School Teacher and Coach," Audio Recording, JudgeRoberts.com, accessed January 6, 2025, https://web.archive.org/web/20060519050816/http://judgeroberts.com/docs/what/KIRKBY-ED.mp3; Biskupic, *The Chief*, 27.

6. Biskupic, *The Chief*, 13.

7. Sheldon Whitehouse, "The Scheme 13: Auditioning," Official Senate Site of Sheldon Whitehouse, March 15, 2022.

8. David Enrich, *Servants of the Damned: Giant Law Firms, Donald Trump, and the Corruption of Justice* (Harper Collins, 2022), 224–225.

9. Paul Harris, "Bush Hits Back as Republicans Erupt over Supreme Court Pick," *The Guardian*, October 8, 2005.

10. Rodger Simon, "Leahy Attacks Bush, Roberts," *Politico*, August 1, 2007.

11. "Roberts Swearing-In as Chief Justice," C-SPAN, September 29, 2005, 14:59.

12. Bob Woodward and Scott Armstrong, *The Brethren: Inside the Supreme Court* (Simon & Schuster, 1979).

13. Kevin T. Baine, ed., *Red Mass Primer* (John Carroll Society, 2011).

14. "Red Mass," John Carroll Society (Archdiocese of Washington), accessed December 23, 2024.

15. Baine, *Red Mass Primer*.

16. Mitch McConnell, "Keynote Address by Senator Mitch McConnell [2018 Kentucky Chapters Conference]," uploaded to YouTube by the Federalist Society, November 6, 2018, 43:50.

**CHAPTER 2. CONCEPTION**

1. "US Supreme Court Docket (Gonzales v. Carhart)," FindLaw, accessed December 23, 2024.

2. "The Republican Party Platform of 1980," The American Presidency Project, July 15, 1980; Charles E. Rice, "Ronald Reagan and the Supreme Court Issue," *Wall Street Journal*, September 23, 1980, 34.

3. *Planned Parenthood v. Casey*, 947 F.2d 682 (3d Cir. 1991), Circuit Judge Alito, concurring in part and dissenting in part.

4. Jim Mann, "'Whizzer' Prefers Obscurity, Press Rulings Focus Attention on White (Justice White's Press Decisions)," *Los Angeles Times*, August 7, 1978, Part I, 5; Joan Biskupic, *The Chief: The Life and Turbulent Times of Chief Justice John Roberts* (Basic Books, 2019), 99–100.

5. See Orrin Hatch, *Square Peg: Confessions of a Citizen-Senator* (Basic Books, 2003), 180.

6. Rebecca Mae Salokar, *The Solicitor General: The Politics of Law* (Temple University Press, 1992).

7. Lee Davidson, "Supreme Court Justices Pay Tribute to the Late Rex E. Lee," *Y Magazine*, Fall 1996; Neil A. Lewis, "The 1992 Campaign; Selection of Conservative Judges Insures a President's Legacy," *New York Times*, July 1, 1992, A13; Letter from John G. Roberts to Henry J. Friendly, February 3, 1983, in *The Papers of Judge Henry Friendly*, Harvard Law School, Special Collections Library, Papers of Judge Henry Friendly, box 220, folder 4. See

generally Brad Snyder, "The Judicial Genealogy (and Mythology) of John Roberts: Clerkships from Gray to Brandeis to Friendly to Roberts," *Ohio State Law Journal* 71, no. 6 (2010), 1149–1243.

8. Maralee Schwartz and Al Kamen, "Starr's 'Political' Deputy," *Washington Post*, September 22, 1989, A25; Jan Crawford Greenburg, *Supreme Conflict: The Inside Story of the Struggle for Control of the United States Supreme Court* (Penguin, 2008), 209.

9. Republican National Convention (RNC), "Republican Party Platform of 1988," American Presidency Project, August 16, 1988.

10. *Planned Parenthood of Southeastern Pa. v. Casey*, 505 U.S. 833 (1992), official transcript of the proceedings before the Supreme Court (Anderson Reporting Company), April 22, 1992, 43, 44, 46, 50.

11. David Siders, "'The Dog That Caught the Car': Republicans Brace for the Impact of Reversing Roe," *Politico*, June 25, 2022.

12. Memo, John G. Roberts to Fred F. Feilding, February 10, 1983, Folder "JGR/Intercircuit Tribunal" (1 of 5), box 29, John G. Roberts Files, Ronald Reagan Library.

13. See Stephen Vladeck, *The Shadow Docket: How the Supreme Court Uses Stealth Rulings to Amass Power and Undermine the Republic* (Basic Books, 2023).

14. Biskupic, *The Chief*, 66; David E. Rosenbaum, "Files from 80's Lay Out Stances of Bush Nominee," *New York Times*, July 27, 2005.

**CHAPTER 3. AMBITION**

1. "Voting Irregularities in Florida During the 2000 Presidential Election," US Commission on Civil Rights.

2. Jeffrey Toobin, "The Absolutist," *New Yorker*, June 23, 2014.

3. Abby Goodnough, "Nominee Gave Quiet Advice on Recount," *New York Times*, July 21, 2005.

4. Leonard Leo, "Leo, Leonard Interview," by Center for Presidential History, Vimeo, July 19, 2018, 1:48:16, https://vimeo.com/280829547.

5. Joan Biskupic, "Supreme Court Is About to Have 3 Bush v. Gore Alumni Sitting on the Bench," CNN, October 17, 2020.

6. Goodnough, "Nominee Gave Quiet Advice."

7. Robert O'Harrow and Shawn Boburg, "A Conservative Activist's Behind-the-Scenes Campaign to Remake the Nation's Courts," *Washington Post*, May 21, 2019.

## CHAPTER 4. OLD MONEY

1. See Orrin Hatch, *Square Peg: Confessions of a Citizen-Senator* (Basic Books, 2002), 130.

2. "Support for Judge Thomas Nomination," C-SPAN, September 13, 1991, 55:02; "Support for Judge Thomas Nomination," C-SPAN, October 9, 1991, 30:54.

3. Ethics and Public Policy Center, "Judicial Activism," C-SPAN, May 18, 1997, 38:05.

4. "Fun and Fancy Rule at Rices' Dance," *Winston-Salem Journal and Sentinel*, May 29, 1938.

5. Margaret Truman, *Harry S. Truman* (William Morrow, 1973), 429.

6. Al Mackey, "Robert E. Lee and Me," Student of the Civil War, February 21, 2021, https://studycivilwar.wordpress.com/2021/02/21/robert-e-lee-and-me (citing Ty Seidule, *Robert E. Lee and Me: A Southerner's Reckoning with the Myth of the Lost Cause* [St. Martin's Press, 2021]); Brent Staples, "Confederate Tributes Are Losing Their Patron Saint," *New York Times*, April 27, 2023.

7. Martin Sherwin and Kai Bird, *American Prometheus: The Triumph and Tragedy of J. Robert Oppenheimer* (A. A. Knopf, 2005), Kindle location 10422 et seq.; Jeffrey J. Crow, "The Paradox and the Dilemma: Gordon Gray and the J. Robert Oppenheimer Security Clearance Hearing," *North Carolina Historical Review* 85, no. 2, April (2008): 188.

## CHAPTER 5. DIRTY TRICKS

1. Roger Simon, "How a Murderer and a Rapist Became the Bush Campaign's Most Valuable Player," *Baltimore Sun*, November 11, 1990.

2. Rick Pearlstein, "Exclusive: Lee Atwater's Infamous 1981 Interview on the Southern Strategy," *The Nation*, November 13, 2012.

3. "Who Are the Nominees?" Committee for Justice, archived August 12, 2002, https://web.archive.org/web/20021013043114/http:/www.committeeforjustice.org/contents/nominees.

4. "History of Lynching in America," NAACP, accessed January 3, 2015.

5. US Senate Committee on the Judiciary, *Confirmation Hearing on the Nomination of Charles W. Pickering, Sr. to Be Circuit Judge for the Fifth Circuit: Hearing Before the Committee on the Judiciary, United States Senate, One Hundred Seventh Congress, Second Session, February 7, 2002* (US GPO, 2003), 104.

6. “Senator Thurmond 100th Birthday,” C-SPAN, December 4, 2002, 1:06:09.

7. Thomas B. Edsall and Brian Faler, “Lott Remarks on Thurmond Echoed 1980 Words,” *Washington Post*, December 11, 2002; Elisabeth Bumiller, “Divisive Words Behind the Scenes; with Signals and Maneuvers, Bush Orchestrates an Ouster,” *New York Times*, December 21, 2002.

8. Email from Ginni Thomas to Brett M. Kavanaugh, “Heritage—Events and Publications—Nov. 6h—Congrats!” November 6, 2002 (on file with author).

9. “DC Court of Appeals Confirmation Hearing,” C-SPAN, January 28, 2003, 52:29.

10. “Why Not Go 24/7 on Estrada?” Committee for Justice, archived July 27, 2004, https://web.archive.org/web/20051101012259/https:/committeeforjustice.org/contents/reading/Whynot.pdf.

11. US Senate Committee on the Judiciary, “Report on the Investigation into Improper Access to the Senate Judiciary Committee’s Computer System,” 108th Cong., 2nd Sess., 2004, https://cryptome.org/judiciary-sys.htm.

12. Gail Russell Chaddock, “‘Memogate’ Opens Window on Judiciary Fights,” *Christian Science Monitor*, March 17, 2004.

13. Jeffrey Toobin, “Where’s Manny?” *New Yorker*, November 25, 2007.

14. Sheryl Gay Stolberg, “Out of Practice, Senate Crams for Battle over Court Nominee,” *Washington Post*, July 8, 2005.

**CHAPTER 6. BIG MONEY**

1. Kert Davies, “Top Ten Documents Every Reporter Covering Exxon Mobil Should Know,” Climate Investigations Center, May 23, 2016.

2. Thomas B. Edsall, “GOP Creating Own ‘527’ Groups,” *Washington Post*, May 24, 2004; “Progress for America,” *SourceWatch* (Center for Media and Democracy), accessed January 2, 2025.

3. Richard A. Serrano and David G. Savage, “Justice Thomas Reports Wealth of Gifts,” *Los Angeles Times*, December 31, 2004.

4. “‘Brilliant’ and ‘Roberts’ Ad Launch,” Progress for America, September 3, 2005, https://web.archive.org/web/20050912124945/http://judgeroberts.com/docs/videos/brilliant.pdf.

5. Lisa Graves, “Five Facts About Rob Arkley, Funder of Luxury Travel for Supreme Court Justices and Groups Packing the Court,” True North Research, November 7, 2023; Jennifer Taub, *Other People’s Houses: How Decades of Bailouts, Captive Regulators, and Toxic Bankers Made Home*

*Mortgages a Thrilling Business* (Yale University Press, 2015), Kindle location 1880.

6. Gary Legum, "Sam Alito Not Only Luxury Fishing Vacation Whore to Ever Serve on Supreme Court: What in the Wide Wide World of Dead Scalia Is A-Goin' on Here?" *Wonkette*, June 21, 2023.

7. Sarah Posner, "The 'Anti-Catholic' Playbook," *The Nation*, September 5, 2018.

8. Viveca Novak and Peter Stone, "The JCN Story: How to Build a Secretive, Right-Wing Judicial Machine," *Daily Beast*, March 23, 2015.

9. Jeanne Cummings, "In Judge Battle, Mr. Sekulow Plays a Delicate Role," *Wall Street Journal*, May 17, 2005.

10. David K. Kirkpatrick, "A Year of Work to Sell Roberts to Conservatives," *New York Times*, July 22, 2005.

11. "2017 National Lawyers Convention, White House Counsel McGahn," C-SPAN, November 16, 2017, 50:15.

12. Evan Vorpahl and Lisa Graves, "Who Is Targeting State Courts," True North Research, April 24, 2024.

13. "Judge Scalia's Cheerleaders," *New York Times*, July 23, 1986; Andy Kroll, Andrea Bernstein, and Ilya Marritz, "We Don't Talk About Leonard: The Man Behind the Right's Supreme Court Supermajority," *ProPublica*, October 11, 2023; Special to *The New York Times*, "The Federalist Society: The Cover of a Pamphlet Published by the Federalist Society; Judge Scalia's Cheerleaders," *New York Times*, July 23, 1986.

14. Mark Joseph Stern, "The Federalist Society Just Proved It's All In for Trump," *Slate*, November 18, 2019; Josh Blackman, "@senatemajldr We have flipped the 2nd Circuit . . . ," X, November 14, 2019.

15. Michael Joseph Gross, "A Vast Right-Wing Hypocrisy," *Vanity Fair*, January 2, 2008.

16. David Warner, "Richard Scaife the Man: His Impact on W. PA." *Pittsburgh-Post Gazette,* April 21, 1981, 6.

17. David Daley, "The Other Memo That Started the Conservative Legal Movement," *The Atlantic*, July 30, 2024.

18. Robert O'Harrow and Shawn Boburg, "A Conservative Activist's Behind-the-Scenes Campaign to Remake the Nation's Courts," *Washington Post*, May 21, 2019.

19. O'Harrow and Boburg, "A Conservative Activist's Behind-the-Scenes Campaign"; Dan Kennedy, "'A Civil Action': The Real Story," *Boston Phoenix*, December 18, 1998.

20. Colin Woodard, "Why Did Trump's 'Judge Whisperer' Buy a House on the Maine Coast?" *Portland Press Herald*, August 18, 2019.

21. "The Conservative Movement Transforming America's Courts," uploaded to YouTube by *The Washington Post*, May 21, 2019, 28:51.

22. David Montgomery, "Conquerors of the Courts," *Washington Post*, January 2, 2019; "The Conservative Movement Transforming America's Courts."

23. "The Conservative Movement Transforming America's Courts."

24. "The Conservative Movement Transforming America's Courts"; O'Harrow and Boburg, "A Conservative Activist's Behind-the-Scenes Campaign."

**CHAPTER 7. CORRUPTION**

1. Stephen Gillers, David Luban, and Steven Lubet, "Improper Advances: Talking Dream Jobs with the Judge Out of Court," *Slate*, August 17, 2005.

2. Gillers, Luban, and Lubet, "Improper Advances." See also Tom Brune, "Roberts Meeting 'Illegal': Legal Ethicists Say White House Interview Jeopardized Judge's Impartiality in a Case on Military Tribunals," *Newsday*, August 18, 2005.

3. Publius [Alexander Hamilton], "The Appointing Power Continued and Other Powers of the Executive Considered," The Federalist Papers: No. 77, April 2, 1788.

4. "2024 Election Calendar," Colorado Secretary of State Jena Griswold, accessed January 2, 2025.

5. *United States v. Fischer*, 64 F.4th 329, 433–434 (DC Cir. 2023); Jodi Kantor, "At Justice Alito's House, a 'Stop the Steal' Symbol on Display," *New York Times*, May 16, 2024; letter from Jamie Raskin and Alexandria Ocasio-Cortez to the Honorable John G. Roberts, Jr., House Committee on Oversight and Accountability, October 4, 2024; Jodi Kantor, Aric Toler, and Julie Tate, "Another Provocative Flag Was Flown at Another Alito Home," *New York Times*, May 22, 2025. See also Matthew D. Taylor, "From the 10/40 Window to January 6th: How Evangelical Spiritual Warfare Violence Shaped the Capitol Riot," American Academy of Religion, archived August 9, 2024, https://papers.aarweb.org/attached-paper/100804-1040-window-january-6th-how-evangelical-spiritual-warfare-violence-shaped; Bess Levin, "Trump Virtually High-Fives Samuel Alito for Refusing to Recuse Himself from January 6 Cases over Flag Incidents," *Vanity Fair*, May 30, 2024.

6. "Lynching in America: Confronting the Legacy of Racial Terror," Equal Justice Initiative, accessed January 2, 2024.

7. David Brock, *Stench: The Making of the Thomas Court and the Unmaking of America* (Knopf, 2024), 315–321; Bob Woodward and Robert Costa, "Virginia Thomas Urged White House Chief to Pursue Unrelenting Efforts to Overturn the 2020 Election, Texts Show," *Washington Post*, March 24, 2022; Shawna Chen, "Report: Texts Show Ginni Thomas Pushed Meadows to Help Overturn 2020 Election," *Axios*, March 24, 2022. See also John Kruzel, "Ginni Thomas's Activism Sparks Ethics Questions for Supreme Court Justice," *The Hill*, March 19, 2022.

8. Tom Norton, "Fact Check: Was Clarence Thomas Lone Dissenter on Trump Jan. 6 Documents?" *Newsweek*, June 17, 2022; Brock, *Stench*, 315–321.

9. Andrew Buncombe, "Who Is 'Coup Memo' Author John Eastman and What Role Did He Play in Pushing Trump's Plan to Derail Democracy?" *The Independent*, June 17, 2022; Kyle Cheney, "Ginni Thomas' West Wing Contacts Raise New Questions for Another Trump Ally: John Eastman," *Politico*, March 26, 2022; see also Heidi Przybyla, "Dark Money and Special Deals: How Leonard Leo and His Friends Benefited from His Judicial Activism," *Politico*, March 1, 2023.

10. Cheney, "Ginni Thomas' West Wing Contacts"; Exhibit F in *John C. Eastman v. Bennie G. Thompson, et al.*, 636 F. Supp. 3d 1078, 111 (C.D. Cal. 2022).

11. Donald J. Trump, "Tweets of January 6, 2021," American Presidency Project.

12. Alyssa Bowen, Evan Vorpahl, and Lisa Graves, "A Year Later, All Known Evidence Still Points to Rep. Lauren Boebert Being the First to Report that Speaker Pelosi Had Been 'Removed' from the House Chamber on January 6," True North Research, January 6, 2022; Trump, "Tweets of January 6"; Eric Neugeboren, "US Rep. Louie Gohmert Asked Trump for a Pardon After Insurrection, Jan. 6 Committee Reveals," *Texas Tribune*, June 23, 2022. This mob that besieged the Capitol included numerous people who Trump knew were armed, due to his objection to using magnetometers. As former White House aide Cassidy Hutchinson testified before the January 6 Committee, Trump shouted, "I don't f***ing care if they have weapons. They're not here to hurt me. Take the f***ing mags away. Let my people in. They can march to the Capitol from here. Let the people in. Take the f***ing mags away" (Cassidy Hutchinson, "Clip of the Sixth Hearing of January 6 Attack on the US Capitol," C-SPAN, June 28, 2022, 2:43). Trump was supremely confident that the

armed attendees were not there to hurt him. Meanwhile, he supported disarming the National Guard. At Trump's request, Acting Secretary of Defense Christopher Miller ordered the National Guard to follow rules of engagement on January 6 that did *not* allow them to have weapons. On January 4, Miller sent a memorandum ordering that "without the Acting Secretary's 'subsequent, personal authorization,' the [DC National] Guard would not be issued batons, helmets, or body armor; could not interact physically with protestors, except in self-defense; and that the Quick Reaction Force (QRF)—40 servicemembers staged in case of an emergency at Joint Base Andrews in Prince George's County, Maryland—could be deployed only as a last resort," according to the official report of the findings made by the United States House Select Committee to Investigate the January 6 Attack on the United States Capitol.

13. Jo Becker and Julia Tate, "Clarence Thomas's $267,230 R.V. and the Friend Who Financed It," *New York Times*, August 5, 2023.

14. Justin Elliott, Joshua Kaplan, and Alex Mierjeski, "Billionaire Harlan Crow Bought Property from Clarence Thomas. The Justice Didn't Disclose the Deal," *ProPublica*, April 13, 2023; Justin Elliott, Joshua Kaplan, and Alex Mierjeski, "Clarence Thomas and the Billionaire," *ProPublica*, April 6, 2013; Emma Brown, Shawn Boburg, and Jonathan O'Connell, "Judicial Activist Directed Fees to Clarence Thomas's Wife, Urged 'No Mention of Ginni,'" *Washington Post*, May 4, 2023; see also the brilliant recap by John Oliver, *Last Week Tonight* on MAX, season 11, episode 1, YouTube, February 22, 2024, 30:20.

15. Andy Kroll, Andrea Bernstein, and Ilya Marritz, "We Don't Talk About Leonard: The Man Behind the Right's Supreme Court Supermajority," *ProPublica*, October 11, 2023.

16. Thomas also failed to disclose the sources of his wife's income for years, as Common Cause uncovered.

17. Lisa Graves, "Clarence Thomas Has No Shame. But You Knew That," *Common Dreams*, February 9, 2024.

18. Rebecca Beitsch, "Raskin, Ocasio-Cortez Demand Answers from Roberts on Alito, Thomas Actions," *The Hill*, October 4, 2024.

**CHAPTER 8. MANIPULATION**

1. John Spong, "The Man in the White Hat," *Texas Monthly*, February 2006.

2. Andy Kroll, Andrea Bernstein, and Ilya Marritz, "We Don't Talk About Leonard: The Man Behind the Right's Supreme Court Supermajority,"

*ProPublica*, October 11, 2023; Tessa Berenson Rogers, "Donald Trump Offers Conservatives a Deal on Supreme Court," *Time*, March 21, 2016.

3. Ron Elving, "What Happened with Merrick Garland in 2016 and Why It Matters Now," NPR, June 29, 2018.

4. Lois Beckett, "NRA Cheers Nomination of Neil Gorsuch, Seen as Gun Rights Defender," *The Guardian*, February 1, 2017.

5. Evan Vorpahl, "Billionaire Charles Koch's 'Americans for Prosperity' Mobilizes for Dan Kelly," True North Research, March 29, 2023; Elving, "What Happened with Merrick Garland."

6. Alana Goodman, "Exclusive: Trump's Supreme Court Pick Neil Gorsuch Founded and Led Club Called 'Fascism Forever' Against Liberal Faculty at His Elite All-Boys DC Prep School," *Daily Mail*, February 1, 2017.

7. Charlie Savage and Julie Turkewitz, "Neil Gorsuch Has Web of Ties to Secretive Billionaire," *New York Times*, March 14, 2017; "NEW: Accountable.US Report Uncovers Conflict of Interest Between Justice Neil Gorsuch and Billionaire Philip Anschutz in Key Environmental Case," Accountable.US, October 2, 2024; Charlie Savage, "Head of Major Law Firm Bought Real Estate from Gorsuch," *New York Times*, April 25, 2023.

8. *Snyder v. United States*, 603 U.S. 1, 21 (2024), (Jackson, J., dissenting).

9. "Median Weekly Earnings $1,227 for Men, $1,021 for Women, First Quarter 2024," US Bureau of Labor Statistics, May 2, 2024.

10. *Snyder v. United States*, 603 U.S. 1, 21–22 (2024), (Jackson, J. dissenting).

**CHAPTER 9. GUNS**

1. "Guns," Gallup Historical Trends, accessed January 2, 2025; "See How AR-15 Style Guns Create 'Explosions Inside the Body,'" uploaded to YouTube by CNN, June 9, 2022, 9:51.

2. "How Many US Mass Shootings Have There Been in 2024," BBC, December 17, 2024; "Past Summary Ledgers," Gun Violence Archive, accessed January 2, 2025.

3. "Firearms Commerce in the United States: Annual Statistical Update 2021," Bureau of Alcohol, Tobacco, Firearms and Explosives, accessed January 2, 2025; Jeffrey M. Jones, "Majority in US Continues to Favor Stricter Gun Laws," Gallup, October 31, 2023; Gabriele Galimberti, "America's Gun Culture Is Unique. My Photographs Can Help Explain Why," *NBC News*, July 4, 2022.

4. Joel Achenbach, Scott Higham, and Sari Horwitz, "How NRA's True Believers Converted Marksmanship Group into a Mighty Gun Lobby,"

*Washington Post*, January 12, 2013; Gil Troy, "The Teen Killer Who Radicalized the NRA," *Daily Beast*, October 8, 2017.

5. "New Report Highlights US 2022 Gun-Related Deaths: Firearms Remain Leading Cause of Death for Children and Teens, and Disproportionately Affect People of Color," Johns Hopkins, Bloomberg School of Public Health, September 12, 2024.

6. "About the Firearms Industry's Trade Association," NSSF, accessed March 24, 2025; "The Gun Industry's Power Broker," Everytown Research & Policy, January 12, 2023; "RE: Supplemental Evidence for MUR 7147," Campaign Legal Center, October 14, 2020.

7. For example, see Brief for National Sports Shooting Foundation, Inc. as Amicus Curiae in Support of Petitioners, *Loper Bright Enterprises v. Raimondo*, 603 U.S. 369 (2024).

8. Mark Hensch, "NRA Makes $1M Ad Buy to Tout Gorsuch: Report," *The Hill*, March 3, 2017; "Supreme Court Nominee Gorsuch—Outdoorsman and Worthy Successor to Scalia," National Shooting Sports Foundation, February 1, 2017; Larry Keane, "Judge Kavanaugh's Supreme Court Nomination Is On-Target," National Shooting Sports Foundation, July 10, 2018; Larry Keane, "Supreme Court Nominee Judge Amy Coney Barrett a Jurist for All Rights," National Shooting Sports Foundation, September 28, 2020.

9. Scott Neuman, "The 'Gun Dude' and a Supreme Court Case That Changes Who Can Own Firearms in the US," NPR, August 14, 2022.

10. *District of Columbia v. Heller*, 554 U.S. 570, 621 (2008).

11. Mark Walters, "Hour 1 [Interview with Alan Gottleib @16:04]," *Armed American Radio with Mark Walters* (podcast), February 14, 2016, 53:53 (min. 16:02, 17:56), http://armedamericanradio.s3.amazonaws.com/02-14-2016_Hour_1.mp3.

12. Josh Sugarmann, "Gun Industry 'Ambassador' Antonin Scalia to Hear Gun Case," *Huffington Post*, May 1, 2010.

13. Stephen Bruce, "'Any Good Hunting?' When a Justice's Impartiality Might Reasonably Be Questioned," SSRN, October 5, 2016, http://dx.doi.org/10.2139/ssrn.2782170; Paul Duggan, "Lawyer Who Wiped Out DC Ban Says It's About Liberties, Not Guns," *Washington Post*, March 18, 2007.

14. "Beretta Group Pledges $1 Million to Benefit the NRA Institute for Legislative Action and Civil Rights Defense Fund," National Rifle Association for Legislative Action, September 3, 2008.

15. Editorial Board, "Ashcroft's Gun Views Now Policy," *Baltimore Sun*, October 1, 2021.

16. Editorial Board, "Ashcroft's Gun Views."

17. Lisa Graves, "Should Violent Domestic Abusers Be Allowed to Possess Guns?" *Grave Injustice*, season 1, episode 2, May 16, 2024, 32:51; Jodi Kantor and Mike McIntire, "The Gun Lobby's Hidden Hand in the 2nd Amendment Battle," *New York Times*, June 18, 2024.

18. Saul Cornell, "Clarence Thomas' Latest Guns Decision Is Ahistorical and Anti-Originalist," *Slate*, June 24, 2022.

19. Saul Cornell, "The Long Arc of Arms Regulation in Public: From Surety to Permitting, 1328–1928," *UC Davis Law Review* 55 (June 2022): 2545.

20. Cornell, "Clarence Thomas' Latest Guns Decision."

21. Graves, "Should Violent Domestic Abusers."

22. Graves, "Should Violent Domestic Abusers."

23. Matt Valentine, "Clarence Thomas Created a Confusing New Rule That's Gutting Gun Laws," *Politico*, July 28, 2023.

24. Valentine, "Clarence Thomas Created a Confusing New Rule."

25. *Garland v. Cargill*, 602 U.S. __ (2024); Miles Kohman, "The Las Vegas Mass Shooter Had 13 Rifles Outfitted with Bump Stocks. He Used Them to Fire 1,049 Rounds," *The Trace*, August 3, 2018.

26. Brief for National Sports Shooting Foundation, Inc. as Amicus Curiae in Support of Petitioners; Jennifer Mascia, "How SCOTUS's Chevron Decision Threatens Gun Regulations," *The Trace*, July 2, 2024.

**CHAPTER 10. ABORTION**

1. David E. Rosenbaum, "Files from 80's Lay Out Stances of Bush Nominee," *New York Times*, July 27, 2005.

2. *NOW v. Operation Rescue*, 726 F. Supp. 300 (D.DC 1989).

3. *Bray v. Alexandria Women's Health Clinic*, 506 U.S. 263, 319 (1993), (Stevens, J., and Blackmun, H. dissenting and citing Cong. Globe, 42d Cong., 1st Sess., 484 [1871]).

4. CBS News.com Staff, "Right to Kill?" *60 Minutes*, March 26, 1999.

5. "Criminal Section Selected Case Summaries," US Department of Justice, archived August 25, 2015, https://web.archive.org/web/20150825044254/http://www.justice.gov/crt/criminal-section-selected-case-summaries; Freedom of Access to Clinics Entrances (FACE) Act, US Code 18 § 248; "NAF Violence and Disruption Statistics: Incidents of Violence & Disruption Against Abortion Providers in the US & Canada," National Abortion Federation, accessed January 2, 2025, www.prochoice.org/pubs_research/publications/downloads/about_abortion/violence_stats.pdf.

6. *Hill v. Colorado*, 530 U.S. 703 (2000); *McCullen v. Coakley*, 573 U.S. 464 (2014); Kalvis Golde, "Anti-Abortion Activists Ask Justices to Overrule Ban on Expressive Activity Outside Clinics," *SCOTUSblog*, November 1, 2024.

7. One Wisconsin Now, "Gov. Scott Walker's State Lawyer Secretly Joined Attorney General Brad Schimel, Department of Justice Lawyers at Hate Group Conference," *Urban Milwaukee*, May 21, 2018; Amy Littlefield, "The Christian Legal Army Behind the Ban on Abortion in Mississippi," *The Nation*, November 30, 2021.

8. Alliance Defending Freedom, "What You May Not Know: How ADF Helped Overturn Roe v. Wade," LinkedIn, accessed January 2, 2025; Ansev Demirhan and Alyssa Bowen, "Meet the Woman Behind the Court Ruling Overturning Roe v. Wade," True North Research, Substack, July 26, 2022.

9. Elizabeth Dias and Lisa Lerer, "The Untold Story of the Network That Took Down Roe v. Wade," *New York Times*, May 28, 2024.

10. Editorial Board, "Abortion and the Supreme Court," *Wall Street Journal*, April 26, 2022; Joan Biskupic, "The Inside Story of How John Roberts Failed to Save Abortion Rights," CNN, July 26, 2022; Josh Gerstein and Alexander Ward, "Supreme Court Has Voted to Overturn Abortion Rights, Draft Opinion Shows," *Politico*, May 5, 2022.

11. Ken Armstrong, "Draft Overturning *Roe v. Wade* Quotes Infamous Witch Trial Judge with Long-Discredited Ideas on Rape," *ProPublica*, May 6, 2022.

12. Armstrong, "Draft Overturning Roe v. Wade Quotes Infamous Witch Trial Judge."

13. Gareth Gore, "Opus Dei and the Moneybags Kid," *Rolling Stone*, September 28, 2024; "History, the Supreme Court, and *Dobbs v. Jackson*: Joint Statement from the AHA and the OAH," American Historical Association, July 6, 2022. See also Heidi Przybyla, "'Plain Historical Falsehoods': How Amicus Briefs Bolstered Supreme Court Conservatives," *Politico*, December 3, 2023.

14. *Dobbs v. Jackson Women's Health Organization*, 597 U.S. 215 (2022).

15. Marge Piercy, "Right to Life," in *Circles on the Water* (Knopf, 1982).

16. Michael Avery and Danielle McLaughlin, *The Federalist Society: How Conservatives Took the Law Back from Liberals* (Vanderbilt University Press, 2013), 26.

17. Avery and McLaughlin, *The Federalist Society*, 26.

18. Andy Kroll, Andrea Bernstein, and Ilya Marritz, "We Don't Talk About Leonard: The Man Behind the Right's Supreme Court Supermajority," *ProPublica*, October 11, 2023.

19. Carla Astudillo and Erin Douglas, "We Annotate Texas' Near-Total Abortion Ban. Here's What the Law Says About Enforcement," *Texas Tribune*, September 10, 2021.

20. Amanda Seitz, "Feds: Hospitals That Denied Emergency Abortion Broke the Law," *Associated Press*, May 1, 2023.

21. Megan Messerly and Adam Wren, "National Right to Life Official: 10-Year-Old Should Have Had Baby," *Politico*, July 14, 2022.

22. "26 States Are Certain or Likely to Ban Abortion Without Roe: Here's Which Ones and Why," Guttmacher Institute, October 28, 2021; T. J. L'Heureux, "Who Are the Arizona Supreme Court Justices? What to Know," *Phoenix New Times*, October 23, 2024; Adam Edelman and Alex Tabet, "Arizona Supreme Court Rules a Near-Total Abortion Ban from 1864 Is Enforceable," *NBC News*, April 9, 2024; "Governor Katie Hobbs Signs Bill into Law Officially Repealing 1864 Abortion Ban," Office of the Governor: Katie Hobbs, May 2, 2024; Todd Richmond, "Wisconsin Supreme Court to Consider Whether 175-Year-Old Law Bans Abortion," *Associated Press*, July 2, 2024; Kyle Khan-Mullins and Carlos Sánchez Mora, "Meet the Billionaire Couple Pumping Their Fortune into Right-Wing Politics," *Forbes*, August 3, 2022; Lisa Graves and Evan Vorpahl, "Snapshot of Dick Uihlein and the 'Fair Courts America' Attack Ad Machine," True North Research, February 13, 2023; Evan Vorpahl, "Dark Money–Fueled WI Supreme Court Candidate's Anti-Abortion Views Span Decades," *Truthout*, March 26, 2023; Susan Davis, Tamara Keith, and Kelsey Snell, "Janet Protasiewicz Won Wisconsin Supreme Court Seat, Giving Liberal Justices Majority," NPR, April 5, 2023; "What Is 'Women Speak Out?'" True North Research Substack, accessed January 2, 2025.

23. Elie Mystal, "How John Roberts Delivered the House to His Fellow Republicans," *Balls and Strikes*, November 16, 2022.

24. Kavitha Surana, "Abortion Bans Have Delayed Emergency Medical Care. In Georgia, Experts Say This Mother's Death Was Preventable," *ProPublica*, September 16, 2024.

25. "AFJ Nominee Report: Matthew Kacsmaryk," Alliance for Justice, accessed January 2, 2025, https://afj.org/wp-content/uploads/2019/12/AFJ-Kacsmaryk-Report.pdf.

26. In 2024, *ProPublica* reported that Justice Clarence Thomas's wife Ginni personally thanked Shackelford for First Liberty's work against Supreme Court ethics reform, emailing him in Trumpian all caps, "YOU GUYS HAVE FILLED THE SAILS OF MANY JUDGES. CAN I JUST TELL YOU, THANK YOU SO, SO, SO MUCH." On the same call where he read out Ginni's email,

Shackelford called Justice Elena Kagan "treasonous" and "disloyal" for supporting an enforceable ethics code for Supreme Court justices. See Andy Kroll and Nick Surgey, "Ginni Thomas Privately Praised Group Working Against Supreme Court Reform: 'Thank You So, So, So Much,'" *ProPublica*, September 4, 2025; Andy Kroll and Nick Surgey, "Inside Ziklag, the Secret Organization of Wealthy Christians Trying to Sway the Election and Change the Country," *ProPublica*, July 13, 2024; "The Inequality Act: Weaponizing Same-Sex Marriage," *Public Discourse*, September 4, 2015; "Nomination of Matthew Kacsmaryk to the Northern District of Texas, Questions for the Record" US Senate Committee on the Judiciary, December 20, 2017; Robert Barnes, Caroline Kitchener, and Ann E. Marimow, "The Controversial Article Texas Federal Judge Matthew Kacsmaryk Did Not Disclose to the Senate," *Texas Tribune*, April 15, 2023; James Finn, "Judge Who Banned Abortion Pill Hid Anti-Trans Christian Extremism from Senate," *Medium*, April 19, 2023; "Brief of *Amici Curiae* 43 Members of Congress in Support of Petitioners," *SCOTUSblog*, accessed January 2, 2025.

27. Ansev Demirhan and Lisa Graves, "Far-Right Players Behind Latest Attacks on Abortion in Emergencies," *Ms. Magazine*, January 1, 2024.

**CHAPTER 11. GOD**

1. Notably, the Leo-tied Judicial Crisis Network ran ads attacking the first Muslim nominee to a federal appellate court in US history. See Adeel A. Mangi, letter to President Joseph R. Biden Jr., AboutLaw.com, December 16, 2024, https://aboutblaw.com/bgA0.

2. Isaac Kramnick, *The Godless Constitution: The Case Against Religious Correctness* (W. W. Norton, 1996), 110–119.

3. "Transcript: JFK's Speech on His Religion," NPR, December 5, 2007.

4. Lisa Graves, "Backgrounder on the Supreme Court, Judge Amy Barrett, Trump Advisor Leonard Leo, and Billionaire Charles Koch," True North Research, October 26, 2020; "Fr. Paul D. Scalia," Saint James Catholic Church, accessed January 2, 2025; Gareth Gore, "Opus Dei and the Moneybags Kid," *Rolling Stone*, September 28, 2024; Evan Thomas, "Washington's Quiet Club," *Newsweek*, March 8, 2001 (updated March 13, 2010); Carol Brzozowski, "Love of God Is Shrouded in Secrecy: Opus Dei Wants Others to Understand Devotion," *South Florida Sun Sentinel*, May 25, 1990 (updated September 25, 2021). See, generally, Gareth Gore, *Opus: The Cult of Dark Money, Human Trafficking, and Right-Wing Conspiracy Inside the Catholic Church* (Simon & Schuster, 2024).

5. "Pulling Back the Curtain: Opus Dei," Robin Morgan, September 26, 2022; "Six Priests Are Reappointed as Pastors or in Special Assignments," *Catholic Standard*, September 16, 2004; "Deacon Mike Coney," St. Catherine of Siena Parish, accessed January 2, 2025; Lisa Graves and Caroline Jones, "Justice Barrett's Ties to Shell and API Are Far Deeper Than Reported; Her Father Could Be Deposed in Climate Change Suits," True North Research, January 14, 2021; Joseph Bottom, "Alito and the Catholics," *CBS News*, January 17, 2006.

6. Betty Clermont, "Opus Dei's Influence on the US Judiciary," *Church and State*, December 21, 2018.

7. Frank Newport, "The Religion of the Supreme Court Justices," Gallup, April 8, 2022.

8. Dahlia Lithwick and Mark Joseph Stern, "We Need to Have a Talk About Leonard Leo's Version of Catholicism," *Slate*, September 23, 2024.

9. The Council on National Policy "has been strategizing to dominate the Supreme Court for decades. . . . They have worked through the Federalist Society, the Heritage Foundation, and the National Rifle Association, all run by members of the CNP." Anne Nelson, "This Powerful Group Groomed Mike Pence for the White House. Impeachment Could Complicate Their Plans," *Salon*, October 25, 2019. See Anne Nelson, *Shadow Network: Media, Money, and the Secret Hub of the Radical Right* (Bloomsbury, 2019); Robert O'Harrow, "God, Trump and the Closed-Door World of a Major Conservative Group," *Washington Post Magazine*, October 25, 2021; Shawn Boburg and Robert O'Harrow Jr., "A Conservative Activist's Behind-the-Scenes Campaign to Remake the Nation's Courts," *Washington Post*, May 21, 2019.

10. Leonard Leo, "2022 John Paul II New Evangelization Award Leonard Leo Remarks," uploaded to YouTube by Catholic Information Center, Washington, DC, November 30, 2022, 22:59.

11. Heidi Schlumpf, "Leonard Leo, Architect of Conservative Supreme Court, Takes on Wider Culture," *National Catholic Register*, January 4, 2024; "Letter from Escriva to Franco," Opus Dei Awareness Network, accessed January 2, 2025.

12. Women of Wit, "An Historian's Reaction to Dobbs v. Jackson Women's Health Organization," *Women in Theology*, July 18, 2022.

13. Hans Nichols, "Scoop: Activist Leonard Leo Pushes to 'Weaponize' Conservatives," *Axios*, September 12, 2024; Nina Burleigh, "Who Is Leonard Leo's Mysterious Dark Money King?" *New Republic*, May 16, 2023.

14. Robert P. George and Jean Bethke Elshtain, eds., *The Meaning of Marriage: Family, State, Market, & Morals* (Scepter Publishers, 2006), 101–102.

15. Richard A. Posner, "Supreme Court Gay Marriage: John Roberts' Dissent in Obergefell Is Heartless," *Slate*, June 27, 2015.

16. "The San People," Exploring Africa, Wayback Machine, https://web.archive.org/web/20190723203638/https://www.exploring-africa.com/en/botswana/san-or-bushmen/san-people, accessed January 2, 2025; Sarah Prager, "In Han Dynasty China, Bisexuality Was the Norm," *JSTOR Daily*, June 10, 2020.

17. Jamie Abrams and Amanda Potts, "The Rhetoric of Abortion in Amicus Briefs," *Missouri Law Review* 89 (2024): 399.

18. Linda Greenhouse and Reva B. Siegel, *Before Roe v. Wade: Voices That Shaped the Abortion Debate Before the Supreme Court's Ruling* (Kaplan, 2010), 77–84.

19. *303 Creative LLC v. Elenis*, 600 U.S. 570 (2023); James Esseks, "In Masterpiece, the Bakery Wins the Battle but Loses the War," News and Commentary, *ACLU*, June 4, 2018.

20. Hila Keren, "The Alarming Legal Strategy Behind a SCOTUS Case That Could Undo Decades of Civil Rights Protections," *Slate*, March 9, 2022.

21. *Burwell v. Hobby Lobby Stores, Inc.*, 573 U.S. 682 (2014).

22. Bruce Gourely, "Supreme Theocrats: The Anti-Freedom, Anti-Life, Biblical Worldview of the Christian Nationalist Majority on the Nation's Highest Court," Americans United for Separation of Church and State, September 3, 2024.

23. "People for the American Way Report in Opposition to the Confirmation of Supreme Court Nominee John Roberts," People for the American Way, August 24, 2005.

24. Amy Howe, "Justices Side with High School Football Coach Who Prayed on the Field with Students," *SCOTUSblog*, June 27, 2022.

25. "People for the American Way Report"; "John Roberts," Ronald Reagan Presidential Library Digital Library Collections Chron File (8/1/1985-8/19/1985) box 66; *Stone v. Graham*, 449 U.S. 39 (1980).

26. Associated Press, "How Will Louisiana's Ten Commandments Classroom Requirement Be Funded and Enforced?" NPR, June 30, 2024.

27. Matt Ford, "The Chief Justice Who Isn't," *New Republic*, October 20, 2022.

28. Sheldon Whitehouse and Jennifer Mueller, *The Scheme: How the Right Wing Used Dark Money to Capture the Supreme Court* (New Press,

2022); Sheldon Whitehouse and Melanie Wachtell Stinnett, *Captured: The Corporate Infiltration of American Democracy* (New Press, 2017).

29. Lisa Graves, "The Koch Brothers: The Extremist Roots Run Deep," *Progressive Magazine*, July 10, 2014; Jane Mayer, *Dark Money: The Hidden History of the Billionaires Behind the Rise of the Radical Right* (Doubleday, 2016); Christopher Leonard, *Kochland: The Secret History of Koch Industries and Corporate Power in America* (Simon & Schuster, 2019); Lisa Graves and Nancy Maclean, "The Billionaire Kingmaker (Still) Dividing the Nation," *Progressive Magazine*, January 3, 2023; Lisa Graves, "Josh Duggar–Led Group Funded via Koch Brothers Freedom Partners Operation," *PR Watch*, August 22, 2015; Ansev Demirhan, "The Same Dark Money Groups That Helped Overturn Roe Are Also Behind Attacks on Abortion Pill," *Ms. Magazine*, February 2, 2023.

30. Stephanie Kirchgaessner and Rachel Leingang, "Kevin Roberts, Architect of Project 2025, Has Close Ties to Radical Catholic Group Opus Dei," *The Guardian*, July 26, 2024; "A Project 2025 Administration Stands Ready to Execute a Set of Drastic, Feasible, and Specific Plans That Would 'Institutionalize Trumpism' and Remake America's Federal Government," Project 2025 Admin, accessed January 2, 2025.

31. David Schultz, "The Roberts Court Takes Aim at the Establishment Clause," *The Hill*, May 31, 2023.

**CHAPTER 12. VOTING**

1. David Daley, *Antidemocratic: Inside the Far Right's 50-Year Plot to Control American Elections* (Mariner Books, 2024), 89 (Kindle).

2. US Senate Committee on the Judiciary, *Confirmation Hearing on the Nomination of John G. Roberts, Jr. to Be Chief Justice of the United States*, 109th Cong., 1st Sess., September 12–15, 2005.

3. Peggy Noonan, *What I Saw at the Revolution: A Political Life in the Reagan Era* (Random House, 1990), 100.

4. Ronald J. Ostrow and James Gerstenzang, "Four Witnesses Dispute Word of Rehnquist," *Los Angeles Times*, August 2, 1986; Robert Lindsey, "Rehnquist in Arizona: A Militant Conservative in 60's Politics," *New York Times*, August 4, 1986.

5. US Senate Judiciary Committee, *Nominations of William H. Rehnquist, of Arizona, and Lewis F. Powell, Jr., of Virginia, to Be Associate Justices of the Supreme Court of the United States, Hearings, November 1971*, 92nd Cong., 1st Sess., Statement by Rep. John Conyers, Jr., 349–359; Adam Liptak, "The Memo That Rehnquist Wrote and Had to Disown," *New York Times*,

September 11, 2005. See US Senate Judiciary Committee, *Nomination of Justice William Hubbs Rehnquist to Be Chief Justice of the United States, Hearings Before the Committee on the Judiciary, July 29, 30, 31 and August 1, 1986*, 99th Cong., 2nd Sess., William Rehnquist, "A Random Thought on the Segregation Cases," memorandum, 324–325.

6. Ian Haney-Lopez, "How Conservatives Hijacked 'Colorblindness' and Set Civil Rights Back Decades," *Salon*, January 20, 2014; Rick Perlstein, *Before the Storm: Barry Goldwater and the Unmaking of the American Consensus* (Bold Type Books, 2001), 461 (Kindle).

7. Daley, *Antidemocratic*, 45; Associated Press, "Reagan Quotes King Speech in Opposing Minority Quotas," *New York Times*, January 19, 1986; Martin Luther King Jr., "I Have a Dream," 1963, aired on *Talk of the Nation*, NPR, 2010, transcribed by NPR, January 16, 2023.

8. *Reynolds v. Sims*, 377 U.S. 533, 377 (1964); *Lane v. Wilson*, 307 U.S. 268, 275 (1939), https://supreme.justia.com/cases/federal/us/307/268.

9. "Many Believe South Will Find Way Out of Latest Difficulty," *Greenville News*, April 3, 1944, 5; Chris Myers Asch, *The Senator and the Sharecropper: The Freedom Struggles of James O. Eastland and Fannie Lou Hamer* (New Press, 2008), 92 (Kindle); "Mike Wallace Interview with Senator James Eastland," C-SPAN, July 28, 1957.

10. Sidney Blumenthal, "Look Away, Dixieland," *The Guardian*, November 7, 2003.

11. Blumenthal, "Look Away, Dixieland." See also "James Baldwin vs William F Buckley: A Legendary Debate from 1965," audio restored by Adam D'Arpino, posted to YouTube by Aeon Video, August 13, 2019; Nicholas Buccola, *The Fire Is upon Us: James Baldwin, William F. Buckley Jr., and the Debate over Race in America* (Princeton University Press, 2019).

12. *City of Mobile v. Bolden*, 446 U.S. 55, 128 (1980), https://supreme.justia.com/cases/federal/us/446/55.

13. "Section 2 of the Voting Rights Act," Civil Rights Division, US Department of Justice, updated April 5, 2023.

14. Ari Berman, *Give Us the Ballot: The Modern Struggle for Voting Rights in America* (Picador, 2016), 147 (Kindle).

15. US Department of Justice, "Correspondence Files of Kenneth W. Starr, Counselor to the Attorney General, 1981-83," Accession #60-88-0498, box 22, record group 60.

16. Joan Biskupic, *The Chief: The Life and Turbulent Times of Chief Justice John Roberts* (Basic Books, 2019), 69 (Kindle).

17. Robert Pear, "Reagan Backs Voting Rights Act but Wants to Ease Requirements," *New York Times*, November 7, 1981; US Department of Justice, "Correspondence Files of Kenneth W. Starr."

18. US House Committee on the Judiciary, Subcommittee on the Constitution, "Voting Rights Act: Evidence of Continued Need," testimony by Bill Lann Lee, March 8, 2006.

19. Representative Lynn Westmoreland, Statement on House Passage of Voting Rights Act, released July 13, 2006, cited in Nathaniel Persily, "The Promise and Pitfalls of the New Voting Rights Act," *Yale Law Journal* 117 (2007): 181.

20. *Northwest Austin Municipal Util. Dist. No. One v. Holder*, 557 U.S. 193 (2009).

21. "Shelby County, Alabama, Installs Marker Commemorating Racial Terror Lynchings," Equal Justice Initiative, July 16, 2020.

22. Lisa Graves, "How Charles Koch Backed the John Birch Society at the Height of Its Attacks on Martin Luther King," *PR Watch*, January 18, 2016; Lisa Graves, "The Koch Brothers: The Extremist Roots Run Deep," *PR Watch*, July 10, 2014; Lisa Graves, "Like His Dad, Charles Koch Was a Bircher (New Documents)," *PR Watch*, July, 8, 2014.

23. "*Shelby County v. Holder*," *SCOTUSblog*, accessed January 2, 2025; brief for the Honorable Congressman John Lewis as Amicus Curiae, *Shelby County v. Holder*, 570 U.S. 529, *5 (2013).

24. "How *Shelby County v. Holder* Broke Democracy," NAACP Legal Defense and Educational Fund, accessed January 2, 2025; "*United States v. Texas, et al.*; *Veasey v. Perry*," Political Participation, NAACP Legal Defense and Educational Fund, accessed January 3, 2025, http://www.naacpldf.org/case-issue/united-states-v-texas-et-al-veasey-v-perry.

25. *N.C. State Conference v. McCrory*, No. 16-1468 (4th Cir. 2016), 10–77; Editorial Board, "North Carolina's Voting Restrictions Struck Down as Racist," *New York Times*, July 29, 2016; Lisa Graves, "Democracy in Peril," *Progressive*, February 7, 2022.

26. Evan Vorpahl and Julia Peck, "Trump's Jan. 6th Speech Incited an Insurrection and a Fanatical Rewriting of State Laws to Subvert Our Freedom to Vote," True North Research, January 4, 2022.

27. "How *Shelby County v. Holder* Broke Democracy."

28. "How *Shelby County v. Holder* Broke Democracy."

29. Catalina Feder and Michael G. Miller, "Voter Purges After Shelby: Part of Special Symposium on Election Sciences," *American Politics Research* 48 (2020): 687–692; "How *Shelby County v. Holder* Broke Democracy."

30. Sheldon Whitehouse, "How to Keep the Supreme Court from Partisanship," *Wall Street Journal*, January 10, 2018.

31. *Rucho v. Common Cause*, 588 U.S. 1–2 (2019), (Kagan, J., dissenting).

32. Lisa Graves, "The Rollback and Ongoing Threats to Voting Rights," Grave Injustice, season 1, episode 3, posted to YouTube by *Courier*, May 23, 2024.

33. Brief of Alabama and 12 Other States, *Louisiana v. Callais, Robinson v. Callais*, September 3, 2024.

34. Paul Brownfield, "Laying Down the Law," *Los Angeles Times*, January 31, 1999.

35. See, e.g., Daley, *Antidemocratic*, 256-263.

36. See generally Robert Bork, "Neutral Principles and Some First Amendment Problems," *Indiana Law Journal* (1971).

**CHAPTER 13. CLASS**

1. US Code 28 (2011) § 453.

2. *Biden v. Nebraska*, 600 U.S. 477 (2023).

3. *Biden v. Nebraska* (Kagan, J., dissenting); Amy Howe, "Supreme Court Strikes Down Biden Student-Loan Forgiveness Program," *SCOTUSblog*, June 30, 2024.

4. *Biden v. Nebraska.*

5. Brief of Elisabeth DeVos, et al., as Amici Curiae, *Biden v. Nebraska.*

6. *City of Grants Pass v. Johnson*, 603 U.S. ___ (2024); Anatole France, *The Red Lily* (Borgo Press, 2002), 72.

7. "Johnson v. Grants Pass," National Homelessness Law Center, accessed January 2, 2024; *Johnson v. Grants Pass*, 603 U.S. ___ (2024), (Thomas, C. concurring); *Johnson v. Grants Pass* (Gorsuch, N., opinion).

8. *Johnson v. Grants Pass* (Sotomayor, S. dissenting).

9. Wendell Potter, *Deadly Spin: An Insurance Company Insider Speaks Out on How Corporate PR Is Killing Health Care and Deceiving Americans* (Bloomsbury Press, 2010).

10. John McDermott, "Small Business Group Under Fire on Funding," *Inc.*, June 25, 2012.

11. Jan Crawford, "Roberts Switched Views to Uphold Health Care Law," *CBS News*, July 2, 2012.

12. Joan Biskupic, "The Inside Story of How John Roberts Negotiated to Save Obamacare," CNN, March 5, 2019; Crawford, "Roberts Switched Views."

13. Lisa Graves, "Chambers of Commerce Exposed by CMD," *PR Watch*, April 4, 2016.

14. *Burwell v. Hobby Lobby Stores, Inc.*, 573 U.S. 682 (2014); *Little Sisters of the Poor Saints Peter and Paul Home v. Pennsylvania*, 591 U.S. __ (2020).

15. Brian R. Frazelle, "Corporate Clout: As the Roberts Court Transforms, the Chamber Has Another Big Term," Constitutional Accountability Center, July 26, 2017; "The Chamber of Litigation, Part II," Public Citizen, March 16, 2017.

16. Lisa Graves, "Chamber of Commerce Exposed by CMD," *PR Watch*, April 4, 2016.

17. Nancy MacLean and Lisa Graves, "Time to Fight," interview by Nitish Pahwa, *Slate*, August 30, 2021; Lewis F. Powell Jr., "Powell Memorandum: Attack on American Free Enterprise System," *Reuters*, August 23, 1971.

18. Rachel Carson, *Silent Spring* (Houghton Mifflin, 1962); Robert Easton, *Black Tide: The Santa Barbara Oil Spill and Its Consequences* (Delacorte Press, 1972); "2005 Essay from Santa Barbara Wildlife Care Network," 1969 Santa Barbara Oil Spill, accessed January 10, 2025, https://www2.bren.ucsb.edu/~dhardy/1969_Santa_Barbara_Oil_Spill/About.html.

19. Julia Peck, Ansev Demirhan, and Evan Vorpahl, "The World's First Climate Denial Conference," True North Research, April 26, 2022.

20. Michael Barera, "The 1981 PATCO Strike," *UTA Libraries Blog*, September 2, 2021; Bart Barnes, "Robert Poli, Who Led 1981 Strike That Led Reagan to Fire Traffic Controllers, Dies at 78," *Washington Post*, September 23, 2014.

21. Joseph A. McCartin, "PATCO, Permanent Replacement, and the Loss of Labor's Strike Weapon," *Perspectives on Work* 10, no. 1 (2006): 17–19; Joseph A. McCartin, "The Strike That Busted Unions," *New York Times*, August 2, 2011.

22. US Senate Committee on the Judiciary, *Confirmation Hearing on the Nomination of John G. Roberts*; *Holly Farms Corp. v. NLRB*, 517 U.S. 392 (1996).

23. Claire Mullins, "A Day in the Life: A Union and Civil Rights Leader," Baltimore Museum of Industry, July 23, 2020; Carol J. Loomis, "The Sinking of Bethlehem Steel," *CNN Money*, April 5, 2004.

24. Gordon Lafer, *The One Percent Solution: How Corporations Are Remaking America One State at a Time* (ILR Press, 2017), location 3729 (Kindle).

25. *Friedrichs v. California Teachers Association*, 578 U.S. __ (2016); *Abood v. Detroit Board of Education*, 431 U.S. 209 (1976).

26. *Janus v. American Federation of State, County, and Municipal Employees, Council 31*, 585 U.S. __ (2018).

27. Ed Pilkington, "Rightwing Alliance Plots Assault to 'Defund and Defang' America's Unions," *The Guardian*, August 30, 2017.

28. Jane Mayer, *Dark Money: The Hidden History of the Billionaires Behind the Rise of the Radical Right* (Doubleday, 2016).

29. Mayer, *Dark Money*.

30. Cited in Lisa Graves, "Inside the Koch Family's 60-Year Anti-Union Campaign That Gave Us Janus," *In These Times*, July 12, 2018.

31. Petition for Writ of Certiorari, *Cedar Point Nursery v. Hassid*, 594 U.S. __ (2021).

32. Scott A. Budow, "How the Roberts Court Has Changed Labor and Employment Law," *Illinois Law Review*, September 13, 2021.

33. *Students for Fair Admissions v. President and Fellows of Harvard College*, 600 U.S. 181 (2023).

34. Amy Goldstein, R. Jeffrey Smith, and Jo Becker, "Roberts Resisted Women's Rights," *Washington Post*, August 18, 2005.

35. Goldstein, Smith, and Becker, "Roberts Resisted."

36. *Ledbetter v. Goodyear Tire*, 550 U.S. 608 (2007).

37. *Corner Post, Inc. v. Board of Governors of the Federal Reserve System*, 603 U.S. 799 (2024).

**CHAPTER 14. POWER**

1. Lisa Graves, "Clarence Thomas Has No Shame. But You Knew That," *Common Dreams*, February 9, 2024.

2. *Fischer v. United States*, 603 U.S. (2024), (Barrett, A., dissenting).

3. Aleks Phillips, "Full List of Capitol Rioters Jailed So Far and the Sentences They Are Serving," *Newsweek*, September 12, 2024; Melissa Quinn, "Missouri Executes Marcellus Williams Despite Questions over Evidence, After Supreme Court Denies Final Bid for Delay," *CBS News*, September 25, 2024.

4. Amy Howe, "In Overnight Orders, Justices Allow Federal Execution to Proceed," *SCOTUSblog*, July 14, 2020.

5. Terrence P. Dwyer, Esq., "SCOTUS Year in Review: Decisions on Qualified Immunity and Fourth Amendment Seizures," *Police1*, December 10, 2021.

6. *SEC v. Jarkesy*, 603 U.S. Slip Op. 1, 2, 38 (2024), (Sotomayor, J., dissenting).

7. "Ten Minute Read: The US Supreme Court's 2022 Business Cases," Quinn Emanuel Trial Lawyers, accessed January 10, 2025.

8. John Nichols, "Which Shall Rule: Wealth or Wisconsinites," *The Cap Times*, October 25, 2015. See, generally, Joseph Ranney, "Chief Justice Edward G. Ryan: A World in Which Nothing Is Perfect," *Wisconsin Lawyer*, September 1, 2002.

**EPILOGUE**

1. "[Resolution] Impeaching Donald John Trump, President of the United States, for High Crimes and Misdemeanors," H.Res. 24, 117th Cong., 1st Sess. (2021); Mitch McConnell, "Read McConnell's Remarks on the Senate Floor Following Trump's Acquittal," CNN, February 13, 2021.

# INDEX

# INDEX

# INDEX

# INDEX

Credit: S. Williams Studios

**Lisa Graves** is one of the nation's foremost experts on the right-wing influence on the US Supreme Court and other levers of power. She leads True North Research and is a cohost of Legal AF. She has served as a senior advisor in all three branches of the federal government, including as chief counsel for nominations for the Senate Judiciary Committee for Senator Patrick Leahy. She is @thelisagraves on Bluesky. She resides in Superior, Wisconsin.